FUSṬĀṬ EXPEDITION FINAL REPORT
VOL. 1: CATALOGUE OF FILTERS

AMERICAN RESEARCH CENTER IN EGYPT REPORTS

Fusṭāṭ Expedition Final Report
Vol. 1: Catalogue of Filters

Volume 8

CATALOGUE OF FILTERS

by

George T. Scanlon

Published for

THE AMERICAN RESEARCH CENTER IN EGYPT, INC.

by

EISENBRAUNS

*Produced for the American Research Center in Egypt
and distributed by*

*Eisenbrauns
POB 275
Winona Lake, Indiana*

© 1986 by the American Research Center in Egypt

Library of Congress Cataloging in Publication Data

Scanlon, George T.
   Fusṭāṭ expedition final report.

   (American Research Center in Egypt reports; v. 8)
   Includes bibliographical references.
   Contents: v. 1. Catalog of filters.
   1. Cairo (Egypt)—Antiquities. 2. Egypt—Antiquities. 3. Ex-
cavations (Archaeology)—Egypt—Cairo. I. American Research
Center in Egypt. II. Title. III. Series.
DT150.5.F87S27   1986   962′.16   86-2185
ISBN 0-936770-13-9 (v. 1)

TABLE OF CONTENTS

PREFACE AND ABBREVIATIONS

The Fustat Expedition of the American Research Center in Egypt (ARCE) excavated the vast site in Old Cairo for an aggregate of twenty-seven months between March 1964 and early November 1980. There were eight full seasons, ranging in duration from two and a half months to five, carried out in the tripartite concession denominated Fustat-A, -B and -C. In the Preliminary Reports of the various seasons, the staff members and Egyptian authorities are cited and thanked, as they are in other volumes of this Final Report. However, should this volume be the only one to reach print or to survive, it is incumbent upon us to recall with the deepest gratitude those persons and institutions without whose efforts at the site or sustaining support this **particular** work would never have achieved fruition. These are, without any prejudice of order:

1) The artists and photographers who translated the filters from finds into published facts.

    1964   Kenneth Pawula, Elinore Pawula, Erik Gronborg
    1965   Elinore Pawula, Deborah Butterworth, Theodora Mackay, Gordon Holler
    1966   Judith Knowlton, Richard Steiner, Dr. Kent Weeks
    1968   Elinore Pawula, Clara Sampson, Sue Booth, Penny Freeman
    1971   Esmat Allouba, Clara Sampson, Elizabeth Rodenbeck, Sophie Ebeid
    1972   Clara Sampson, Elizabeth Rodenbeck, Dr. Thierry Bianquis
    1973   Clara Sampson, Dr. Thierry Bianquis
    1978   Elizabeth Rodenbeck, Dr. Doris Abou-Seif Behrens, Jean Tifft
    1980   Clara Sampson, Joseph Guirgis

2) The Egyptian authorities who granted us the concession, assisted in the organization of the field work, and permitted us access to and division of the finds.

    a. Directors-General of the Islamic and Coptic division of the Antiquities Service: Drs. Anwar Shukri, Muhammad al-Mahdi, Gamal Mehriz; Messrs. Abd al-Rahman Abd al-Tawwab and Sulayman Ahmad Sulayman.

    b. Inspectors from the same division: Messrs. Fahmy Abd al-'Alim, 'Asim Abd al-Rahman, Ahmad Makkawi, Midhat al-Munabawi, Abbas al-Shinnawi, Abd al-Hafidh Diab and Sayed Abd al-Maksud.

    c. Directors of the Islamic Museum in Cairo: Mme. Wafeya Izzi and Dr. Abd al-Ra'uf Yusuf.

3) The personnel of the ARCE office in Cairo, particularly the Directors during the period of excavations at Fustat: Mr. John Dorman, Drs. Paul Walker and James Allan.

4) The Smithsonian Institution through whose Foreign Currency Program we were supported in our endeavors no matter how rough the political and professional waters; and

5) Those who provided the Fustat Expedition with hard currency support: Princeton University Museum of Art, the Kelsey Museum of the University of Michigan, the Corning Museum of Glass, the Ashmolean Museum of the University of Oxford, and the anonymous donors through whose efforts objects have been forwarded from Fustat to the Akron Museum of Art, the Oriental Institute of the University of Chicago, the Archaeological Museum of the University of Missouri, and the East Asian Art Museum in Stockholm.

A large number of the filters herein described and catalogued have already been published in one form or another. Yet other reported archaeological data and objects from the Fustat Expedition help us to achieve real and associative dating. As these are constantly referred to throughout this study it is necessary to supply a list of their abbreviations for ease of citation. Unless otherwise noted, the present author is responsible for the articles, and *JARCE* denotes the *Journal of the American Research Center in Egypt*:

Anc./Ancillary	"Ancillary Dating Materials from Fustat," *Ars Orientalis*, VII (1968), pp. 1-17
F.F./Fat. Fil.	"Fatimid Filters: Archaeology and Olmer's Typology," *Annales Islamologiques*, IX (1970), pp. 31-51
FEPR '64	"Preliminary Report: Excavations at Fustat," *JARCE*, IV (1965), pp. 7-30
FEPR '65-I	"Fustat Expedition: Preliminary Report 1965. Part I," *JARCE*, V (1966), pp. 83-112
FEPR '65-II	"Fustat Expedition: Preliminary Report 1965. Part II," *JARCE*, VI (1967), pp. 65-86
FEPR '66	(with W. B. Kubiak) "Fustat Expedition: Preliminary Report 1966," *JARCE*, X (1973), pp. 11-25
FEPR '68-I	"Fustat Expedition: Preliminary Report 1968. Part I," *JARCE*, XI (1974), pp. 81-91
FEPR '71-I	(with W.B. Kubiak) "Fustat Expedition: Preliminary Report 1971. Part I," *JARCE*, XVI (1979), pp. 103-124
FEPR '71-II	(with W.B. Kubiak) "Fustat Expedition: Preliminary Report 1971. Part II," *JARCE*, XVII (1980), pp. 77-96
FEPR '72-I	"Fustat Expedition: Preliminary Report 1972. Part I," *JARCE*, XVIII (1981), pp. 57-84
FEPR '72-II	"Fustat Expedition: Preliminary Report 1972. Part II," *JARCE*, XIX (1982), pp. 119-129
FEPR '73	"Fustat Expedition: Preliminary Report. Back to Fustat-A 1973," *Annales Islamologiques*, t. XVII (1981), pp. 407-436

FEPR '78	"Fustat Expedition: Preliminary Report 1978," *JARCE*, XX (1983), in press
Fustat-Arts	"Fustat and the Islamic Arts of Egypt," *Archaeology*, vol. 21, n. 3 (June 1968), pp. 188-195
Fustat-Glass	(with R.M. Pinder-Wilson) "Glass from Fustat: 1964-71," *Journal of Glass Studies*, vol. 15 (1973), pp. 12-30
Numismatics	(with Th. Bianquis and A. Watson) "Numismatics and the dating of Early Islamic Pottery in Egypt," *Near Eastern Numismatics, Iconography, Epigraphy and History: Studies in Honour of George C. Miles*, ed. D.K. Kouymjian (Beirut: 1974), pp. 163-173
Pits	"The Pits of Fustat: Problems of Chronology," *Journal of Egyptian Archaeology*, vol. 60 (1974), pp. 60-80
R.G./Recent Glass	"Recent Glass from Fustat," *Bulletin d. Soc. Arch. d'Alexandrie*, no. 43 (1972-73), pp. 81-89
Reconsiderations	"Fustat: Archaeological Reconsiderations," *Colloque International sur l'Histoire du Caire* (Cairo: 1972), pp. 415-428
Shard Count '68	"The Fustat Mounds: A Shard Count 1968," *Archaeology*, vol. XXIV no. 3 (June 1971), pp. 220-233

Two other publications, the one in a major, the other in a minor conspectus, are crucial to the study of Egyptian filters and are abbreviated as follows:

Olmer	Pierre Olmer, *Les Filtres de Gargoulettes*: Catalogue Général du Musée Arabe du Caire (Cairo: 1932)
Grube-Keir	Ernst J. Grube, *Islamic Pottery . . . Keir Collection* (London: 1976)

Finally, it must be understood that this manuscript was virtually complete when funding for the 1980 season, which allowed us to investigate Fustat-C, became available. Rather than revamp the typology, it has been considered better to describe the important filters from that season in Appendix D, while intercalating all examples typologically in the Table of Registered Filters.

INTRODUCTION

The filter exists to deter the entry of insects and other possibly harmful materials of irreguar shapes (generally between a crumble and a lump) into liquids intended for human consumption. Equally the filter should discourage the passage of such sediment as has collected within the volume of the liquid which does not contain coagulants. The accretion of the impurities within the contained liquids lends inexorably to the rejection of the vessel. Hence the containers must be cheap, rather light-weight insofar as the liquid itself supplies the balancing weight, generally porous if coolth is desired, and of an easily stored and replicable shape. In the periods anterior to Islam, exceptional filters were punched in metal and glass vessels; but the vast majority of filter bottles, both before and after the advent of Islam in the Middle East and North Africa, were manufactured of local ceramic clays.

So utilitarian an object would not be subject to much technological development let alone be made to bear the imprint of artistic impulse. Yet one witnesses the almost idiosyncratic development of filter design in Islamic Egypt, so much so that the evolution of filter patterns assumes chronological significance in the archaeology of Muslim Egypt. This evolution paralleled the maintenance of simple utterly utilitarian filter vessels, objects which are made and marketed to the present day throughout the Nile Valley. (Neither in Spain nor Sicily, where filter design exhibited a lesser, but equally cogent, development, did the industry survive as anything more than a source of folkloric interest.) The medieval Egyptian craftsman went so far so to decorate the external surface of the vessel (incising, glazing and lustering) as well as achieving such variations of shape and filter placement that these attributes can be cited to ascertain not only more accurate dating but the contemporary criteria of taste.

In his monumental catalogue of the ceramic filters in the Islamic Museum of Cairo, Pierre Olmer provided the base for all subsequent discussion of the subject.[1] A shorter animadversion on types, chronology and place of manufacture appeared eight years later in the Maspero *festschrift*.[2] The present author has contributed two studies to the subject: in one he sought to prove that on the basis of archaeological evidence proceeding from excavations carried out at Fustat by the American Research Center in Egypt (ARCE) Olmer could be accepted as a sure guide for the Fatimid range of filters;[3] and in the other to bolster Olmer's hesitant chronology for the pre-Fatimid period and to demonstrate that the filters themselves can be considered safe archaeological criteria in undisturbed loci.[4] The validity

---

[1] Olmer; particularly his Introduction and bibliographical survey.

[2] Pierre Olmer, "Le decor des filters de gargoulettes de l'Egypte Muaulmane," *Melanges Maspero III: Orient Islamique.* (Cairo: 1935-40), pp. 33-39.

[3] Fat. Fil.

[4] Ancillary.

of the last contention was tested in two further articles where filters or filter fragments were put in relief against associated datable evidence from the same or comparable loci so as to strengthen the chronological *dicta* posited in the earlier studies.[5]

However, the materials studied in the last four articles came from the first four seasons of the excavation (1964, '65, '66 and '68), whereas the Fustat Expedition/ARCE accomplished a further four full (1971, '72, '78 and '80) and one shorter (1973) season at the site. A great deal of new evidence came forth which must of necessity be fitted into the published frame-work and which alters, corroborates or deepens the typological and chronological asservations of Olmer and the present author. It is our purpose here to present this new material in such a form as to illustrate the archaeological finds as such *and* the modifications noted above; *but* without an undue repetition of published examples. The repetitions will be limited to those bolstering a development or design concept; and a full list of registered ARCE filters will be appended for those seeking the entire conspectus.[6] As only one of our examples (Fig. 179) is possibly from Nubia, we concur with Olmer that the filters were made either in the Qena-Ballas area or at Fustat itself.[7]

[5] Recent Glass and Pits.

[6] The most important, but not exhaustive, sources for published filters are in the various Preliminary Reports (cited as FEPR '64, etc.), Ancillary, Fat. Fil., and Pits. Further examples are cited in Grube-Keir, pp. 123-127 and 351-356. It is interesting that so far ranging a bibliography of the genre, published in 1976, should fail to cite our Fat. Fil, published in 1970; more particularly fig. 6 therein duplicates two examples in the Keir Collection.

[7] Olmer-Maspero, p. 35 f. The Fustat context can be proven by the waster in Bahgat and Massoul, *La Ceramique Musulmane de l'Egypte* (Cairo: 1930), pl. LIX bis, no. 123.

CATALOGUE OF FILTERS

Category A. The Pre-Fatimid Period
ca. 700-1000 A.D.

Although Olmer was quite clear about the general characteristics of his Tulunid filters, he was a bit wary of what lay on either side of the group. We are a little less so, because of evidence proceeding from a stricter archaeology. (It must never be forgotten that Olmer's typology is based almost exclusively on stylistics. Whereas this is methodologically respectable for the Fatimid, Ayyubid and Mamluk periods in that the various decorative devices found on the filters of these periods can be duplicated in objects from other metiers; e.g., blazons and epigraphic devices in Nashhi script; one is landed very much in a quandary for the earlier periods where there is little or no duplication, except for the vaunted Samarra-C stucco style.) Though our group can be typed on such criteria as vessel shape, filter placement, decorative devices on filter and/or vessel body, we have pratically no sharp breaks, rather a 'continuing' evolution with a most muted tempo of disappearance. When a commodity is mass-produced, the early, easy crudity (simple, punched holes) may continue through an entire epoch and disturb an otherwise lambent chronology. What intrigues us about the filters of this early period is how quickly, almost simultaneously, decoration is imposed on simple mechanics of utility (cf. the 'pinpoint' in fig. 7 a-d) and full design itself becomes the fact of the matter, lifting the vessel almost to the pitch of artistic expression.

I. The 'simple/mechanical'. Three characteristics unite this group, which initiates the Islamic series, and no doubt continues a method well-established long before in Egyptian ceramics: dead red or buff-brown clay, convex filter, and placement of the filter at the base of the neck.

A. THE UNRIBBED NECK. Possibly the oldest type, where the only differential is in how the filter is made: either of random holes or a design accomplished in the process of execution.

> Fig. 1. The holes are small: round or ovoid. The filter is only slightly wider than the body, and is of about the same thickness as the wall of the bulbous body. The locus of its discovery is discussed in Pits, p. 68; 8th century continuing into the early 9th.

> Fig. 2. The same type of holes are repeated, but here they are executed in a rough helical fashion. Four large holes are pierced at the 'corners' of the design, as it were, and a fifth one at the center. These latter would seem to facilitate the

filtering as can be seen from the underside in Pl. I-a. The convexity of the filter is more pronounced, and the body is more bulbous. As we lack a base, we cannot be certain if it contained a convexity similar to that of Fig. 1. Because of two blue-glass vessels in the same find-spot, we are constrained to see this vessel-filter shape continuing into the 9th century.

Fig. 3. The same rough helical design, with the holes being more uniformly square. Though the entire filter is convex in shape, the outer 'ring' is indented slightly. We lack a body; hence it is difficult to give certainty to the placement. The clay is red rather than reddish. However, the simplicity and mode of making the design make one opt for the early period, but with a trail-off into a later one. 9th-early 10th century.

B. THE RIBBED NECK. The essential difference is in the placement of the holes, all of which are round and comparatively large.

Fig. 4. The random piercing indicates that little attention was paid to the pattern, though the vessel itself retains a classical elegance. The convexity of the filter is not as pronounced as that obtaining in A-I-A above, and the convexity of the base is not as obvious. It was found in the same pit as the small terra-cotta figurine illustrated in Ancillary, text fig. 1. 8th-early 9th century.

Fig. 5. There are more holes than in the preceding example, though they are as randomly pierced. The shape is different in that there is a single ridge more than half-way up the body proper, giving the impression that the body was turned in two parts. There is a definite convexity on the underside of the base. Part of the neck is missing, but the over-all shape is ascertainable. Because of glass and schist vessels discovered in the same pit, we would assign this filter bottle to the 9th century.

Fig. 6. This very elegant water-bottle has a shape unique in our typology in that its flaring rim is just slightly wider than its shoulder-body joint. The neck is very lightly ribbed as compared to Figs. 4 and 5. The clay is more buff-brown than reddish brown, but the brown wash slip external turned reddish brown on firing. The eleven holes are not evenly dispersed but they do make at least a ringlet. The contents of the pit where this vessel was discovered are discussed in Pits, pp. 65-68, and it would seem to lie decisively in the 8th century, though the circlet motif continues into the 9th-10th century as witness the filter fragments to be seen in Pits, pl. XVI-9, FEPR '68-I, pl. XXVI-d, and FEPR '68-II, pl. XVI-b.

II. The 'simple/mechanical' with imposed decoration. Four examples of this type were discovered in 1968 and have been published twice: Pits, pl. XVII-1, 2 and 3 and pl. XXI-1; and in Ancillary, figs. 4 and 5. All are of buff-brown clay; all the filters are slightly convex; and all are placed at the jointure of neck and shoulder. On the basis of one, the height and flair of whose neck is ascertainable, the complete vessels might have been quite similar to that of Fig. 6. The necks were generally ribbed, but often sparingly.[8] The key to the type is that a symmetrical design has been 'pin-pointed' or incised (or both) onto the already symmetrical pattern of simple circular piercings: the process whereby art is superimposed on mere utility. This particular pitch of the process runs parallel with the introduction of *artfully* designed filters (Type III below), but would seem not to have survived much beyond the middle of the 9th century. All are reproduced here to permit the reader to see how Type A-II grows out of Type A-I.[9]

> Fig. 7-a, b, c. All from the same locus (Pits, pp. 69-71) and all datable to 8th-early 9th century.

> Fig. 7-d. From a locus the contents of which are discussed in Pits, p. 74, n. 34; and FEPR '68-I, p. 84. The candelabra-effect is unique, if intentional, in the iconography of this period. 9th century.

III. Early 'decorative' filter. The group represents the first known attempt of the Egyptian filter as decoration as opposed to filter as utility. There can be no doubt that it was so conceived because unlike groups A-I and A-II, the design 'hooks onto' the vessel rather than being smoothly joined to it (almost a continuing curve of the shoulder) as can be seen most strikingly in Figs. 1 and 2. Further, these decorative filters are concave, and are made of the Qena/Ballas white clay, which because of impurities can fire into tints ranging from the ecru to the slightly grey and greenish. But all the vessels are thin-walled, as compared to those of red or buff-brown clays. Although our earliest dated examples are without necks at all, two slightly later ones indicate that the filter was, of course, made separately and placed *along* the neck of the vessel, which itself sometimes carried an epigraphic or abstract incised external design.[10] Generally, these vessels tended to have thick, flat bases to compensate for the relative thinness of the body proper.

In the interesting vessel shown in Fig. 8 the lost filter was placed approximately half-way along the neck, and sufficient of the *spring* remains to assume it was concave. (The placement of the filter can be checked in its photograph in Pits, pl. XV-3.) Though there is no external incised decoration, there is a slight ridging at the shoulder-neck jointure to relieve the austerity. It was found in the same locus as Fig. 6, and can be assumed as being of the 8th century. (Kelsey Museum: Reg. No. 68-10-13)

A. OPEN-WORK WITH SURFACE SCRATCHING. That such fine and strong designs should evolve so quickly remains something of a mystery. Two factors distinguish this group: fine, large fully open-worked designs, and sufficient width of the surface lines of the design to permit additional decorative scratching. The technique has been noted by Olmer (pl. LXXIX-A), but he was unable to attribute it to any particular era (Olmer, p. 105). On

---

[8] Ancillary, fig. 5. This is the neck of Fig. 7-c herein.

[9] Another interesting variant can be seen in FEPR '68-I, pl. XXVII-a, second from left, bottom row. The context was 9th century.

[10] The latter stylistic can be seen on vessels of the same clay, of the same date, and all equally thin-walled; cf. Pits, pl. XV-2, 8 and 9; and Fustat-Arts, p. 191. Some of these vessels had plain and/or stepped finials on the handles.

archaeological grounds we are rather certain, that the origin of the type is definitely pre-Tulunid.

Pl. I-b   An incomplete filter, and one lacking any neck. But it is large and definitely concave. It was found in the estopped pit which contained the famous lustered glass goblet containing the name of Abd al-Samad b. Ali, grand-uncle of Harun al-Rashid and governor of Egypt in 155 A.H.[11] *Pace* Olmer, the design would seem at best anepigraphic. 8th century.

Pl. I-c   Again our example is incomplete and lacks a neck; but it is an almost exact duplicate of Olmer, pl. LXXIX-A. Because of its find-spot and its decorative technical resemblance to the filter in Pl. 1-b, it can be dated analogously, as can that of Olmer. Here the epigraphic possibility seems clearer, and we may have an orthographic variant of the term "*al-'izz*," "glory." The object has been published and its find-spot discussed, FEPR '65-II, fig. 2-b. 8th century.

Fig. 9.   A very fine leaf-form filter, attached some distance below the rim of the vessel. The interior of the leaf is 'opened-up' for practicality but not so much as to deny sufficient surface for short and elongated scratched decor. The filter was found in a partially, but not wholly disturbed, pit whose other contents included sufficient glass and pottery evidence to point to 9th-10th century dating. Stylistically one would put this filter in the earlier sequence of the locus: 9th century.

Fig. 10.   A direct, larger variation of Fig. 9. The design is definitely V-shaped. Inside the incipient triangle is a leaf form bounded by two winding vine forms (part of one is missing). Broad and narrow circles connect the design elements and the whole pattern to the inner neck of the vessel. Most of the surface of the filter is scratched with some pin-pointing of the leaf-form. Externally the neck is incised twice with a rectangular register of abstract design, in the spirit of that of the white-ware ewer illustrated in Pits, pl. XV-8. Among the associated evidence from the same find-spot as this filter, was a very fine small Samarra lustre bowl. Again we would assign this object to the 9th century.

B. V-SHAPED LATTICING. The same characteristics of clay and filter placement obtain here as for the previous type. But now there is a diminution towards the complete disappearance of any scratching of the surfaces which make up the pattern. The designs are so simple and strong that they need no further embellishment to call attention to themselves.

Pl. 1-d   This filter has been published and discussed in Ancillary, fig. 7-b. The lattice is composed of a triangle within a triangle, all surfaces of which have incised

---

[11] The contents of the particular pit are fully discussed in FEPR '65-I, passim and Fustat-Arts, p. 191. The two white-ware pitchers to be seen in Pits, pl. XV-8 and Fustat-Arts, p. 191 came from the same source, proving how early these thin-walled, beautifully shaped vessels were in every day use in Islamic Egypt. They did not appear in any of the pre-700 A.D. strata of the various cuts into the streets of Fustat; this should be significant for the pottery profile of post-Classical Egypt, cf. Numismatics.

<table>
<tr><td></td><td>parallel lines along their lengths. The side panels are not attached by larger or smaller rings, as in type A-III-A, but by incipient fleurons, here a little too hesitant in expression to be as successful as those in Fig. 11 and Pl. II-a below. As all of the other objects from the same undisturbed find-spot can with confidence be put before 900, we may assume a 9th century dating for this filter, and, considering the developmental nature of the next two examples, one would put it around the middle of that century.</td></tr>
<tr><td>Fig. 11.</td><td>Here is the simple diamond lattice with fully articulated fleuron shapes in the side panels. Two sets of two parallel scratched lines along the lengths of the V conclude the surface manipulation. The filter is placed rather high along the neck of the one-handled vessel which lacks a body. The find-spot suggests a Tulunid dating, slightly later than Pl. I-d, slightly earlier than Pl. II-a, because of the development of the lattice. We would suggest a date 850-900.</td></tr>
<tr><td>Pl. II-a</td><td>This filter has been published and the contents of its find-spot fully explained, *Pits*, fig. 9. It is the development of the lattice which is interesting in that it was possibly the model for the Fatimid lattices cited by Olmer, pls. XII-C and XVII-C. The simple diamonds of Fig. 11 have had their interstices broadened to give an effect of two arrow-heads and this one aspect relates our filter to Olmer's, pl. XLVIII-C. However his side-panels lack our finished, lace-like fleurons. There are traces of the upper parts of a possibly Kufic inscription incised externally on the neck.[12] On the whole, one would place it after Fig. 11 and before the Fatimid filter stylistics triumphed. Early 10th century.</td></tr>
</table>

C. TRIANGLE LATTICE. It could be that this type might have had a parallel development with the V-lattice. Now the triangle is absolute, allowing for *three* side panels for jointure with the band which attaches to the inner side of the neck.

<table>
<tr><td>Pl. II-b</td><td>The filter is slightly chipped, but the design is so symmetrical as to be almost rigid. The large inner triangle is subdivided by another triangle, and the resulting four inner triangles are each defined by a thin-walled triangle. Each outer panel is composed of two intersecting wide-surfaced roundels, each with a triangular center abutting the large inner triangle, and the intersecting roundels are hinged to the defining outer band by a thin-walled triangle. What interests one in addition to the obvious triumph of the triangle, is that the surface of the roundels and that of the inner large triangle are scratched with lines and dots, a technique which throws us back into the world of A-III-A. But the disciplined division of the design points forward to a certain Fatimid technical rigour. It is then recidivist and anticipatory; but those strongly articulated thin-walled triangles would seem to be the stronger</td></tr>
</table>

---

[12] For an example of the complete inscription on the neck of a filter bottle, cf. Pits, fig. 6 which is from the same source as Fig. 6, herein, hence 8th century. The example from Pits, presently in the Kelsey Museum (Reg. No. 68-10-7), has a simple finial on the handle.

element. As the filter was a surface find, stylistics are crucial. It is concave in profile, as can be seen in Ancillary, fig. 4-a. Ca. 900.[13]

Fig. 12.   The inner and outer aspects of this filter have been published (FEPR '65-II, fig. 6-c and Ancillary, fig. 4-b), but only now together. Once again we have a beautiful enunciation of both triangle and panels. The latter are simply thin-walled vine or fleuron elements, whilst the former is a pre-echo of those flat panels with a sort of jumbled mock Kufic slashing. It is this last quality which distinguishes our example from Olmer, pl. XLVIII-B, whose center is a fuller, aery repeat of the panel motif. (Our center is more in the spirit of Olmer, pl. LXXVIII-A.) Externally the neck has a not unusual inscription band, but it is also elegantly ribbed so as to call attention to the placement of the filter and the tapering of the neck. Though it lacks a body, the neck and filter attest the high artistic and technical achievement of the pre-Fatimid ceramist in this genre. The find-spot would indicate a 9th-early 10th century dating, and for reasons similar to those relating to Pl. II-b, we would opt for a dating ca. 900.

D. QUADRANT LATTICE.   The idea is simplicity itself; the difficulty is seeing it developing from the V and triangle lattices, or having it evolve simultaneously with them. Like all the examples in the broad category of A-III, these are concave and are placed between the rim and the neck-shoulder jointure.

Pl. II-c   Though the filter is incomplete, the full design can be ascertained. The design area is divided into four, and the division surfaces have double parallel lines incised. Each quadrant is carved into an apparent double fleuron, or two fleurs-de-lys with a shared section. There is a certain verve in the cutting, but no symmetrical certainty; withal there is nothing remotely comparable in Olmer. The piece has been published (FEPR '68-II, fig. 8) and the contents of its find-spot discussed. 9th-10th century.

Pl. II-d   Two motifs are at work in this filter: in opposite quadrants there are a series of triangular holes in lines of diminishing number: in the other two a design of slashes which is balanced even though it appears random, perhaps an incipient floral motif is intended. The object has been published Ancillary, fig. 6-d), and from evidence associated with it we can assign it to the 9th-10th century.

E. LATTICE IN PARALLEL REGISTERS.   This group is of compelling interest in that one motif, the lyre or heart shaped cutting, clearly stems from the spirit of Samarra-C stucco decoration.[14] So pervasive was this style that we find it obtaining in so utilitarian a category

---

[13] Thus we would amend the dating proposed in Ancillary, p. 10 and n. 19, opting now for ca. 900 rather than 800 A.D.

[14] For the clearest analysis and illustration of this stucco development, cf. K.A.C. Creswell, *Early Muslim Architecture*, II (Oxford: 1940) pp. 234-242, 287f. and pls. 52-58 and 72-75. For the local expression in the wood and stucco of the Mosque of Ibn Tulun, cf. ibid., pp. 343ff. and pls. 101-114. The application

as the filter, whose decorations to date have not seemed to parallel motifs from other artistic pursuits. There can be no thematic doubt that this group is firmly Tulunid, and the archaeological evidence corroborates Olmer's surmise (pl. XLVIII). However none of our examples duplicates his lovely circular band about the central lattice.

Pl. III-a/Fig. 13. This filter has been published: FEPR '58-I, fig. 15 and its find-spot discussed therein. Suffice it here to note the elegant ribbing of the neck, the placement towards the rim, and the incised abstract design external, comparable to those on Figs. 10 and 14. The central register of the lattice has a symmetrical abstract cut design, as though striving for the beveled effect. The outer registers are each composed of a simple fleuron, or a roughened version of the fleur-de-lys. 9th-10th century.

Fig. 14. Two of the motifs in the central register are similar to those in that of Olmer, pl. XLVIII-A. As our sample is broken, we cannot be certain of the composition of the one side register, but the other would indicate a more open design (of circles or vine elements) on either side of a flat uncut asymmetrical surface, itself duplicated in the Olmer example. The filter profile is concave and sufficient of the side exists to ascertain a placement along the neck of the vessel. Associated finds point to a date rather early in the 10th century.

Pl. III-b This filter has been published: FEPR '65-I, fig. 3a. Within the category it is something of a *chef d'oeuvre*: The central register is a "repeat variation" of the Samarra-C element, while the side panels are strongly enunciated pierced roundels on either side of an uncut elliptical shield. The centers of the roundels are furthered *filtered* with smaller sets of circles and the entire composition is anchored to the outer rim of the lattice by very light filigree work. These side panels take up elements encountered singly in the patterns of the V and triangular lattices. It is incomplete and there is no indication of where it would have been placed vis-à-vis the neck of the vessel. Further, it is anamalous in that its profile is flat rather than concave. However, by virtue of its design elements and artifacts associated with its find-spot (most particularly the cut and tonged glass to be seen in FEPR '65-I, figs. 4a-c), we feel confident that it is pre-Fatimid, indeed that it was made sometime before 950 A.D.

Pl. III-c/Fig. 15. A beautiful variant with four parallel panels: the inner two attempting the beveled effect and reminiscent of the motif in Pl. III-a and Fig. 13; the outer ones duplicating those in Fig. 14. The profile is a bit flat, but the placement is towards the neck. Externally there is the abstract incised design in the spirit of those of Figs. 10 and 13: a design bordered above by a single ribbing and below by a two-step telescoping. The filter has been published

---

and later development of the style is best surveyed in Richard Ettinghausen, "The 'Beveled Style' in the post-Samarra Period," *Archaeologia Orientalia in Memoriam Ernst Herzfeld*, New York (1952), pp. 72-83.

(FEPR '65-I, fig. 3 d); again on stylistics and shape we would place it before the Fatimid canon of filter design. Before 950 A.D.

F. PARALLEL LINE LATTICING. Stylistically this type may be out of strict rotation, but its very simplicity makes it something of a "rogue" within the pre-Fatimid lattice categories. However, it precedes and may be the prototype for the open-work lattices of the Fatimid period and after; cf. Olmer, pls. XXI and XXII.

> Fig. 16. A very rough and simple design of meshing triangles aligned between parallel lines. The limit of the design is not marked, not even by a simply incised circle. The profile is rather flat, but the placement is clearly along the neck rather than at the jointure of neck and shoulder. This filter was found in the same pit as Fig. 9, but a meter above. One may with safety assign it a dating of ca. 900 A.D.

IV. Hatch-work surfaces. This is a very broad group, which gains a certain unity because of two criteria; the filter is placed along the neck of the vessel, and a good deal of the design surface, i.e. the part left by the filter itself, is emphasized by incised hatching. The designs themselves may be "flat" geometrical, lattice geometrical, or zoomorphic. All of these types set the scene for the Fatimid "renascence," and all would seem eventually to end up convex in profile and placed at the jointure of the neck and the shoulder of the vessel. Most can be placed securely in the 10th century, and constitute a transitional artistic thrust which might be termed "continuing Tulunid."[15] There is no external decoration, and ribbing and stepping practically disappear. Olmer published only two examples with hatch work incising (pls. LVIII-E and LXXVIII-E), and assigns both to the Tulunid period, though he says nothing about the placement of the filter. Thus, a stricter archaeology helps toward a somewhat clearer chronology. Because of the *possible* contemporaneity of Type A-V (infra), the problem becomes one of discrimination of design elements. At the present pitch of research, there is no guarantee that one or other of the filter designs did not continue into the early 11th century.

A. FLAT GEOMETRICAL. This group is best described as having more "surface" than filter, per se. Artistically it is something of a come-down after the bravura of the lattice filters of Type A-III.

> Pl. III-d/Fig. 17. The pattern is fully geometrical but not strictly symmetrical. Six flat polygonal surfaces, all with incised hatchwork, predominate, with a central pattern of six triangles attending a central one. These latter and the interstices at the rim between the polygons all have slashed openings, which may or may not be pseudoepigraphic. The entire composition is incorporated by two incised circular lines. As can be seen in Pl. III-d, the filter is placed towards the rim of the vessel and the handle has a simple finial.[16] A

---

[15] Ancillary, p. 15 f.

[16] A similar handle can be seen in Pits, fig. 6. The filter is missing but it was placed comparably to Fig. 17 herein; but the former vessel had an incised inscription external.

rather fine fragment of a 10th century Chinese procelain bowl (FEPR '71-II, fig. 15) found with this filter in a generally undisturbed portion of a sanitation canal would indicate a comparable dating for the filter. 10th century.

B. LATTICE GEOMETRICAL. Here more openings are attempted, giving a lattice-like effect, therefore reducing the areas to bear hatch-work.

Fig. 18.   A partial filter, but sufficient remains to give the sense of the pattern. A central rectangle of three panes is attached at the sides by fleuron-type openings to a comparatively wide circular register. The inner rectangle contains sets of three vertical and horizontal slashings in the middle panel, with zig-zag lines in the bounding panels. These latter would seem to be the incipient striated zig-zag border of the Fatimid decorative canon.[17] The circular band contains (six?) asymmetrical flat surfaces with incised hatchwork, each banded by a leaf-like fleuron on one side and a diamond opening on the other. Again there is the single incised line enveloping the entire design. The filter would appear to have been almost concave in profile, and placed along the neck of the vessel. Though the locus evidence is not conclusive, on stylistics alone we would assign this filter to the 10th century.

C. ZOOMORPHIC HATCHWORK. The animals are drawn so that the major outlines of the body become slashed holes. The rest of the surface of the body is left unincised. The surround of the animal is then slashed in various ways, and the remaining surface is covered with incised hatchwork. The model is clearly Olmer, pl. LVIII-E, which he assigns to the Tulunid period. All considerations are complicated by the fact that filters with zoomorphic hatchwork are both concave and convex and are placed both along the neck and at the neck-shoulder jointure. Further it is difficult to specify the species of the quadruped, but our three examples are parallels of Olmer's. The Fatimid zoomorphic filters are more specific as to species.

Pl. IV-a/Fig. 19.   This filter has been published and its find-spot discussed; Pits, fig. 8. The design is far more straightforward than Olmer's, though the head is missing here. The filter was placed mid-way along the neck. 9th-10th century.

Fig. 20.   Here there can be no doubt as to shift of placement and profile. The head of the quadruped more nearly resembles that of Olmer. There is a slight ridging external, a characteristic not common to the filters of Type A-IV. The analysis is further complicated by the presence in the pit where the filter was found of a copper coin of the Abbasid governor Al-Sari b. al-Hakam (200-205 A.H./815-820 A.D.). However, as there were no decorative filters of the 9th century placed at the neck-shoulder jointure and none was convex in profile, we would place this zoomorphic filter in the 10th century.

[17]Fat. Fil., p. 42.

Pl. IV-b/Fig. 21. This filter has been published, FEPR '65-I, fig. 3b. It is convex
in profile and is at the jointure of neck and shoulder. It was found in the
same context as Pl. XXII-b. For the same reasons as noted for Fig. 20,
we suggest a 10th century dating.

V. Filigreed effect. This is perhaps a debatable grouping, more dependent on archaeological evidence than on design factors. The very tight filigree pattern in full domination
cannot be associated with filters placed elsewhere than at the neck-shoulder jointure.
However, as an *element* of the design, it does occur in filters of the 10th century, some
of which are definitely placed along the neck, a reality which we have seen dates the pre-
Fatimid range. It represents a thin slicing into the body of the filter, as distinct from the
slash patterns we will see below. The slicing can have the effect of continuous "runny"
lines, or rather closely meshed but asymmetrical narrow gauge openings. The overall patterns are of the large geometrical panels which may also contain, even attend, slash work
and the zoomorphic. The placement of the filter varies; and the entire group must be
seen as both anticipating the Fatimid canon and continuing parallel with the establishment
of that canon.

A. FILIGREE GEOMETRICAL. The close lace-like filigree attends the more dramatic
slash portions, rather like a persistent sub-melody. But these filters are clearly different
from those where the slash patterns are the all-in-all of the full design.

Pl. IV-c/Fig. 22. This filter has been published (FEPR '64, fig. 3 f); here we can
see that it is convex and placed at the jointure of neck and shoulder. The
filigree section is below a full horizontal panel of pseudo-Kufic slash work
and on either side of a vertical half-panel of the same. The filigree section
is continuous and reminiscent of the Greek letter *pi*. Simple lattice triangles complete the composition. The filter was found beneath the stone
flooring of an early Fatimid domicile, hence we assign it to the late 10th
century.

Fig. 23. A very interesting medley of elements; a square central area with incurving
sides, composed itself of three panels—a central one with slash pattern,
the two bounding ones of filigree "runny" lines about a centered slash
motif. The remainder of the filter surface thus becomes four ellipses, of
which two are of the slash pattern, the others contain simple slashed parallel
lines. Its profile is convex, and it is placed at the neck-shoulder jointure.
There is a rib-like break in the profile externally. This filter was found
in the same locus as that of Fig. 17 and Pl. III-d, whose profile is concave
and whose placement is along the neck. Hence during the 10th century,
the profile and placement become less certain guides to the dating. As
has been averred, in such cases the archaeological evidence becomes more
telling. 10th century.

Pl. IV-d/Fig. 24. Compositionally this filter returns us to the world of the V-shaped
lattice, type A-III-B. Within the V we have a division into two wide and

one narrow panels. The wide ones contain a slash pattern of what can be taken as the stenographic motif for the term "baraka," separated by upright parallel slashes.[18] As these are separated by the narrow filigree motif, they may be construed as aspiring to "mirror" one another, a device more prominently associated with *tiraz* bands in Islamic textiles. Bounding the large central area are two arcs of straight filigree. Though the neck is incomplete, there can be little doubt that the profile is concave. This filter has been published (Ancillary, text fig. 6b); the dating from material associated with its find-spot is admittedly uncertain. It is more in the 10th century tradition, but the presence of the "baraka" motif places it within the Fatimid portion of that century. The filigree and the concavity look backward, as it were; hence one feels safer in attributing the filter to the latter half of the 10th century: a true transition piece.

Fig. 25. This filter has a design of three parallel panels: a wide central one of slash elements, probably of the "baraka" shortening, bounded on either side by arc-ed filigree panels. It has the same inspiration as Olmer, pl. LXXVIII-E, though the latter has a central double panel of mirrored "baraka" symbols. Our example is considerably smaller in radius. It is convex in profile and placed at the neck-shoulder jointure. It was a surface find, so its dating is problematical. Because of the filigree work, we would place it in the last part of the 10th century.

Pl. V-a/Fig. 26. The design of this filter has been published: Ancillary, text, fig. 5b. It is a dramatic improvement on the previous sample, but in the same style. Here the central panel is of a beautiful "baraka" symbol repeated thrice between doubled parallel lines. The curving vertical is elegantly toothed; the filigree boundaries are more pronounced but still arc-shaped. Ours is of the same general type as Olmer, pls. LXXVIII-D, and E but neither the uprights nor the filigree are so beautifully executed as our example. The filigree again leads us to put the example in the latter half of the 10th century.

B. ZOOMORPHIC MOTIFS WITH FILIGREE ELEMENTS. The perfect example of this category is to be found in Olmer, pl. LXII-A. It is utterly free of any slash elements and the filigree is so surely executed that one has a sense of design. As with the animals in the hatch-work category, A-IV-C, the body of the animal is generally left free of any surface decoration. The unreserved areas are rather hastily composed of filigree and slash motifs, but not in such a way as to give a sense of symmetry. Though our first two examples are unique, neither has the artistic finish of Olmer, pl. LXII-A.

---

[18] This possibly symbolic device is often seen on Fatimid ceramics; cf. *La Ceramique Egyptienne de l'Epoque Musulmane* (Basel: 1922), pls. 20, 22, 60, 71 and 85; and for a debased variant, cf. Bahgat and Massoul, op. cit., pl. A-9. It can also be seen in Fatimid lustre glass; cf. C. J. Lamm, *Mittelalterliche Glaser und Steinschnittarbeiten aus dem Nahen Osten*, II (Berlin: 1930), tafs. 34-8 and 37-10. A fragment of lustre glass with an identical repeat pattern was discovered in the ARCE excavations in 1978, Reg. No. 78-9-1, presently in the American University in Cairo.

Fig. 27.   Here is a quadruped with long ears and a short tail. It is in position of stride, passant to the left. Between the ears and again between the front legs are slash lines but not nearly of either the elegance or violence we have noted heretofore. The filigree elements are very thinly sliced and demonstrate no palpable pattern. Indeed, the seeming vigour of the animal is set off by the imprecision of the rest of the design. As the profile is concave and the placement along the neck, we would place the filter in the 10th century. However, the find-spot was slightly disturbed (under the fallen vault of a storage room hewn in the *gabal*); and it was found with another filter (Fig. 44) with a slash pattern, but glazed, an almost certain sign of a Fatimid atelier. It would seem, then, more judicious to assign this example to the latter part of that century.

Fig. 28.   This filter is incomplete, but stylistically it compares easily with Fig. 27 in that we have a quadruped with little surface decoration, and both slash and filigree elements. However, this animal is short-eared and with no definition of left and right front and rear legs. The tail is awkwardly indicated, but might be long and probably bushy. The filigree is almost lattice-like, and there is one "baraka" slash section. The profile was concave and placed along the neck of the vessel. Materials associated with the filter in its undisturbed find-spot allow a 10th century dating.[18a]

Category B. The Fatimid Period
ca. 1000 - ca. 1200 A.D.

In his strictly stylistic analysis, Olmer seems not to have made a mistake in his assignments to the Fatimid period. This was the high-point of inventiveness, when filter designs approached the exuberant variety found in stucco, wood and ceramic objects. Certain design elements, clearly originating in the previous period, were now elegantly finished and incorporated in what can only be termed the Fatimid "canon" of filters; while newer ones were so briskly syncopated as to achieve an "air" immediately identifiable as Fatimid. Novel, more ebullient vessel shapes were introduced, and a taste for glaze and external lustre finish becomes evident. As there was no diminution of architectural inventiveness throughout the

---

[18a] After this manuscript was completed, the author received information from Dr. George Bass about the cargo in the shipwreck at Serce Liman, Turkey. A number of filter vessels were found, and Dr. Bass kindly supplied photographs and drawings of the more important ones. Three examples were clearly of Category A, more particularly of Types A-V-A and A-V-B herein. All had the filter placed *along* the neck with design elements appropriate to our chronological ordering before 1000 A.D. However the numismatic evidence points to a dating within the first quarter of the 11th century. None of our Type B-I ("continuing" patterns with the filter at the junction of neck and shoulder) was found. As these materials have not been completely analyzed and but one published (G. F. Bass and F. H. van Doorninck, Jr., "An 11th century shipwreck at Serce Liman, Turkey," *IJNAUE* (1978), fig. 10), the only route to reconciling the two "field," as distinct from "stylistic," datings is to consider a longer "inventory life" for our Type A-V. The same seems to hold true for the glass and glazed ceramics, all of which *appear* to us to be clearly 10th rather than 11th century on the basis of undisturbed loci at Fustat.

era or in the quality of the attendant decoration, it is difficult to assign strict chronology within the period. The same is true archaeologically, though the associative numismatic evidence of undisturbed loci containing filters pointed more to the 11th than to the 12th century.[19]

The filters are now all convex in profile, and, the height and width of the neck notwithstanding, they were all placed at the jointure of the neck and shoulder of the vessel. Both the walls of the vessel and the thickness of the filter itself tend to be thinner than those of the 9th-10th century, and there is little emphasis on external ribbing.

Three design categories originated earlier in the 10th century, but surely carried on well into the 11th on the strength of our archaeological evidence. These may be seen as distinct from but contributive to the grander Fatimid "canon," though unlike the latter, it is almost certain they did not continue into the 12th century. Thus it is incumbent upon us to assign two broad categorizations to the filters of the period: continuing and canonical, albeit the latter is statistically and artistically overwhelming.

I. "Continuing" patterns. These are visually kin to the filters in groups A-V-A and A-V-B, but with differences subtle enough to suggest development or archaeological evidence to permit 11th century dating. The most usual vessel shape is that of Fig. 29, which is really a 9th-10th century shape but where the filter has slipped down to the neck-shoulder jointure.[20] (Compare this shape with those of Fig. 8 herein and Fat. Fil., fig. 2 to achieve a sense of the subtle shift of vessel shape and filter placement.) The filter space is rather small.

A. FILIGREE RADIAL.   Though here the filigree would seem to be freed of slash elements, as obtained with filters of group A-V, a hook-like slash motif has evolved, lending itself to radiating and radiant patterns, but without affording any but a slap-dash effect.[21] Two examples from the ARCE finds have been published (Ancillary, figs. 4-c and d; Pls. V-b and c herein), and three more bear discussion:

> Fig. 30.   A photograph of this filter has been published (Ancillary, fig. 3-b), but with the drawing and profile we can appreciate its placement and the hook-like motif. It is clear, too, that the profile was definitely convex and that because the filter space was comparatively narrow the body of the vessel ballooned out correspondingly, something of a break with the more usual vessel shape. (Neither of the two other published examples with radial pattern and hook motif has a comparable ballooning out; cf. Ancillary, text figs. 4-c and d.)

---

[19] This point is most cogently argued in FEPR '65-II, pp. 82 f. and Fat. Fil., pp. 37 f.

[20] This vessel was found in 1972 in the upper reach of pit B-D in XXI'-5; cf. FEPR '72-I, Plan I. The contents of this pit have been discussed in Numismatics, p. 172, from which it can be deduced that the filter vessel is of the 10-11th century. (Reg. No. 72-10-34 in the Ashmolean Museum, Oxford.)

[21] That an over-all filigree effect can be pleasing see Olmer, pl. XXI-D. He would have this example Ayyubid (p. 34), but it would seem to be definitely of the 10th-11th century on the basis of its kinship to his pl. LXXIX-E, which he eschews dating, but which is again 10th century, since the filter profile is concave.

This filter was found in the same locus as that of Pl. V-a and Fig. 26; late 10th-early 11th century.

Fig. 31.   This undistinguished filter is a surface find, but its similarity to those in Ancillary, text figs. 4-c and d (Pls. V-b and c herein), and the central motif of Olmer, pl. LXXIX-C gives one no hesitancy in placing it in this grouping and assigning it the same chronology. Though badly rendered, there is the same hook-motif, convexity of profile and placement at the neck-shoulder jointure. Late 10th-early 11th century.

Fig. 32.   Though there is no true symmetry in the execution, one has here the dominance of the hook motif. A novelty is in the central raised convex nodule or button, an element one generally associates with the post-Fatimid filters. That it lacks distinction is obvious when compared with the central filigree of Olmer, pl. LXXIX-E. In its find-spot there were many fragments of FFS pottery, which when added to its distinct complexity of profile and placement, permit an 11th century dating, more likely the first half.

B. DOMINANT SLASH. We have seen the appearance of this design element emerging in the Tulunid period in groups A-IV and A-V, but there associated with other elements or technical aspects (profile and placement) which told more strongly when seeking a chronological sequence. Slash filters with all kinds of ancillary motifs (pseudo-epigraphic, hatch-work, striated zig-zag lines, etc.) were manufactured in abundance well past the threshold of the 11th century, as evidenced by their association with canonical filters in undisturbed loci.[22] Exceptionally some were glazed. Artistically the type never achieved any distinction, though the vessel containing the filter may have been interesting either in its shape or its external decor. However, the variations are so manifold, as though pure whim dictated, that impeccable categorization is almost impossible. Thus, we have opted for broad geometrical differences and a miscellaneous group which fits stylistically if not organically. To avoid costly repetition, we have followed certain rules in our choice of illustration herein:

a.   If a filter exactly duplicates one in Olmer, we list it in the appended Table of Finds; or else illustrate it by photo or drawing should its external decoration or placement dictate;

b.   If a drawn pattern has been published, but not the filter profile, we furnish herein a photo of the pattern and the profile;

c.   If a filter pattern has been published as a photo, we furnish a drawing of the drawn pattern and the profile herein;

d.   If both drawn pattern and profile have been published, we herein supply a photo of the pattern.

1. Central triangle. The geometry is achieved by sets of slash lines alone or in pairs, the jointure arcs are left plain or simply decorated. The central triangle is then treated in a manner ranging from the simple inchoate to the overly slashed with the ancillary motif

---

[22] The explanation in Fat. Fil., p. 39 f and notes, holds good for the majority of slash pattern filters found subsequent to 1966.

noted above. The profiles are almost all convex and placement is at the jointure of neck and shoulder of the vessel.

Fig. 33.   While the neck of the vessel is expressively strong, the filter is simplicity itself. Among the associated finds were glass weights of the Fatimid Caliphs al-Hakim and al-Mustansir. 11th century.

Pl. V-d/Fig. 34.   A very simple attempt at a striated zig-zag line. Other materials from the locus strengthen assigning the filter to the 11th century.

Fig. 35.   This is comparable to Fat. Fil., fig. 1-e, with again a short single rough striated line. It was found with Fig. 38 and the archaeological context puts it in the 11th century.

Pl. VI-a/Fig. 36.   Pattern published in Fat. Fil., fig. 1-d. The contents of its find-spot were mostly Fatimid, but of uncertain date. However, by analogy with other filters of this type found in proven 11th century contexts, we so date this example.

Pl. VI-b   A filter vessel, complete except for its handle. Both its drawn pattern and profile have been published (Fat. Fil., fig. 2). Its locus yielded no other material, but by analogy we can date it to the 11th century.

Pl. VI-c/Fig. 37.   The drawn pattern has been published (Fat. Fil., fig. 1-b). As with the last example, two short striated lines identify the pattern. Though a surface find, by analogy it can be assigned to the 11th century.[23]

Fig. 38.   Found in the same locus as Fig. 35, and easily dated to the 11th century. The departure is in the suavity of the neck, with very finely defined external ribbing below the rim and the balancing break between the shoulder and the body proper: an altogether exceptional shape for a filter vessel during the Fatimid period.

Fig. 39.   This filter exhibits the shift to the three zig-zag striated lines in the central triangle. The neck reminds one of that of Fig. 38, but lacks the rather elegant ribbing. This was found in the exposed pit of a trial trench which contained three other Fatimid filters: Pls. X-a, XIII-b and XVI-d. All are of the 11th century.

Pl. VI-d/Fig. 40.   One of twelve Fatimid filters found in a single pit in 1965, the contents of which have been fully studied in Fat. Fil., p. 38 (therein referred to as Pit 2), and which have been assigned to the 11th century. The slash elements can be seen to get rather wide, reducing the central triangle. The filter pattern has been published.

Pl. VII-a/Fig. 41.   This filter is from the same find-spot as the above and has been published (Fat. Fil., fig. 1-a). Here the slash pattern practically obliterates the sense of the central triangle. 11th century.

Pl. VII-b/Fig. 42.   The triangle almost reasserts itself. The circle in the center would

---

[23] An almost exact duplicate of this pattern was found in 1964. It is definitely 11th century: cf. Reg. No. 64-4-76 in the Typological Table of Registered Filters herein.

seem to defeat the utility of the filter, but as we have seen the nodular "button" in Fig. 32, the element might have been employed here. Though a surface find, we may by analogy with other similarly styled filters put it in the 11th century. The drawn pattern can be seen in Fat. Fil., fig. 1-f.

Fig. 43.   Here a newer variation appears: a triangle within a triangle, or almost so. The small area left for decoration is given over to thinly sliced zig-zag lines and small holes. The evidence from the find-spot is indecisive, but would seem to be more generally Fatimid than earlier. Also, by analogy we can place this sample within the 11th century grouping.

Fig. 44.   All the external surfaces of the vessel are covered with a tawny brown vitreous glaze. The central triangle carries two filigree-like squiggly slicings. The neck and body are comparatively thin-walled and the vessel had a single handle. It was found with Fig. 27 and helps to date both to the very end of the 10th century. In our opinion, the glazing makes it almost certain that it is Fatimid.

Fig. 45.   Here the triangle is intensively "designed," but without any obvious design as such. It is comparable to Olmer, pl. LXXVIII-A, though it lacks the latter's three borders of striated zig-zag. The concavity of the profile is quite pronounced. The contents of its find-spot afforded no sharp chronological certainty, though the evidence speaks for the 10th century. The filters in Pl. IV-a and Figs. 50 and 51 were found with this example, and the latter in particular makes us opt for the late part of that century.

Pl. VII-c/Fig. 46.   This pattern has been published (FEPR '64, fig. 3-c) and is, like Fig. 45, comparable to Olmer, pl. LXXVIII-A, though without the borders. It was found below the paving within a secondary construction, which itself might be considered early Fatimid. Taking all the stylistic and dating arguments for this group into account, it would seem safe to assign this example to the last part of the 10th century.

Pl. VII-d   Both patterns and profile of this filter have been published (**Ancillary**, text fig. 6-a). There it was defined as possibly Tulunid, but a re-assessment of the contents of the find-spot (which included Pls. IV-b and XXII-b) and the adjacent undisturbed area, plus a consideration of the hook-motif on two of its three borders, would make it rather a late 10th-early 11th century model. The hook-motif as a border can be seen in Olmer, pl. LXXVIII-D, which he deems Tulunid, but which we see as being late 10th century. The motif is present again in Fig. 48, and since it is absent within the canonical series, we may assume it does not continue long into the 11th century.

Pl. VIII-a/Fig. 47.   A most interesting filter in that the inner triangle is subdivided into one large with slash motifs and three smaller ones with hatch-work scratched into the surface. The drawn pattern appears in Fat. Fil., fig. 3-b. There is a pronounced convexity of the profile. By analogy and consideration of the evidence from the find-spot, this filter may be assigned to the early 11th century.

2. Central quadrangle. Except that a true or quasi-quadrangular space dominates the pattern, the same rubrics as noted for the central triangle above obtain here.

Fig. 48.   This filter has been damaged, but sufficient remains to consider it as rough-hewn. Two narrow slashes define two sides of the quadrangle and the other sides consist of four smaller but wider slashes which take definition from the circularity of the full filter. The central quadrangle contained either filigree slice effects or pseudo-epigraphic elements. A local imitation of a Chinese porcelain bowl of the 10th century was found in the undisturbed fill which contained this filter.[24] Thus it would be prudent to consider this sample as emanating from the late 10th century.

Fig. 49.   Two narrow and two wide slashes define an asymmetrical quadrangle, which contains indeterminate filigree-slice and slash motifs. Though an improvement on Fig. 48, the pattern cannot claim any artistic quality. The general shape of the vessel remains and the convexity of the filter recalls Fig. 44, though this example is unglazed. There is likewise the trace of a single handle. We would therefore argue a comparable dating: the very end of the 10th century.

Fig. 50.   This filter's central area is more truly a trapezoid than a filter. The two short adjacent sides are effected by double slashes, while the longer sides are each composed of a zig-zag striated line ending in a slash. This latter feature related our filter to those of Olmer, pls. LXXVIII-A and B. He would have these models in the Tulunid period, but because of the arguments cited relative to the filters in Pl. IV-a and Fig. 45 herein, found in the same locus as this one, we are prone to place it at the end of the 10th century. (An interesting variant in shape is the single ribbing external.)

Fig. 51.   A more regular quadrangle in the center, but with the same general characteristics of pattern of Fig. 50. The find-spot is the same as that of Fig. 50 (and of Pl. IV-a and Fig. 45), and the same reasoning obtains for placing this sample at the end of the 10th century.

Fig. 52.   A rather small filter with a finely designed symmetrical dominant quadrangle. The latter is divded into three panels horizontally, a hatch-work scratch pattern occupying the upper and lower sections, while the central one contains a somewhat indeterminate slice-and-slash motif. The quadrangle is anchored to the filter circle at its points with narrow intermediate connecting lines on each side. While the evidence from the find-spot was not conclusive, by analogy with the filters in Figs. 48-51, we would place this one at the end of the 10th century.

Pl. VIII-b/Fig. 53.   This filter has been published (Ancillary, text fig. 6-b). It is exactly the same as Fig. 52, except that the central panel of the quadrangle has perhaps more filigree-slice than slash elements. The intermediate contact lines are clearer. The evidence from the find-spot was chronologically

---

[24] Cf. FEPR '68-II, pl. XVIII-b and fig. 2.

equally inconclusive as that for Fig. 52, but by the same arguments we would assign this filter also to the end of the 10th century.

Fig. 54.　　One sees in this sample a variation within the pattern of Figs. 52 and 53 in that the central panel is an obvious pattern of almost parallel squiggly slice-lines, and that the contact lines of the other filters have here become the small ringlets which are so much a design element of the canonical filters. The locus of its discovery has been fully discussed elsewhere;[25] suffice it here to assign it a late 10th-early 11th century dating.

3. Central pentagon. An interesting development no doubt co-terminous with those slash filters with central triangles and quadrangles. Important, too, in that the central shape anticipates pentagonal designs within the Fatimid canon; cf. Olmer, pls. IX-A and C.

Fig. 55.　　Though our filter is incomplete, it is almost an exact duplicate of Olmer, pl. LXXVIII-C, with a central panel of thin sliced pseudo-epigraphic elements bounded by two trapezoidal panels with surface scratched hatching. Even the intermediate contact lines with the filter circle are similar. Though Olmer would have his example from the Tulunid era, we, by analogy with the filters with triangles and quadrangles, defined by slashes, would place ours at the end of the 10th century; and, on the basis of the find-spot, possibly of the early 11th century. It is an excellent example of the "continuing" filter pattern.

4. Miscellaneous dominant slash. As with all attempts at archaeological typology, some examples will fight exact categorization, though one element or two of the design pattern will indicate inclusion somewhere within the broad rubric. In the three following examples the strand of similarity is the slash motifs, though a true geometry is never quite achieved.

Pl. VIII-c　This is an "inclusive" filter, in that there is no "slashing off" of a central geometrical design area, which is in itself further subdivided or contains further slash patterning. There is a tripartite division: a central unsymmetrical rectangle with what appears to be pseudo-epigraphic slice elements, bounded by two arc panels containing the hook motif. This latter element relates the sample to Olmer, pl. LXXVIII-D, which he claims is Tulunid. The contents of the find-spot included quite a number of 10th century items,[26] but also three items of the 11th century: a glass *jeton* of al-Hakim, another of al-Mustansir, and a fragmentary canonical filter (Fig. 77). Thus it would seem judicious to assign this filter (whose drawn pattern and profile can be seen in FEPR '68-II, fig. 18-a) to the middle of the century, with its convex profile and placement arguing for a date sometime after 950 A.D. However, it is wiser to admit it as a 10th century typological enigma.

[25] Pit B-D in XXI'-5, cf. discussion in n. 20 supra. Fig. 29 herein is from the same locus.

[26] These include three pieces of 9th-10th century glass (Fustat-Glass, fig. 44 and FEPR '68-II, fig. 16 and pl. XXIII-b and c) as well as two "Fayyumi-type" bowls of the 10th century (ibid., figs. 17-a and b).

Pl. VIII-d The drawn pattern and profile of this filter has been published (Ancillary, text fig. 5-c). The comparatively short neck has a single rib external, this and the pattern recall the filters of Figs. 23 and 25 and Pls. IV-d and V-a. Again it is of the "inclusive" type, the pattern divided into three horizontal panels divided by striated zig-zag line which relates it in totality to Olmer, pl. LXXIX-D. As with his example, the upper and lower panels are mirrors of one another, an element we have seen earlier as associated with filigree filters. No doubt all three panels contained the stenographic "baraka" symbol. The find-spot would seem to have been disturbed, but the zig-zag dividers place this filter (and Olmer's) very close to the canonical series. Hence, we would differ with Olmer and place both his example and this at the Fatimid end of the 10th century.

Pl. IX-a The drawn pattern and profile have been published (Ancillary, text and fig. 5-a). An extraordinary and strange development out of the slash technique. A quatrefoil of open elliptical leaf shape dominates the inclusive pattern, the spine of each leaf shown as an elongated line growing out of a wider jagged, saw-tooth base. This is a clear but better sculpted derivative of the motif in Olmer, pl. LXVII-C, which is quadrangular in spirit rather than inclusive. Unlike the interstitial design which is scratched hatching, ours is composed of slash-work. It is difficult to determine whether the center circle was once closed by a nodular button. Once again the contents of the find-spot were chronogically inconclusive. However, since the spine shape is reminiscent of that of the lustre design on the external of Olmer's pl. A of his Introduction (no. 8577/167) which is clearly Fatimid, we sense that this element is more important than the slash pattern of the interstices, and opt for a late 10th century dating. Withal, like the previous two filters, it must be more truly seen as a chronological engima within the "continuing" series.

C. CENTRAL "KNITTING" PATTERN. This term is an adaptation of Olmer's explanation of the design, further analyzed in Fatimid Filters, p. 41. Because the pattern is accompanied by lustre painting external in one of his examples (Pl. A of his Introduction, no. 8577/167), he gives his samples a sure Fatimid dating. The barrette-like shape of the connecting lines, the fact that some examples are covered in a vitreous glaze, and that there is an attempt to define the knitting by a central zig-zag line strengthen the attribution. The natural development of the simple pattern was towards a "ruching" (complex knitting) effect which in turn resulted into a true *fleuronne*. The same rules for illustrating the Dominant Slash category apply here.

Fig. 56. The original vessel had one handle and was externally glazed a bright turquoise. The barrette effect is clear and the knitting is defined by a squiggly zig-zag line. It is a very good approximation to Olmer, pl. XLIV-A. The find-spot has been designated Pit 2. Since some find-spots for this type of filter contained evidence from the last decade of the 10th century, we may assume its genesis then (it is not at all anticipated in any of our groups previous to 1000 A.D.), but allowing its *floruit* after the turn of the century, to which date we assign this example.

Fig. 57.   The same as Fig. 56, except that the zig-zag line is discontinued. The vessel had a single handle. The find-spot also contained the canonical filters in Pl. XVII-d and XIX-b, allowing us to put this example into the early 11th century.

Pl. IX-b/Fig. 58.   This filter's drawn pattern has been published (Fat. Fil., fig. 3-c). Here there is pronounced discontinuity of the knitting line, and one can perhaps see an attempt at indicating ruching: if so, it is extremely rudimentary. The evidence from the find-spot was not conclusive, so we are forced by analogy with the group as a whole to suggest an 11th century date.

Fig. 59.   This is very much in the style of the filter in Pl. IX-b. The move towards ruching is more pronounced. As it was discovered in the *sibakh* layer there can be little absolute surety of date. But on analogy alone, we would place it in the 11th century.

Pl. IX-c/Fig. 60.   A very important piece, in that the external surface is lustred on a turquoise tin glaze, and thus falls into the Fatimid sequence of lustred filter vessels first noted by Olmer in Pl. A of his Introduction and discussed within that section. The filter pattern itself is in the spirit of the preceding two examples, and about as roughly executed. The lustre decoration would seem to be of reversed heart shaped leaves with a motley leaf-and-vine decor within.[27] The upper interstitial design cannot be comprehended, except that it is in reserve. This was a surface find, but by analogy with our other finds and by comparison with Olmer's example, we can safely assign it to the 11th century.

Pl. IX-d/Fig. 61.   This published filter (Fat. Fil., fig. 3-d) may be considered a failed effort at ruching, just as the following one is successful. However, it has a vitreous turqoise glaze external, which affords it a certain importance. As it was found in the *sibakh*, its date cannot be fixed with certainty; withal, by analogy with others of its type from more certainly dated loci, it would seem to emanate from the 11th century.

Pl. X-a/Fig. 62.   As can be seen from the published pattern (Fat. Fil., fig. 3-e), the central zig-zag line is quite distinctly scratched. The novelty is that there are two barrettes instead of the usual three on either side of the design. It is from the same find-spot as Fig. 39 and Pls. XVI-d and XIII-b; like them, it can be assigned to the 11th century.

Pl. X-b/Fig. 63.   The type reaches its *fluorit* in this superb pattern of two triangular motifs (cf. Fat. Fil., fig. 3-f): one of three elliptical leaf-forms with the

---

[27] This motif of the heart-shaped leaf with interior motival development can be gleaned from *La Ceramique Egyptienne* (in n. 18 supra), pls. 5-9, 12, 24, 63 and 66; Bahgat and Massoul, op. cit., pls. VIII-7 and XXXIII; and 'Abd al-Ra'uf Yusuf, *Khazafun min al-'asr al-fatimi wa asalibhum al-fanniyah* (Cairo: 1962), passim.

spines reminiscent of those of Pl. IX-a, and an oppositely sited one containing three knittings and zig-zag striated lines; all with a central shared circular center which might have been capped by a nodular button. With it was found an incomplete Fatimid bowl whose vitreous glazing (manganese and white) had a rippled effect. This would help to support what would otherwise be an analogical dating to the 11th century.

II. "Canonical" patterns. Any perusal of Olmer would demonstrate that this range of filter pattern was clearly the dominant and most varied in the history of the metier. There is a fineness and sureness of execution, with little of the impromptu which attends so much of the "continuing" range; an almost dictated symmetry of design, with a clear preference for the geometrical, or, at the very least, a sense of geometrical repeat; a zoomorphic and epigraphic ambient whose components are clearer in origin than that attempted in the 9th and 10th centuries; and a *pulling-together* of design elements which were rather fugitive in the immediately preceding category, e.g. the squiggly zig-zag becoming a more symmetrically integrated striated zig-zag line. Profile and placement remain as before; any novelty in the pattern itself must be viewed as a simple rearrangement or reordering of discrete design elements within the accepted rubric. [28]

A rough categorization was attempted in Fat. Fit. In general, it will be adhered to herein, though with amplification and further subdivision. The broadest divisions will be seen to be the geometrical, the zoomorphic, the epigraphic, and the miscellaneous. Chronologically, we can be certain of those filters described in Fat. Fil. (p. 38) as emanating from Pits 1 and 2. Some filters found after that publication and emanating from comparably secure loci, (viz. the seven filters in fig. 12 of Pits), and others which can be almost securely dated by analogy with these and those from Pits 1 and 2 will be assigned to the 11th century. But as noted in the introduction to this section, we can never be absolutely certain that the patterns were not continued, indeed continuously evolved, in the 12th century. Such a distraction must obtain when discussing the dating of surface finds.

The rules governing illustration of the canonical range will parallel those noted for the filters in the dominant slash category, B-1-B.

A. GEOMETRICAL

1. Circular inclusive patterns without border. These filters proceed from simple but varied mesh-patterns, through intricate star and star-and-knot patterns (Olmer's "etoile"), towards a distinctive geometrical flower design (Olmer's "fleuronne"). Olmer sees the mesh design without the striated border (pl. XXI) as being Ayyubid (op. cit., p. 34); but one was found with a definite Fatimid canonical example, so it would seem safer, unless noted to the contrary, to see most of the entire group, so easy to manufacture, as simply continuing into the 12th century.

---

[28] Thus, for some tastes, these canonical patterns seem tighter, indeed aesthetically colder, than those which appear immediately subsequent to the Fatimid epoch. The argument is most puissantly visible in the "peacock" filter (Olmer, pl. LXIII-A), which he insists is Ayyubid on iconic analogy with the silk textile in the Musee de Cluny: Olmer, pp. 80 f. However, one is left with a lingering doubt as to exactly which part of the 12th century we may *safely* assign either the textile or the filter.

a. Mesh

Pl. X-c/Fig. 64. This is practically a perfect duplicate of Olmer, pl. XXI-B, only the outermost interstitial opening is different. The mesh itself is of asymmetrical hexagons, rather poorly executed. Its drawn pattern has been published (Fat. Fil., fig. 10-f); and by its association with Fat. Fil., fig. 9-a and c, in the same find-spot, we may assume it to be Fatimid of the 11th-12th century.

Pl. X-d/Fig. 65. The drawn pattern of this sample has been published (Fat. Fil., fig. 11-a); it would seem to be a clumsy effort of circularly linked sets of circlets, giving the effect of the roughest interstitial polygonality. Olmer's pl. XXI-F and the central mesh of his pl. XXII-E are far more successful essays. Ours is a surface find; hence we suggest a date in the 12th century, but more than possibly before the Ayyubid conquest.

Pl. XI-a/Fig. 66. Again the drawn pattern has been published (Fat. Fil., fig. 11-b). The mesh is composed of very small diamonds each with a smaller hole in its center; all the elements so linked as to give an interstitial cruciform effect. As this is also a surface find, we would assign it to the pre-Ayyubid 12th century, and feel strengthened in doing so by appeal to the identical interstitial cruciform effect to be noticed in two other mesh filters (Fat. Fil., figs. 11-e and 12), both of which carry the telling striated zig-zag intermediate border.

b. Mesh with intermediate dividers.

Pl. XI-b/Fig. 67. One may see this filter as an attempt to elevate design elements to be seen in Pls. X-c and XI-a. As there does not seem to be any firm distinction between diamonds and hexagons (cf. drawn pattern in Fat. Fil., fig; 11-d), the interstitial effect is nebulous at best. What is distinctive is the thin circular divider effecting separation of simple bead-like border from the internal circular mesh. In the more elegant examples this narrow divider will be a wider one containing the zig-zag line. As the find-spot was in the fill between two walls of a domicile which was dated to the 11th century, we can posit the pattern as originating then and probably continuing into the 12th century.

Pl. XI-c/Fig. 68. As this filter has two thin dividers, it could be seen as an advance over the preceding one. The center mesh is composed of diamonds and circlets, the middle circle of circlets, and the outer border is composed of radiant spokes, each of which is of three conjoined circlets. Though it is a surface find, it is the interstitial cross of the central mesh (cf. FEPR '64, fig. 2-e) which moves us to see the full pattern as emerging out of the Fatimid canon, hence pre-Ayyubid in spirit.

c. Star and star-and-knot patterns.

Pl. XI-d/Fig. 69. The drawn pattern of this surface find has been published (Fat. Fil., fig. 5-e). It is basically a six-pointed star composed of the familiar barrettes, but without any knotting or ruching. As it lacks these characteristics, it is unlike anything in Olmer, but by analogy with others within this sub-category, we can see it as Fatimid and most probably of the 11th century.

Pl. XII-a/Fig. 70.   This represents the natural variation of the filter above, in that the barrettes are supplied each with an arrow-like knit, but still maintaining the star effect. The center surface is poorly executed with a hint of ruching. As the drawn pattern has been published (Fat. Fil., fig. 6-b), it remains to point out the anamoly of the profile, which is concave, and hence departs in this one respect from the canon. However, it can be seen as a firing error, in that the round pattern as a whole simply fell. The find-spot would dictate an 11th-12th century date.

Pl. XII-b/Fig. 71.   One may see (from the drawn pattern in Fat. Fil., fig. 5-d) an improvement of the barrette-and-knit of Pl. XII-a in two respects; between the barrettes is a tiny triangular continuation of the central surface, and within this latter a set of six diamond openings, two of which have disappeared but are ascertainable. The neck of the vessel is classic and one handled, the latter being slightly ribbed on its outer surface. All the material associated with the find-spot (including Fig. 72) points to an 11th century dating.

Pl. XII-c   In the same spirit as the preceding, except that the execution of the inner circle of diamond holes has been botched. The drawn pattern has been published (Fat. Fi., fig. 6-c); and, though the object was a surface find, by analogy with the last filters, we can assign it to the 11th-12th century.

Pl. XII-d/Fig. 72.   There are three interesting aspects about this filter: it is of red clay[29] rather than the more usual buff whitish; it has a lightly incised design external (cf. Fat. Fil., fig. 5-e), a factor we last came upon in the early 10th century; and the small triangular protuberance has so grown in terms of the barrette that we have what is almost a trefoil fleuron. Its find-spot was identical to that of Pl. XII-b and, for the reasons that obtained there, we assign this filter to the 11th century.

Fig. 73.   Again a rather bungled attempt, but one no doubt intended to duplicate Olmer, pl. XXIX-B. The diamond openings have moved to the inner periphery of the design, and the inner surface, quite mal-proportioned, has simple linear scratches, possibly meant as ruchings of the knitted center. A surface find which we may by analogy assign to the 11th-12th century.

Pl. XIII-a/Fig. 74.   A more successful essay of the pattern, uncharacteristically in red clay, wherein the star pattern of the diamond holes has more clarity, though the interstitial triangular protuberances are not of uniform dimension. There can be no doubt that this model is of the 11th century, since

---

[29] Not quite so unusual, as a series of red ware filter vessels with external decoration can be confidently assigned to the Fatimid period; cf. Appendix B infra and Pits, pl. XVI-2 and 3.

it was found in Pit 2 (Fat. Fil., fig. 5-a and p. 38) with eleven other filters, one of which is of the developed star pattern seen in Pl. XIII-c.

Fig. 75.   A very lithe variation of Olmer, pl. XXIX-B, where the knot-holes are replaced by slit lines, and the diamond holes become more ellipsoidal in shape. A surface find, but, again by analogy, one we may assign to the 11th-12th century.

Pl. XIII-b   A very successful example of the knotted barrette and central pattern of flame-like elliptical holes, as can be seen more clearly in the published pattern (FEPR '66, fig. 1). It was found in the same spot as Pl. X-a, Fig. 39 and Pl. XVI-a, and like them is of the 11th century.

Pl. XIII-c   A splendid variation on the knot-knit theme, where the large interstitial design becomes a pattern of Y's with suffragan diamond holes. It arouses further interest in that the basic hexagonal star has here become septagonal. It is again from Pit 2 (Fat. Fil., p. 36 and fig. 5-e) and is a close relative to Pl. XIII-a from the same find-spot, hence almost certainly of the 11th century.[30]

d. Flower designs.

Pl. XIII-d/Fig. 76.   A very fine example of the simplified flower design arising from the barrette and the extended interstitial protuberance. We end here with a very fine quatrefoil, each part of which is a trefoil. The inner divisions become quite simply extended diamond forms. It is an artlessly simple but aesthetically satisfying pattern, fitting perfectly into the proportionate lineaments of the neck and shoulder, offset by a low handle which does not rise to the height of the neck. It is really unlike anything in Olmer, though one finds echoes, as in pl. IX therein. As the elegance is distinctly Fatimid, so the find-spot confirms an 11th century date, containing as it does the zoomorphic filter in Pl. XXI-d.

Pl. XIV-a   As can be seen from the published pattern (Fat. Fil., fig. 6-a), we have a basically solid quatrefoil imposed on a four barrette star, with traces of knitting apparent as small circular holed extensions of the knot. Each of the surfaces of the quatrefoil has a flame-like elliptical opening attendant to the very center of the design, with three holes towards the extremity of the leaf. This last feature also obtains on the octofoil in Olmer, plate B of his Introduction, which he assigns to the Ayyubid period on the basis of the external decoration. Notwithstanding, the entire *conception* of our filter is a development of Fatimid elements. Further, its find-spot would indicate an 11th-12th century date.

---

[30] This filter is an almost exact duplicate of Olmer, pl. XXX-A, except that the central nodular button is missing. The hexagonal model can be seen in Olmer, pl. XXIX-D, except that the diamond shapes are solid. He would assign these filters to the Mamluk period, but our archaeological evidence speaks volumes for a Fatimid origin of the design pattern of the entire group B-II-A-1.

Fig. 77.   A fine radiant flower which when complete had twenty-one serrated petal-leaves. The central pattern is of a helical knit-ruching. One has the impression a flower rather like a peony or chrysanthemum was intended as is more obvious from the complete filter in Olmer, pl. XLV-D, which has twenty-five serrated spiny leaves. The theme was repeated in Fig. 90, this time with a surround of incised zig-zag line. The find-spot contained many examples of 10th century pottery and glass and the filter of Pl. VIII-c. However, as has been discussed with that sample, note had to be taken of the Fatimid glass weights present in the pit. Hence whereas there can be doubt that Fig. 90 is Fatimid of the 11th century, we may imagine the present filter and Olmer's pl. XLV-D as preliminary exercises, but certainly within the Fatimid canon. Though the central knit-ruching gives one pause, we would see the present example as of the very early 11th century. Further as Olmer is uncertain as to the date of his pl. XLV-D, we would give it a comparable chronology.

2.   Circular inclusive patterns with border.   Here in a typological sense we find the incised zig-zag circular border asserting itself as a full design element. It both encloses and punctuates; it is a firmly canonical motif. The patterns themselves generally parallel those noted in the broad category without border (B-II-A-1) with the same strictures applying.

a. Mesh.

Pl. XIV-b   The published pattern (Fat. Fil., fig. 13-a) shows a cruciform grill mesh of square holes, with the design at the cross missing. The border is a perfect example of the incised zig-zag continuous line. It is because of this latter characteristic as well as of the fineness of the cutting of the unique central pattern which gives us no pause in assigning it to the Fatimid canon, probably of the 11th century.

Pl. XIV-c/Fig. 78.   With the neck and filter intact, sufficient of the other parts remained to allow this restoration. The vessel lacked any handle, was quite thin-walled in body, and was covered with a turquoise vitreous glaze except at the bottom of the vessel, the ring foot, and the interior of the neck. Its filter pattern is like Olmer, pl. XXII-C, except for the striated zig-zag border separating the central pattern from the outer circlet of circles. The find-spot stamps it as undeniably Fatimid of the 11th century.

Pl. XIV-d   This is a slightly smaller but more finely executed duplicate of the preceding filter, as can be seen by comparing the published patterns, Fat. Fil., figs. 11-e and 12. Thus, though it is a surface find, we have no hesitancy in assigning it also to the same 11th century.

Pl. XV-a   As can be seen from the published pattern (Fat. Fil., fig. 11-f), this filter is Olmer's, pl. XXII-C with the addition of an intervening striated zig-zag border, then completed by a radiant pattern of spoke-ends each with three aligned tiny holes. Though this latter element will become a characteristic of Ayyubid and Mamluk filters, the central pattern is simply too canonical to put it so late. As it was found in the foundation fill of a room of a

Fatimid house, with that of Fat. Fil., fig. 10-a, we would place it in the pre-Ayyubid 12th century.

Fig. 79. This is an almost perfect duplicate of Olmer, pl. XXII-D, except that the roundel with the hexagonal openings has been replaced with a Norman shield-shape.[31] However, though Olmer would have his example Ayyubid, we feel that the dominant central pattern and the inner border of an incised zig-zag line strongly suggest a pre-Ayyubid 12th century dating.

Pl. XV-b A canonical mesh roundel can be seen in the center of the published pattern of this filter (Fat. Fil., fig. 13-a), but it is surrounded, after the intervening characteristic zig-zag border, by the more Ayyubid spoke-end element to be noted in Pl. XV-a. The contents of the fill of the find-spot point to the Fatimid period, so once again we are prone to place the example in the pre-Ayyubid part of the 12th century.

Pl. XV-c The published pattern shows a radial mesh, an interval border of zig-zag, and the outer spoke-end border to be seen in Pls. XV-a and b. It was found with the truly canonical filter in Pl. XVI-c, though the contents of the locus were not uniformly chronologically integral, nothing was post-Fatimid. Hence we are inclined to assign this filter to the 11th-12th century.

Fig. 80. This, again, is a chronologically enigmatic filter. The central mesh which has a central nodular button is certainly Ayyubid in feeling, but the surrounding zig-zag border and circle of small circlets is canonically Fatimid, just the reverse of the situation with filters in Pls. XV-a, b and c and Fig. 79. The decisive factor would seem to be the portion of the moulded decoration external which contains a portion of a Naskhi inscription, a decorative feature which Olmer associates with the Ayyubid hegemony. However, Creswell notes a single line of Naskhi in a window grille in the Mosque of Al-Salih Tala'i, built at the finale of the Fatimid period.[32] Would this novel epigraphic style have made a lightening leap into the world of ceramics? The find-spot helps us to no certain conclusion, except to place it immediately before or during the Ayyubid governance of Egypt. It would appear safer to simply allow the filter a date sometime in the second half of the 12th century.

b. Star and star-and-knot patterns.

Fig. 81. A very well executed example of the canonical circular geometrical pattern, but with a subtle conceit: the hexagonal sets of openings at the very center are not attended by a star of twelve openings, but one of eleven, with

---

[31] For a discussion of this shape which first appears as a scutcheon on the Bab al-Nasr in Cairo, cf. Creswell, *Muslim Architecture of Egypt*, I (Oxford: 1952), p. 168 f and pls. 49-50. It occurs quite frequently in Mamluk pottery; cf. FEPR '64, frontispiece upper left and our "Some Mamluk Ceramic Shapes from Fustat," *Diamond Jubilee Volume of the Islamic Museum*, (Cairo: 1979), passim.

[32] Creswell, op. cit., p. 285 and pl. 108-c.

eleven triangular openings at the outer interstices of the central pattern. Then we have the characteristic inner border of zig-zag, the intervalent circle of circlets, and a final zig-zag border. As this is a surface find, we may postulate an 11th-12th century dating.

Fig. 82. A hexagonal inner star pattern with the interstitial Y openings, hence very much like Olmer's pl. XXX-A and related to Pl. XIII-c herein, which however is septagonal. Here we have a surround of zig-zag and an outer border not of circlets but of thin-sided triangles. Again a surface find, but because the inner pattern is like that of Pl. XIII-c, a very definite 11th century model, and the indicative zig-zag border, we can assign the filter to the 11th-12th century.

Fig. 83. A simple pentagonal star, with a central knitting with traces of ruching: all bordered by the familiar striated zig-zag line. The filter was discovered in the fill beneath the paving of a room in a Fatimid domicile, and can be assigned to the 11th century.

Fig. 84. An incomplete filter but one whose central pattern is an hexagonal star with alternate barrette knotting, with a simple zig-zag border. No doubt it was meant to duplicate Olmer, pl. XLIII-A. Its find-spot has been fully explained (Pit 1 in Fat. Fil., p. 38), and it is definitely of the 11th century.

Fig. 85. Again incomplete, but of the same general pattern as the previous sample. Though a surface find, we may, on the surety of the previous dating, assign this pattern to the 11th century.

Pl. XV-d A complete example of the hexagonal star pattern with knotting, no doubt what Figs. 84 and 85 were tending towards. The center design is imprecise; but the incised zig-zag line border is characteristic. This too was from Pit 1 (Fat. Fil., p. 38 and fig. 4-a), and is definitely of the 11th century.

Pl. XVI-a An imprecisely realized septagonal star with central knitting and a trace of ruching (Fat. Fil., pl. 4-c). The striated zig-zag line completes the pattern. Both this element and its find-spot point to an 11th century dating.

Pl. XVI-b A beautifully realized septagonal star with alternate knitting, with the central ruching emphasizing the heptagonality (Fat. Fil., fig. 4-e). Both the previous filter and this one are animadversions of Olmer's pl. XLIII-E. This fact and the zig-zag defining border permit us to assign an 11th century dating.

Pl. XVI-c Here the zig-zag border surrounds a central pattern of a nine-pointed barrette star with alternate knotting. The center knitting carries a trace of ruching (Fat. Fil., fig. 4-f). To these elements we may add the evidence from the find-spot and declare this fine example to be of the 11th century.

Fig. 86. This incomplete filter is very much in the spirit of the preceding one, but, if complete, would have had a ten-pointed star with alternate knotting and a comparable center knotting with rudimentary ruching and a zig-zag border. The dating from the find-spot is not more conclusive except to aver that the object is Fatimid, which by motival analogy with the preceding five filters would seem to be true. 11th-12th century.

Pl. XVI-d As can be detected from the published pattern (Fat. Fil., fig. 4-d), this is almost a miscellaneous example within the category. The interior openings are diamond shaped so cut as to give an imperfect hexagonal star, and the lines between are slightly extended into the space between the barrettes. It is difficult to consider the scratching at the center as ruching, since it would seem that an undecorated *solid* surface was desired. As it was found with Fig. 39 and Pls. X-a and XIII-b, there can be no doubt that it is of 11th century vintage.

c. Flower designs.

Pl. XVII-a The published pattern (Fat. Fil., fig. 4-b) shows a quite small incomplete four-pointed fleuron with four intermediate protuberances with small holes, and another small hole at the very center. Whereas here it dominates, it will form part of a larger harmony as in Fig. 101 and Pl. XIX-c. The shape of the neck and the zig-zag border mark it as canonically Fatimid, though it is a surface find. 11th-12th century.

Pl. XVII-b/Fig. 87. Though incomplete, there is no doubt that this is but a slight variant of the central four-pointed fleuron (FEPR '64, fig. 2-c). But here the fleuron and its zig-zag border are off-set from the rim of the design by five tiny circlets, affording the entire design an effect of supple lightness nicely balanced by the forthright handle. It is quite in the style of Olmer, pl. IX-B. The find-spot confirms it as Fatimid, 11th-12th century.

Fig. 88.   Though incomplete, the pattern is ascertainable: a cinque-foil with two small holes in each leaf, simple latticing in the interstices, and a striated zig-zag border. It is unlike any single example in Olmer and is a surface find, but it breathes the air of the Fatimid canon. 11th-12th century.

Fig. 89.   This filter is very much in the spirit of Olmer, pl. XLVI-B, except that the intermediate flower design there is ten petalled, whereas ours has only eight, and that his central fleuron has been replaced by an octagonal star, though most unsymmetrically realized. It was found in the foundation fill of a Fatimid domicile, hence we may put it in the 11th-12th century.

Fig. 90.   A radiant flower of sixteen-serrated petal-leaves, very much in the spirit of Fig. 77. But whereas that filter was reminiscent of Olmer, pl. XLV-D, ours is more like his XLV-A, in that it has the striated zig-zag border. But it lacks the beautiful central fleuron; instead it has a most imprecise center unaccented except for what appears to be some sort of helical ruching. Both this filter and Fig. 77 represent how finely delicate a cutting of the filter was achieved in the Fatimid period. The find-spot permits a dating of the 11th century.

3. Triangular patterns. A very simple pattern wherein the central triangle is defined by a border of zig-zag bands, sometime the whole surrounded by a zig-zag border, thus leaving

three arc-ed or cusped areas. These latter and the inner triangle therefore carry the decoration. It is interesting that Olmer has but one example of the type (pl. V-A), but the center motif is highly developed. Our series of ten filters exhibits a greater sense of variety and motival development.

a. Central lattice and triplet circlets. The inner triangle is a diamond lattice of greater or less delicacy of cutting, while each of the cusped areas contains three joined circlets each with a small opening. Of our five examples, two have been published (Fat. Fil., figs. 7-a and d); the first was from Pit 2 (ibid., p. 38) and definitely of the 11th century; the other (Pl. XVII-c herein) was a surface find but had the more elegant outer surround of zig-zag. As our other three were surface finds, we are perhaps wiser in seeing the pattern continuing into the 12th century.

Fig. 91.   Of the same pattern as Fat. Fil., fig. 7-a, but not so well cut. A surface find; 11th-12th century.

Fig. 92.   Again the same pattern as Fat. Fil., fig. 7-a, but this example has the usual single handle intact. Surface find; 11th-12th century.

Fig. 93.   Though the lattice is passable, the circlets are not as nicely defined as in Fat. Fil., fig. 7-a. Surface find; 11th-12th century.

b. Central lattice and ruching in the arcs. This latter almost looks like the filigree work of the earlier period; but it may really be seen as imperfect approximations of the flower-like effects to be seen in the cusped areas of Olmer, pl. XII-C, which contains a beautiful knot lattice. Our two examples lack such finish of execution.

Pl. XVII-d/Fig. 94.   The pattern has been published (Fat. Fil., fig. 7-b). The rather elegant neck of the vessel has the top of a single handle in situ. The find-spot also yielded the filters in Fig. 57 and Pl. XIX-b, all of which can be dated to the 11th century.

Pl. XVIII-a   As can be seen from the published pattern (Fat. Fil., fig. 7-c), the combinations of elements is surrounded by a border of a striated zig-zag line. As this is a surface find, we sense the possible continuation of the design into the 12th century.

c. Divided central triangle and circlets.

Pl. XVIII-b   The pattern and neck profile have been published (Fat. Fil., fig. 7-a and FEPR '64, fig. 3-c), the latter showing a double handle on one side, a unique feature. The central triangle is very poorly executed, the desire being to achieve three diamond and three triangular surfaces by incised lines, each of the former pierced with three small openings and the latter with larger openings. Each of the arcs has four circlets instead of three. Its find-spot points to an 11th century dating.

d. Central fleuron/flower.

Fig. 95.   This very lovely pattern is a simple variation of Olmer, pl. XII-A. The encircled central fleuron is attended by single circlets in the interstices, and the cusped area contains ruching rather than his four circlets. As it was found within a street fill attendant to a Fatimid domicile, we assume it to be of that period; 11th-12th century.

Pl. XVIII-c/Fig. 96.   This trefoil superimposed upon a central triangle, all elements outlined by zig-zag borders and all interiors diamond-latticed, duplicates Olmer, pl. X-B, except that one of his outer interstices has three small holes rather than one. The filter was found in Pit 1 (Fat. Fil., p. 38 and fig. 7-f) and can be securely dated to the 11th century.

4. Rectangular patterns. The dominant design is contained within a four-sided border of incised zig-zag lines; the border may be straight, curved or bent inwards to form an odd octagon. The four arcs or cusps are then filled with the subsidiary joined circlets, and, in the odd instance, the total design may be bordered by an outer band of zig-zag. The real decorative development is thus within the rectangular space, and Olmer's sixteen examples (pls. VI, VII, XIII, and XIV for the straight sided, and IX for the curved) demonstrate the variational skill of the Fatimid craftsman: there is not an uninteresting or sloppily executed example among them. Our seven examples complement and extend the category.

a. Straight sided rectangle.

Fig. 97.   The central square is divided by a cross of zig-zag at a 45° angle to the central square, and the interstices are filled with diamond lattice-work. It is similar to Olmer, pl. VI-D, except that his interstices have a different geometrical filling. Four circlets in each of the cusped areas completes the pattern. The find-spot permits us to assign an 11th century date.

Pl. XVIII-d   The published pattern (Fat. Fil., fig. 8-d) shows a wonderful oddity for the canonical range: no band of zig-zag lines. The square, punctuated by four small holes at the corners, is divided by a thin-lined cross at 90° angle to the square. Within the quadrants so formed are four rectangular surfaces each touching the outer square at a 45° angle. The central intersection bears a small quatrefoil, each leaf of which has a tiny hole, each central leaf being echoed by a protuberance at the opposite angle. Thus except for the absence of zig-zag bordering, this filter is a duplicate of Olmer, pl. XIV-D. Though a surface find, it can be dated to the 11th-12th century.

Fig. 98.   This overall pattern is more like Olmer, pl. XIV-D, but unlike it in that the quadrants each contain a square-ish rather than a rectangular motif, with irregularly cut protuberances at each angle of the quadrant. The circlets in one arc are very poorly executed. This one-handled vessel can be put into the 11th century from the evidence of its find-spot as well as by its stylistics.

Fig. 99.   Divided into parallel horizontal registers, the central pattern is really an imperfect realization of Olmer, pl. VI-A. The difference is in the lowest of the three registers: instead of an inner bounding border with zig-zag, we have a set of small triangular openings, affording an odd, asymmetric, unbalanced effect, though the frame is rigidly rectangular. The four circlets in his arcs have become three in ours. The thin-walled neck has a graceful fullness at mid-height. This is a surface find, but it can be dated to the 11th-12th century on stylistics.

b. Curve sided rectangle.

Pl. XIX-a   A splendid example of the canonical filter, clean cut and arresting. A quatre-foil (Fat. Fil., fig. 8-c) is set at 45° to the curve sided rectangle. The leaves and sides have the characteristic wavy line, but inner interstices and the elliptical outer arcs contain portions of the fleuron motif: the circlets have disappeared. Thus the spirit of this filter is closer to Olmer, pl. IX-C, than to his other curve sided example, pl. IX-D. The find-spot provided little exact chronological data, but there can be no doubt that this is a Fatimid product: 11th-12th century.

Fig. 100.   Again an extraordinarily pure, simple design, but quite different from either of Olmer's examples. The center fleuron has a circular border of incised zig-zag, which is set so that it is tangent to the curving sides of the rectangle, the whole then surrounded by an outer border containing the wavy line, our only example within this category. The outer elliptical cusps contain a triplet of circlets, and single circlets fill the triangular interstices between inner circle and outer rectangle. Another interesting feature is the external ribbing of the neck. As this was a surface find, it should be more safely considered 11th-12th century.

c. Bent sided rectangle.

Pl. XIX-b   From the published pattern (Fat. Fil., fig. 8-b), one senses a motival confrontation: either the central cross dominates, or is there to accent how the rectangular sides are "bent," thus allowing the strange rectangle-octagon to command attention. Withal, the inner "quadrants" are diamond-shaped with a very thin line to divide the opening. The only other decorative element is the small-holed protuberance to be seen throughout. A similar treatment of the bent sided rectangle can be seen in Olmer, pl. VIII-A. As the filter was found with those in Fig. 57 and Pl. XVII-d, we can place it in the 11th century.

5.   Diamond and fleuron patterns.   This might be considered a variant of the rectangular patterns. However, it is the presence of the fleuron in both of our examples which necessitates a sub-category.[33]

a. Fleuron accessory.

Fig. 101.   This filter was incomplete, but its pattern can be ascertained as a variant of Olmer, pl. XVIII-C, but without the latticing within the divided diamond. The encircled fleurons penetrate the latter and are meant to be tangent to the outer surround border of zig-zag. The latter element defines

---

[33] A single fleuron, all that remained of a larger design (and *not* the central pattern as in type B-II-A-2-c), was found in 1964 in a locus definitely of the 11th century, which helps define the motif as canonical. (Reg. No. 64-5-10; Akron Art Museum.)

the diamond and the division into equilateral triangles. Small-holed protuberances within the interstices diminish the open area of the filter. Though a surface find, we can assign it to the 11th-12th century on the strength of its decorative elements.

b. Fleuron equal.

Pl. XIX-c/Fig. 102. The diamond is here so contracted that the borders of the fleuron touch, though these same borders are incomplete relative to the round border enclosing the entire pattern (Fat. Fil., fig. 8-a). The diamond does have latticing, but the outer interstices are much reduced; in each there is the small holed protuberance. It is easiest to think of the pattern as a combination of Olmer's pls. XVIII-C and E. As it was found in Pit 2 (Fat. Fil., p. 38), it can be placed securely in the 11th century.

6. Pentagonal patterns. Though the sides would be straight as well as curved, Olmer's single example (pl. IX-C) is the latter, which reduces the area of the outer arcs, if the filter size remains standard.

Pl. XIX-d Both the pattern and the ribbed profile of the neck have been published (FEPR '64, fig. 3-d and Fat. Fil., fig. 8-e). Though the filter is damaged, we can see a cinquefoil set within the curved sides of the pentagon: the leaves of the former and the sides of the latter being defined by wavy lines. Our example differs from Olmer's in two ways: the internal interstices are latticed, and the outer ellipses contain two rather than three circlets. As the filter was found beneath a secondary pavement, we can assign it to the 11th-12th century.

7. Radial patterns. It could well be argued that there is little difference between this category, and those with star patterns, with or without borders. However, two considerations must be brought into the argument: in this category the entire radiant or a goodly number of the spokes are made of bands containing incised zig-zag lines; and it is often difficult to decide whether the radial is the dominant or sub-dominant theme of the pattern, as was the case with the diamond vs. the fleuron in type B-II-5. At all events, it will be the spoke division of the filter circle which will govern the categorization.

a. Four-spoked.

Pl. XX-a The published pattern (Fat. Fil., fig. 10-b) shows a simple cross of zig-zag bands. The interstices are subdivided into two by thin lines, making for a subtle eight spoke effect, but not such as to overwhelm the four spoke.[34] Each of the newer spaces is filled with an oddly shaped circlet with a small hole. The find-spot would allow an 11th-12th century dating.

Pl. XX-b/Fig. 103. This is the first of a cache of filters discovered in 1968, comparable to those of Pits 1 and 2 in 1965. The patterns are all published; and they may all be dated securely to the 11th-12th century, though from

---

[34] A similar effect is achieved by having barrettes in the interstices; cf. Fat. Fil., fig. 10-a. This filter was found in the same spot as Pl. XV-a herein.

other evidence in the pit the earlier century would seem more probable (cf. Pits, pp. 76 f.). In this example, the cross is not perpendicular; in the two obtuse angles we have a fleuron and two circlets in each; in each of the very acute angles a single circlet. The whole pattern is surrounded by a border containing the usual wavy line. This is a filter design in the spirit of Olmer, pl. XVIII-F, though both the fleurons and the interstitial elements are different.

b. Five spoked.

Fig. 104. A very simple pattern with latticing between the spokes, exactly like Olmer, pl. III-B. The neck is rather elegant, and has a single handle. The find-spot as well as the design characteristics point to 11th-12th century.

c. Six spoked. All four of our examples were found in 1965, two in Pit 1, one in Pit 2 (Fat. Fil., p. 38), the last was a surface find. The pattern is exactly like that of Olmer, pl. III-C, except that his has a central nodular button and a surround border of zig-zag. There is, however, a slight difference within our samples in the handling of the neck.

Fig. 105. Here the neck is almost a straight rise from the shoulder, and the published example would seem to be the same. This filter comes from Pit 1 (Fat. Fil., p. 38); hence is 11th century.

Fig. 106. This neck is higher and more sinuous in profile than the preceding example. The profile of the surface find, though incomplete, would seem to have the same curvature. The illustrated example comes from Pit 2 (Fat. Fil., p. 38); both can be dated to the 11th century.

d. Seven spoked.

Fig. 107. Though our fleuron is a cinque-foil rather than a quatre-foil, this pattern is a duplicate of Olmer, pl. V-C. The find-spot clearly points to the 11th-12th century, thus confirming the stylistics.

e. Eight spoked. The true eight spoked radiant can be seen in Olmer, pl. V-B. Our three examples might be considered a four spoked radiant superimposed at a 45° angle on a four pointed star. It is because the radiant is over the star that we would distinguish the pattern from the eight pointed star to be found in Fat. Fil., fig. 10-e and Fig. 89 herein, and because of the zig-zag line within the four spoked. Our three examples are practically identical and all come from almost certain 11th century contexts. All the vessels were one-handled and high-necked; the slightly larger filter will be illustrated.

Pl. XX-c/Fig. 108. As the other two examples were from Pit 2 (Fat. Fil., p. 38 and fig. 10-d), this somewhat larger sample comes from a comparable chronological context. The pattern is somewhat lopsidedly executed, but is nonetheless ascertainable.

8. Parallel vertical panels. The pattern is usually divided into two outer cusps containing small-holed circlets by two bands with incised zig-zag lines. This leaves a wide central panel which can be subdivided in various ways and organized through various design elements: zig-zag bands, latticing, fleurons, flat diamonds, further parallel vertical bands, etc. As the verticality dominates, there is no need for the outer surround band. The variety of

of treatment can be gleaned from Olmer, pls. XV, XVI, XVII, and XVIII-A and B (though some of his examples do have the outer border of zig-zag which gives a cramped feeling to the achieved pattern). For the grouping as a whole, the Fustat Expedition contributes thirty examples, giving it pride of place quantitatively within our survey of Fatimid canonical filters.

a. Central lattice. The simplest composition has been published (Fat. Fil., fig. 8-f); as have the two variants: where the dividing band of zig-zag has been doubled (ibid., fig. 9-b), and the outer circlet panels have been replaced by fleurons (FEPR '64, fig. 3-a). Of the four examples of the simplest version, two were found in Pit 2 and one in Pit 1 (Fit. Fil., p. 36), the fourth in an equally provable 11th century context. All examples came from one-handled vessels.

    Fig. 109.   There is a slight outward canting at the rim which adds distinction to the shape of the neck. As this was found in the covered canal leading from a latrine, it can like the domicile be dated to the 11th century.

    Pl. XX-d   A very interesting variation wherein the side panels are dominated by encircled fleurons, and the interstices are filled by approximate demi-fleurons, thus making the whole unlike any composition in Olmer. Though it is a surface find, the filter may be assigned to the 11th century on its stylistics alone.

b. Central lattice and dividers. These dividers are bands with zig-zag lines which vary in number and position.

    1. Double and joint, perpendicular to vertical dividers. This pattern has been published and since it derived from Pit 2, the series can be considered as 11th century (Fat. Fil., p. 36 and fig. 9-d). Three of the four others of the series can be dated from comparable loci, and the last, though a surface find, so dated on stylistic grounds. A variation can be seen in Olmer, pl. XV-A.

    Fig. 110.   The shoulder of this vessel foretells a more bulbous body than any other in the canonical series. It was found with Pl. X-c and Fat. Fil., fig. 9-c.

    2. Double spaced, angled to vertical dividers. Such a pattern makes for a central diamond lattice, itself composed of diamond openings. The remainder of the central panel becomes mini-lattice. The basic pattern has been published (FEPR '64, fig. 3-b), and its find-spot allows an 11th century dating.

    Fig. 111.   A slightly larger central lattice than the published one, leaving too small a space for mini-latticing; one sees instead what appears to be a portion of a fleuron. The object is a surface find, but on stylistics it can be related to the 11th-12th century.

    3. Triple and joint, perpendicular to vertical dividers. Again the variant pattern has been published, and, because it emanates from Pit 2, can be dated to the 11th century (Fat. Fil., p. 36 and fig. 9-e). Another filter proved a variant.

    Fig. 112.   Though the example is damaged, we can see that sufficient remains to gauge the design of the central panel, and to see the side panels had replaced the circlets with a filigree-like semi-barrette element. The filter was a surface find, but the central panel permits us to date it to the 11th-12th century.

4. Triple and spaced, angled to vertical dividers. This gives rise to two equilateral triangular lattices.

Pl. XXI-a The published pattern (Fat. Fil., fig. 9-f) is identical with that of Olmer, pl. XV-C, except that the remaining space of the central panel, after the triangular lattices have been defined, is treated as a filigree rather than being given over to small triangular fillers. As the filter is from Pit 1, it can be dated to the 11th century.

c. Flat diamond lattice. As the published pattern shows (Fat. Fil., fig. 9-a, and FEPR '65-II, fig. 2-a), there is nothing quite like it in Olmer. Our four examples vary only in the fineness of the cutting of the flat diamonds, each of which is small-holed. Fig. 9-a in Fat. Fil. is from Pit 1, so can be dated to the 11th century; two others are surface finds and might be better assigned to the 11th-12th century.

Fig. 113. A very finely cut center panel, and a very elegantly classical neck shape with the usual one handle. The find-spot has been discussed (Pits, p. 76 and fig. 12-d); 11th century.

d. Triple division into rectangles. The central panel is divided laterally, and each rectangle can be treated differently. In our published example (Fat. Fil., fig. 9-c), each rectangle is composed of a quatrefoil formed at the interstices of an incised X crossing. As it was found with Fig. 110 and Pl. X-c herein, it can easily be dated to the 11th-12th century.

Fig. 114. Except for the outer band with incised zig-zag, we have a duplicate of Olmer, pl. XVII-D. As the crossings within the rectangles are composed of double lines, we have a more interesting filter than the latter. The find-spot, beneath the stone paving of a room, points to an 11th century date.

e. Cross bands. Such a pattern of crossed bands of zig-zag leaves four spaces for decoration, while the outer panels retain the circlets.

Fig. 115. The crossing is not entirely symmetrical, but the idea is in force. Latticing returns to fill two of the small spaces, and slight holed protuberances were meant to fill the others. Though a surface find, on the basis of the more firmly dated example in Fig. 116, we may assign this filter to the 11th-12th century.

Fig. 116. This is a duplicate of Olmer, pl. XVIII-A, except that our example has five circlets in each outer panel rather than four. The crossing is more ably executed than in the preceding filter, though the encirclement of the two fleurons is somewhat scanted. The find-spot has been fully discussed (Pits, p. 76); 11th century.

f. Miscellaneous. These filters fall outside strict categorization. Except in one instance, we have vertical division, with the central panel left for thematic development. In short, they seem "one-of-a-kind" filters on the basis of present evidence, though all can be seen as embodying the strictures of Fatimid canonical.

Pl. XXI-b The published pattern (FEPR '64, fig. 2-b) shows much similarity to Olmer, pl. VI-A, but whereas his effect is rectantular as in our group B-II-A-4, ours is more ladder-like. As our example is incomplete, we might allow this to be a defect in what was otherwise intended to be a rectangular pattern. The locus of discovery allows an 11th-12th century dating.

Fig. 117.   This is a slightly damaged example, but its kinship to Olmer, pl. XV-D, is quite obvious. The central panel is divided into two by a single band perpendicular to the vertical dividers, and then the two spaces are subdivided by bands angled to these same dividers. The four spaces thus left are filled with small holed protuberances. A surface find; 11th-12th century.

Fig. 118.   This rather simple filter is unlike anything in Olmer. The central panel is itself subdivided into two vertical panels divided by a vertical band of zig-zag. The achieved pattern—four bands of circlets puncuated by three bands of incised zig-zag lining—can be looked at as being either lateral or vertical in intent. The find-spot also contained Fig. 121; both can be dated to the 11th century.

Fig. 119.   As all three panels are crossed by a divider of zig-zag, the filter does not strictly fall into the B-II-B-8 group, but neither can the pattern be considered strictly radial, B-II-B-7. It is a composite, with interest focussing on the four outer panels, each divided into two triangles, and each of the latter containing one circlet. There is nothing exactly similar in Olmer, but it is in the spirit of other Fatimid canonical filters. The find-spot allows an 11th-12th century date.

B. ZOOMORPHIC. One can detect how the Egyptian craftsman delighted in rendering the human and animal world from scanning Olmer, pls. LII-LXVI, of which most of the examples are Fatimid. The working space of the filter was actually too small to allow perfect fidelity of lineament, but there is throughout a fanciful verve of depiction and caricature. On the one hand there are truly rendered fish forms, while on the other we have such grotesques as birds growing forth from a pierced trefoil, Olmer, pl. LVII-A. Practically all the figures are disported within the typical canonical lattice work, which may or may not be surrounded by the usual band of zig-zagging. The range of our examples is restricted when compared to that of Olmer, but in a number of cases we add significant variations of pattern.

1. Human approximations.

Fig. 120.   A very poorly delineated human form holding a goblet which is triangular in section, seated within a lattice but with no border band. The head is strangely misshapen, and may possibly be meant to be in profile. Olmer's pl. LXIV-A could be a model, though his pl. LXV-A has an equally misshapen head but contains two goblets within the pattern. The theme is a familiar topic of Fatimid art, indeed this example and all of the same type in Olmer might be considered a somewhat proletarian rendering of the courtly drinking-scene.[35] The find-spot has been thoroughly discussed (Pits, pp. 76 f.); 11th century.

---

[35] The bibulous ruler and/or courtier is a theme omnipresent in all the minor arts of the Fatimid period.

2. Animals.

a. Elephant.

      Fig. 121.   Though slightly damaged, the pattern is quite discernible: an elephant passant to the left within the usual lattice with a surround border of zig-zag. The trunk is elongated and its extremity is turned toward the body and the left ear is upright. It was found together with Fig. 118 and can be dated to the 11th century.[36]

      Fig. 122.   A more Babar-like elephant, but otherwise a duplicate of Fig. 121. It is a surface find, hence it may be of a later date: 11th-12th century.

b. Gazelle. This very odd and sprightly animal has been so denominated by Olmer, p. 74 and pl. LVIII-C.[37] Of our three examples, two came from datable *loci*, which would permit us to differ from Olmer, who argues for an Ayyubid dating, and insist that the characteristics are all Fatimid canonical, making his example and our three of that period.

      Pl. XXI-c The pattern has been published (Fat. Fil., fig. 6-e). Though a surface find, it can be related both to Olmer, pl. LVIII-C and the next two filters. 11th-12th century.

      Pl. XXI-d This pattern has also been published (Fat. Fil., fig. 6-f). It was found with the example in Pl. XIII-d and Fig. 76 and can be dated to the 11th century.

      Fig. 123.   The animal depicted here is rather fuller in the body than Olmer's pl. LVIII-C, but it is of the same genre of design. The find-spot is discussed in Pits, pp. 77 f. along with the six other canonical filters found with it; 11th century.

c. Lion. Because of the articulated tail, Olmer would have these oddly staring creatures (pl. LIV) thought of as lions.

      Pl. XXII-a A very small portion of the filter pattern is intact, but its published design

---

Though its first expression is to be found in the carved panels from the Fatimid palace presently in the Islamic Museum of Cairo and in ivory panels in the Louvre and the Bargello, we must look to pottery for the nearest examples of this motif in filters, for which cf. *La Ceramique Egyptienne*, pls. 51, 52, 55 and 83. Though it dropped out of the filter makers range in succeeding periods, it was continued in underglaze painted and sgraffiato pottery, in the Ayyubid and Mamluk period, for which cf. ibid., pls. 86 and 124, and Bahgat and Massoul, op. cit., XXXIV-4 and LI-8.

[36] That the elephant appeared slightly earlier in the filigree effect filters of type A-5-B is proven by a filter which Olmer overlooked but which can be seen in Bahgat and Massoul, op. cit., pl. LVIII-15. The finest representation of the elephant is to be seen on the famous lustre-dish, now in the Benaki Museum in Athens. It is interesting to note that within the same quadrant as our Fig. 121 there was a pit with disturbed contents (G in XXVI-25) which yielded a shard of Mamluk sgraffiato ware on which is depicted an elephant's head with extended trunk. The latter has tusks, too, which all filter depictions lack; cf. FEPR '72, II, fig. 8.

[37] Grube believes this animal is possibly a hare. The three he describes in the Keir Collection are all of this category (nos. 78, 79 and 80), and can be securely dated to the 11th-12th century. The fourth example (no. 81) has a different lattice work and lacks any band of zig-zag; but the rendering of the animal is clearly Fatimid and thus the piece may be assigned a comparable dating; Grube-Keir, pp. 123 f.

(Fat. Fil., fig. 6-d) contains the tail and the surround band of zig-zag. As it was found in Pit 1 as described in Fat. Fil. (p. 38), it is easily assigned to the 11th century.

d. Hare/rabbit. It is interesting that whereas the hare was brilliantly represented in practically every other medium of Fatimid art,[38] it was not distinctly depicted in the realm of the filter.

    Pl. XXII-b The portion of the pattern which remains of this broken filter has been published (Ancillary, fig. 5-d). However, in the light of at least two characteristics of Fatimid canonical filters, viz. the lattice work and zig-zag lines or bands of definition, it is necessary to reconsider the Tulunid dating therein assigned. The reference to Olmer, pl. LXIII-B and C, is a trifle misleading in that the latticings there are different, and the borders of filigree and slash-ruching differ from zig-zag lines. The other evidence from the find-spot and adjacent areas is not absolutely conclusive; nevertheless, we would see this filter as originating in the first half of the 11th century.

e. Peacock. Olmer's pl. LIII shows peacocks with varying degrees of precision in rendering the crown and fan. Again the small size of the filter allowed for very little ornamental clarification. But these canonical animals start the process which ends in the magnificent peacock to be seen in the large filter of the Ayyubid period (Olmer, pl. LXIII-A).

    Fig. 124. A rather animated peacock with pronounced crown; in the usual lattice with border of zig-zag. Its find-spot has been amply discussed (Pits, pp. 75 f) and it can be assigned to the 11th century.

C. INSCRIPTIONAL/EPIGRAPHICAL. Most of the "pious sayings" displayed in Olmer, pls. LXXIV, LXXV, and LXXVII-B (with the exception of LXXIV-C) are written in what may be taken as a "cursive Kufic," wherein the connectives *flow* rather than straiten, and thus seem to be, at least to Olmer, an incipient Nashki. While it is true that these samples lack the ornate compositional grace of Olmer's great Kufic filter (pl. LXXVI-A), they are in separate elements quite distinct from the Naskhi filters of the following periods. As all are in the usual canonical lattice-work and some have the identifying surround band of zig-zag, one would dispute this Ayyubid dating and put all his nine samples in the Fatimid era. From our excavations we have two which duplicate Olmer's types.

    Pl. XXII-c This is a duplicate of Olmer, pl. LXXVII-B, whose inscription is left unread. It could be "man haff taff" which might mean "he who lifts [this water jar] will find it brimming." Our example lacks the zig-zag surround of Olmer's. The published pattern (FEPR '64, fig. 2-e) is less clear than Olmer's example. It is a surface find; 11th-12th century.

    Pl. XXII-d The filter is the same as Olmer, pl. LXXV-C, and the inscription is identical, as can be scanned from the published pattern (Fat. Fil., fig. 13-d).

---

[38] Cf. FEPR '65-II, fig. 5-a for a fine representation of the hare in moulded stucco, and fig. 7-b in an FFS green-glaze bowl. Both of these were found in the same season as our poorly executed example in Pl. XXII-b.

The dating from the find-spot is problematical; but on stylistics one may assign it to the 11th-12th century.

Category C. The Ayyubid and Mamluk Era
ca. 1200 - ca. 1500 A.D.

With the destruction of Fustat in November 1168, the fate of Fatimid control of Egypt was sealed. By 1170 the family of Ayyub, of Kurdish descent but in the employ of the Zangids of Syria, maintained de facto rule of Egypt under the direction of Salah al-Din. The lands of the Nile (by the end of the century the area between the First and Second Cataracts had become nominally Muslim) returned to the Sunni orthodox hegemony, and, using Egypt as his financial springboard, Saladin began his organization of the Counter-Crusade.[39]

Although no exact convulson of taste is noticeable in the arts and architecture, there was a rather quick transformation of taste, due principally to the ingress of influences from Syria, Saljukid Anatolia and, at an intervening "remove" best exemplified by the potters of Raqqa and the migrant metalsmiths of Mosul, of Iran. The Fatimid canonical was essentially eclipsed by 1200, though discrete design elements are employed in the new filters. The filter itself became generally larger, and the patterns *stronger* in effect. Indeed, in this transformation of taste, one senses the imposition of straightforward vigour, even of monumentality, in place of the small scaled and refined. A quick scan of Cairene architecture of the 13th and 14th centuries nullifies any charge of "unimaginative"; nevertheless there is now a comfortable conservatism defining the aesthetic expression of the era. The new robust "academicism" subsumes filter design and integrates it more signally to the artistic range of glazed ceramics, metalware, glass and architectural decoration.

As with so many art historians, Olmer chooses the introduction of Naskhi script to mark the chronological shift.[40] In the absence of firmer archaeological evidence, this must be accepted, though exactly how *early* in the Ayyubid era he places his examples remains vague. A further difficulty arises when we attempt assigning a Mamluk designation as distinct from a Ayyubid one. A variable guide is motival relativity with precisely dated examples from other metiers of artistic production. But this again leaves the art historian foundering, for whereas there is a span of but ninety years for the Ayyubid craftsmen to demonstrate artistic taste, the Mamluks patronage encompasses two hundred and sixty-seven. Though the output of the Cairo workshops was prodigious in the 13th century, can one, short of archaeological evidence, correctly distinguish between an Ayyubid aesthetic in 1200 and a Mamluk one in 1300? In sum, we *feel* Olmer is generally correct in his ascriptions, though we *know* he begs the more compelling questions of transition, continuity and novelty.

The Fustat excavations can add little to the solution of the above queries. The evidence

---

[39] For the most recent exposition of the Ayyubid consolidation of control of Egypt, cf. Andrew Ehrenkreutz, *Saladin* (New York: 1972), passim. The Egyptian Muslim conquest of the Lower Nubian Christian Kingdoms is excellently chronicled in W. C. Adams, *Nubia* (London: 1977), pp. 547-592.

[40] Olmer, pp. 9-11. A slightly earlier appearance in Cairo can be seen in a stela in the Mosque of al-Tala'i'; cf. Creswell, op. cit., p. 285.

from the datable contexts cannot be carried beyond 1200, and very rarely to that point. By far, the greatest quantity of artifacts are to be found in the accumulated mounds above the archtectural remains, and these mounds have been found to be unstratified, as distinct from undisturbed pits and flooring fills.[41] Such examples as we have registered (less than half of those recovered, most of which were repetitive in pattern or incomplete), are surface finds or from disturbed loci within otherwise datable remains. The patterns generally parallel those of Olmer's typology, and the novelties have elements which relate the whole filter to his design corpus for the stated era.

Three design categories stand out: the epigraphic, (though curiously absent from our finds) the heraldic, and the zoomorphic, and all are easily distinguishable from their Fatimid canonical counterparts. (To date no human depiction on a filter after ca. 1200, has been published). The remainder proceed from abstract or abstract-geometrical concepts which are rarely executed with the delicacy observable within the similar ranges of the preceding era. At times the haphazard is effected, something unthinkable in the canonical range. Thus it becomes a problem to find a reasonable modus of distinction for any but the three categories noted above.

One sense of an a priori total break in design demonstrates itself in the absence of the surround and/or defining band with the incised zig-zag wavy line. If one asks what replaced so categorical an element, one approaches a possible line of attack in differentiating the filters with designs other than the epigraphic, the heraldic and the zoomorphic. There is a group with no surround of the inner pattern no matter how varied the latter may be; another contains a radial surround, each spoke of which contains a number of pinholes; and a third group is based on surrounds which contain bands of triangular cuts. A greater degree of order is obtained if we hold for argument's sake that the inner pattern of the three great groups give definition irrespective of the surround; and in all others the surround or its absence is the key to categorization.

With very few exceptions, the filters of this period continue the convexity of profile of the Fatimid era and are placed at the jointure of the shoulder and neck of the vessel. Quite a few of the vessels are glazed, and many carry external moulded decoration, both glazed and unglazed. There is a definite shift in vessel shape, with a tendency to echo metal types. Very few of the water bottles are handled, and the base tends to be ring-shaped, thicker in profile than the vessels of the immediate past. Whereas before the button-nodule was a rarity, it becomes almost the norm in the Ayyubid-Mamluk centuries. Finally, though the filters tend to be wider in diameter than the earlier ones, some exceptional ones are very small, in which case the interest shifts from the filter per se, to the shape of the vessel.

I. Radial central patterns without an obvious surround. In the Fatimid period a well conceived and executed central pattern was articulated by setting it off from the vessel itself by some sort of "break," either circlets or a band of zig-zag. A rather large group of filters

---

[41] A sense of the quantity of glazed ceramics alone in these mounds can be gleaned from our Shard Count '68. A possible exception to the rule was the large mound in Fustat-A, which was partially analyzed in 1973. It proved to be neither a tip-heap of Bahgat's excavations nor one disturbed by illegal scavenging; cf. FEPR '73, pp. 422-432.

appears now without a comparable distancing motif. The central pattern is the "all" of the design, as in the case of our first types C-I-A and C-I-B. The elements of the design are large rectangularly shaped holes punctuated by "sets" of rather small pinhole type of aperture. Often these are composed of concentric band-like arrangements, with the outer band seeming to be a surround, but which itself is not cut off from the area of the jointure, thus giving the effect of a radial design. Though there is development and evolution within the design context, only two dominants are obvious, e.g., the large opening and the sets of small pinholes. True symmetry is the quest, but the result is often poorly executed and unpleasing.

A. TWO ELEMENT SINGLE BAND.

> Fig. 125. There are six large nail-head like apertures punctuated by six "sets" of pinholes, each of four cut in a diamond motif. This single band surrounds a nodular button. A surface find; 13th-14th century.

B. TWO ELEMENT DOUBLE BAND. The judicious difference in this group is the number and placement of the pinholes vis-à-vis the larger apertures.

1. Single small-hole punctuating outer band.

> Fig. 126. Though there are twelve large openings in the outer ring, there are seven in the inner. Such asymmetry points to rather sluggish execution of an otherwise formal design. The two very small dots next to the off-center central pinpoint is further proof of the poor quality. However, the major idea is carried out: a single small hole between the larger ones in the outer ring. A surface find: 13th-14th century.

2. Single small-hole punctuating both bands.

> Fig. 127. The overall pattern looks symmetrical: twelve outer and six inner large openings separated by single pinholes in both bands. However, the large openings are not equal in size. The vessel was coated with a greyish yellow glaze, including the inner surface of the neck. A surface find: 14th century type of siliceous glazing.

> Fig. 128. A variant of the above: there are twelve large apertures in the outer band, but there are eight rather than six in the inner. Three intervalent spaces lack the pinhole, and one outer aperture was so poorly cut that it becomes continuous with the inner one. Surface find: 14th century on the analogy with Fig. 127.

3. Double small-hole punctuation outer band.

> Fig. 129. The outer larger apertures are something of a novelty in that the center of each is widened but not consistently around the band of eleven openings. The latter number is an indication of a failure at symmetry, as though the filter were cut without plan. There are two pinholes in each of the intervals, but none between the eight apertures of the inner band. A surface find: 14th-15th century; it is a poorer variant of the supposed model for Fig. 128.

4. Quadruple small-hole motif punctuating outer band.

   Fig. 130. It is clear that a diamond pattern of four pinholes comparable to those in Fig. 125 between the larger apertures was envisioned. It was unrealized in that in two instances the diamond motif was not achieved and in another only three pinholes were sunk. The outer band of eight apertures is balanced by an inner one of six: all around the central small-hole. A surface find: 14th-15th century.

5. Pyramidal small-hole motif. These are two-band patterns, but one is composed of motifs of six small holes arranged in a pyramidal fashion. These "sets" of small holes stand alone without the interpretation of large openings.

   Fig. 131. The outer band is composed of ten pyramidal "sets" with alternating reverses of base and tip. The inner band lacks any pinholing; unlike the outer band it is very poorly cut: There were meant to be twelve large openings, but there are really eleven and an incipient one. In place of the central single small hole, there are two oddly shaped openings, clearly a mistake in pattern. However, this inner band is reminiscent of the "filigree" filters of type A-V-A and A-V-B, of the 10th century, relative to the hook-like nature of the large openings. It was found in the sieve of a pit whose contents were not consistently datable, but which did contain the filter in Pl. VIII-d. However, the pyramidal motif of small holes cannot be associated with any earlier type of filter. We are prone to assign it as early as possible within the norms of this part of our typology: ca. 1200.

   Fig. 132. Here the five unevenly spaced pyramidal sets form the inner band with tips towards the central small hole. The outer band is poorly planned in that there are thirteen rather than twelve apertures, with double pinholing in the interval. This filter is further an oddity within the Ayyubid-Mamluk canon in that it is placed along the high neck of the vessel, which has a very prominent rib *below* the placement of the filter. As this is a surface find, and as the shape of the neck is so anamolous, it is only by motival analogy with Fig. 131 that we assign it a 13th-14th century date.

6. Two element triple band.

   Fig. 133. Another failed attempt at symmetrical variation on the theme of small holes punctuating three bands of large openings. What was intended was a series of 4/8/16: the inner band punctuated by a single pinhole in the interval, the middle one by the diamond motif of four in the alternate spaces, and the outer by double pinholes. What was produced fails in the outer band in that there are nineteen quasi-rectangular openings, so that the symmetrical composite pattern is destroyed. A surface find: 13th-14th century on the analogy of the group as a whole.

II. Cruciform motif without a surround. This motif is definitely a carryover from the Fatimid canonical mesh designs, type B-II-A-1. Thus the group would seem to be easily placed within the earliest part of the Ayyubid period.

> Pl. XXIII-a/Fig. 134. This pattern has been published (Fat. Fil., fig. 11-c), and it is clear there that the mesh effect has not been effected by eyelets or circlets but by the small holes familiar to us in type C-I-A and C-I-B. The whole exterior of the portion remaining is covered with a darkish green siliceous glaze, and has a single handle, again proof of a carryover. The moulded band of rinceau on the shoulder is another transitional motif. From a piece of pottery dated 556/1161 found in another part of the same building where this filter was found, it would seem the locus has a history extending into the finale of Fatimid power and perhaps further.[42] It may with safety be dated before 1200 and after 1160.

III. Star patterns without a surround. This group is as complicated as the foregoing and as difficult to analyze into elements. Towards the end there is an attempt to make spokes of the star into radial bands containing pinholes, but not quite to the extent of having *all* the elements form a radial band with pinholes. Such ambiguities arise once again from imperfection of execution. Unlike the star patterns of Fatimid filters, there is little proof that the pattern was drawn out beforehand so as to achieve desired symmetry. The size of the filter does not vary very much from that encountered in types C-I and II, but the nodular button appears more frequently.

A. NO EXTRA DECORATION. The emphasis is on the star and no other decorative "openings" are added.

> Fig. 135. A nine-spoked star is achieved by cutting nine narrowly rectangular openings, punctuated by triangular holes at the edge of the pattern. This affords nine V-like spokes. The center is plain except for a central pinhole. As the filter is quite small (less than 3 cm in diameter), interest attaches to the vessel shape. It lacks the high neck associated with Fatimid vessels, being shorter and less straight. The body "bulge" comes closer to the base and there is no proper shoulder or handle. The base is sharply ring-footed and its interior concave, very much like the Fatimid models. This last feature seems an aspect of continuity, permitting a date within the last half of the 12th century. The find-spot was a test trench and chronologically inconclusive.

B. TREFOIL SPOKES WITH FURTHER DECORATION, NO CENTER PATTERN.

> Fig. 136. A more symmetrical six-part star has been executed by having the six rectangular openings proceed from the rim of the pattern to a point of

---

[42] FEPR '64, pp. 23 f. and pl. XV-40.
[43] FEPR '64, p. 11.

contiguity with the central opening. The surfaces left are each made into a trefoil by two triangular cuts at the rim. Finally each trefoil petal is cut by a further triangle with its tip between those cut at the rim. The neck of the vessel and the filter placement are as anamolous as those of Fig. 132. As our filter is a surface find, it is only by motival association with Fig. 135 that we assign it to the 13th-14th century.

Fig. 137.   Except for a single flaw (one trefoil becoming a quatrefoil), this is a lovely and sinuous pattern. The four defining openings are not cut straight and give a "water-wheel" effect to the resulting flower. Each petal has nine small triangular openings in a diamond motif. A nodular button commands the center. As this example was found in the *sibakh*[43] layer, above architectural remains, we may assign it to the 12th-13th century.

Fig. 138.   The four defining rectangular openings are now divided by surfaces, each pierced by five pinholes. Thus the star is composed of four narrow spokes and four trefoils. The latter are plain except for a small round hole cut in the middle foil. The central portion of the pattern is plain except for a small nodular button. The shape is transitional in that the neck and base are like those of Fatimid filter vessels, while the body has a pronounced break from curving to straight at almost midpoint between neck and base. Like Fig. 135, this was a trench find and can likewise be dated to the last half of the 12th century.

Fig. 139.   An incomplete, asymmetrically cut pattern of seven trefoils around a central nodular button. Each trefoil has a diamond motif of nine pinholes, making it rather similar to the petal pattern in Fig. 137. The exterior of the vessel was covered by a mottled green siliceous glaze. This fact, plus the motival analogy with others in this group lead us to put it into the Ayyubid period before 1200, though it is a surface find.

C. TREFOIL SPOKES AROUND CENTRAL PATTERN.

Pl. XXIII-b   The published pattern (FEPR '64, fig. 2-d) shows an odd combination of the central element of Fig. 128, except that the large apertures here are triangular, and the outer section of Olmer's pl. XXXII-A, except that it has six trefoils while ours has four. Or it must be seen as a combination of Figs. 137 and 138 plus the central motif. It is a very poorly executed specimen: the decoration on the petals varies from six to nine pine-points. The seven (rather than four, six or eight) apertures in the central motif add to the awkwardness of the design. A surface find; 13th-14th century.

D. CENTRAL STAR DOMINANT.

Fig. 140.   Here the star is essentially the pattern. Incised lines proceeding from the

---

[42] FEPR '64, pp. 23 f. and pl. XV-40.
[43] FEPR '64, p. 11.

central hole divide the star into six diamonds, each pierced with a single small hole. The inner solidarity of surface is mitigated by the great number of randomly sunk holes in the areas left between the points of the star and the rim of the pattern area. Again this is a poorly executed filter in that one point of the star does not touch the rim of the filter. This is a surface find; but the vessel had a handle and the neck has the characteristic Fatimid straightness of line. One sees too the inspiration in the canonical star motif of Olmer's pl. XXVII-A and B. Before 1200.

Fig. 141.   The same pattern except that the entire star is defined by pinpoints on a star surface which is attached to the rim at six points, yielding six cusped open areas. Then each diamond is cut by an inverted V-opening and one small hole. The nodular button at the center has a small hole pierced through it. Though the surround is different, Olmer's pl. XXVVI-A is clearly a relative of our pattern. Our example was found in the *sibakh*, but the extreme convexity of profile leads us to assign it to the 13th-14th century.

E. STAR AND ROUND SHIELD.

Fig. 142.   This is very much in the spirit of Figs. 135 and 136 and is a better cut version of Olmer's pl. XXXIV-C, in that the central roundel shield is better executed. The latter contains two radial bands of six and twelve small holes attendant to a small nodular button. Though a surface find, it would seem on the strength of Olmer's example to be purely Mamluk; 14th-15th century.

IV. Spoke-radial surround.   This is perhaps the most distinctive motif of the post-Fatimid canonical range. What had simply punctuated a pattern of large apertures, now becomes a flat comparatively wide band with narrow longish tapering openings betwixt. These "spokes" serve to connect the central pattern to the edge of the design, *distancing* and setting off the latter, which become as large as the radial patterns without surround in groups C-I, C-II and C-III. Thus, a grouping is achieved which contains a wider variety of central patterns.[44]

It is well-nigh impossible to plot the evolution of the motif, because it appears associated with canonical motifs (cf. Fat. Fil., figs. 11-f and 13-a and b as proceeding from figs. 11-a and 12 therein; Pls. XV-a, b and c proceeding from Pls. X-d and XIV-c herein); and because attempts are so crudely executed in the later periods.

---

[44] These include the superior groupings of epigraphic, heraldic and zoomorphic patterns. These latter are treated separately herein, irrespective of the surround motif; the distinction proceeds more from familiarity than strict logic.

A. INCIPIENT.

Fig. 143.   Had the pinholing been applied to all the spokes our type might have been seen in its pristine stage. The cross of pinholing, taking in the central design, affords the entire pattern an inexpungable clumsiness. The eight inner triangular openings were meant to be balanced by twelve outer tapering ones; instead we have thirteen, yet another instance of poor execution. A surface find; 13th-15th centuries.

Fig. 144.   A good example of ten wide spokes each with four pinholes, but very unevenly executed. The nodular button may be taken as the central pattern. (The single pinhole at its base may be considered an error of execution.) A surface find; 13th-15th centuries.

B. WITH RADIAL CENTRAL PATTERN.

Fig. 145.   A very interesting example because of the external ribbing of the neck, a feature we have generally associated with pre-Fatimid filter vessels. A central design of seven tapering large holes punctuated by single smaller ones between has a radial surround of fifteen spokes each with three pinholes. A single small hole is punched at the center of the filter. Though discovered among the remains of a Fatimid domicile, it is clearly later. However it is similar to Pl. XV-c, only lacking the zig-zag surround; one feels safe assigning it to the period before 1200.

Fig. 146.   Very much in the spirit of the foregoing filter. The eight inner spokes each has two pinholes, and the outer fourteen each has three. It was found in a pit whose contents were disturbed; however, by motival analogy with Fig. 145 we may assign it a comparable dating, before 1200.

C. CRUCIFORM MESH CENTRAL PATTERN.

Fig. 147.   This filter is similar to that of Pl. XXIII-a and Fat. Fil., fig. 11-a, except that it has a radial surround of fifteen spokes each with three pinholes, which in turn relates it to that of Pl. XI-c herein. Though a surface find, we may assign it to the same date as its congeners: before 1200.

D. CENTRAL STAR PATTERN.

1. Six-spoked.

Fig. 148.   A very poorly cut example. The central star is composed of three wide and three narrow spokes. Each of the former is pierced by three holes, and one at the inner end of each of the latter. The surround is composed of sixteen spokes each with five or six pinholes. A surface find; 13th-15th centuries.

Fig. 149.   A slightly better executed variation of Fig. 148. The wider spokes of the inner star have six small holes pierced in each surface with three more badly placed about the center of the filter surface as a whole. There are fifteen spokes in the outer surround, each with five or six pinholes. A surface find; 13th-15th centuries.[45]

Fig. 151. Another variant in that each of three wide inner spokes has nine small holes pierced so as to yield a pyramid. There are seventeen spokes in the outer surround, each with five or six pinholes. There is a central nodular button on this surface find; 13th-15th centuries.

2. Ten-spoked.

Fig. 152. This is really a five pointed star reminiscent of the barrette style, with a five spoked radiant superimposed with each of the latter spokes bearing a small and a tapering hole. The surround radiant has twenty-eight spokes, each with five pinholes. Such an increase would seem to put this range of filter beyond the Ayyubid period; 14th-15th century.

3. Three trefoils and interstitial pinpoint mesh.

Fig. 153. This may be considered a nine-pointed star, but each trefoil is internally defined by four pinholes in a diamond motif. Unsymmetrically executed, but the intent is clear. The surround is composed of twenty-five spokes each with five pinholes. A surface find; 14th-15th century.

Fig. 154. An exceedingly inept execution of a variant of the foregoing filter. The three parts of the inner star are defined by sets of double parallel lines of pinholes. Then any further definition is simply dissolved. The surround is composed of twenty-one spokes each with three or four pinholes. A surface find; 15th century.

4. Four trefoils and interstitial pinpoint mesh.

Fig. 155. This is essentially a twelve pointed star, but divided internally by sets of pinholes in such fashion as to indicate trefoils. The pattern is strong but unevenly executed. The surround contains thirty spokes each meant to have four pinholes. This filter was found in the disturbed contents of a sanitation pit; 14th-15th century.

5. Three quatrefoils and interstitial pinpoint mesh.

Fig. 156. A well-cut exemplar, but not symmetrical in all its decorative details. Each of the three leaves is meant to be pierced by three sets of four pinholes arranged in a diamond motif. The space between the leaves is taken up by a large triangle with its apex at the rim of the whole central pattern, and its surface decorated with three pinholes. There are thirty-four spokes in the

---

[45] A vessel with a similar filter was found in Nubia at Kasr al-Wizz. Its shape (Fig. 150 herein) is especially interesting as no other vessel with so narrow a base has been found in Fustat, or published to date. Unlike our examples of type C-IV-D-1, the bottle from Nubia has a finial type central button. Notwithstanding these characteristics, the vessel is of Egyptian manufacture. It bears Kasr al-Wizz Reg. No. 65-10-65 and is in the Islamic Museum, Cairo. Cf. George T. Scanlon, "Excavations at Kasr al-Wizz: A Preliminary Report I," *Journal of Egyptian Archaeology*, vol. 56 (1970), p. 46 n. 3 for a discussion of others found at Faras.

surround, each with four pinholes. The profile of filter is highly convex, and there is a very slight shoulder ribbing external. The find-spot was disturbed, but on shape and quality of design we may assign the filter to the 13th-14th dynasty.

E. CENTRAL ENTRELAC PATTERN.

Fig. 157.   This filter is in the spirit of Olmer, pl. XLII-B, but less intricate. There are pinholes in the interstices of the design and on the surface of the weave. This motif is similar to the entrelacs employed elsewhere by the Mamluk craftsman, without being as concisely executed. Each of the twenty-nine spokes of the surround contains four pinholes. Again the locus was disturbed, but the shape of the neck and convexity of the profile stamp the filter as Mamluk: 13th-14th century.

F. CENTRAL CONVEX-CONCAVE PATTERN.

Fig. 168.   The circle of the inner design is chorded, giving a shield shape with sides alternately concave and convex. Barrettes attach this to the outer surround. The surface thus achieved is outlined by pinholing and is punctured by eight round holes. The twenty outer spokes each contain three or four pinholes. This is a surface find, but it is clearly in the lineage of Mamluk design; 14th-15th century.

G. MISCELLANEOUS.

Fig. 159.   The spokes of the outer radiant are not straight, but are rather round-sided. The purpose was to allow each of the twelve surfaces to contain four pinholes in a diamond motif, though this is not perfectly accomplished. A plain narrow surface separates this surround from the inner radial pattern of seven circlets about a largish central circular hole. The outer surface of the vessel carried a milky blue-white siliceous glaze which, added to the resemblance of the central radial design to Pl. XV-b, points to a date around 1200, though the filter is a surface find.

V. Surround(s) of triangular cuts. Whereas the radial spoked surround with pinholes seems to be a continuation of, or at the very least a development from, a Fatimid stylistic, the present rubric would seem to lie entirely within the subsequent era. There is a thematic, though not necessarily a chronological, development of the idea from a single band at the edge of the filter to a double band of triangles to a combination of the latter into a sharp sawtooth motif ending in the latter's separation from the central pattern by an intermediate flat band which itself hears incised lines affording a whorl effect. In these last developments we have a true "framing" of the central pattern. If one peruses the examples in categories C-I and C-III, one can see an "inner" element moving to the "outer" surround, a process one encounters so often in Mamluk architecture where a structurally functional element becomes decorative and vice-versa. The filters in this category seem to be generally more intelligently executed, so that the designs as a whole convey a firmness of presentation no matter how lacking in imaginative variation. From the latter stricture one excepts the zoo-morphic group, the surround notwithstanding.

A. SINGLE BAND SURROUND OF TRIANGIULAR CUTS.

Fig. 160. This fragmentary filter is analagous to Olmer, pl. XXXV-B, and like it probably had a central radiant of triangular holes around a finial button. The interesting departure here is the moving of the pinpoints from the spokes to the flat immediately inner band. The same holds true of the pinholes of the intermediate band of triangular punches. Though found at the base of a wall of a Fatimid domicile, the filter is clearly post-Fatimid and may be assigned to the 13th-14th century.

B. DOUBLE BAND SURROUND OF TRIANGULAR CUTS.

Fig. 161. The original pattern had a surround band of thirteen triangular cuts at the edge punctuated by a like number of diamond (double triangle) cuts. The center was left free of design except for random pinholing. Rather poorly executed. Found in a trial trench; 13th-15th centuries.

Fig. 162. Here the double band of nineteen triangles each is imperfectly realized, but one can see in it the genesis of the saw-tooth band. The central radiant pattern of five spokes punctuated by five largish triangular holes is equally asymmetrical. A surface find; 13th-14th century.

C. SAW-TOOTHED SURROUND. This is accomplished by taking the two bands of triangular holes in the surround and *meshing* them symmetrically. The surround thus achieved either attends the central pattern or is distanced from it by an intermediate flat band with incised lines in a whorl attempt.

1. Immediately attendant to central pattern.

Fig. 163. A surround of twenty-four teeth enclose a circle divided into six parts by pinholes. Each of the sections is randomly pinholed, yielding an overall distinguished pattern. A surface find; 14th-15th century.

Fig. 164. An interesting design and executed with some finesse. The central simple entrelac is akin to Fig. 157, and like it has the outline, interstices and sur-face decoration with pinholes. The surround is now of thirty-two teeth. A surface find but obviously Mamluk; 13th-14th century.

2. Intermediate flat band.

a. Fleuron central pattern.

Fig. 165. Between the central quatrefoil fleuron, so reminiscent of the motif from the Fatimid range, and the thirty-four pointed saw-tooth of the surround, there lies a wide band which is decorated by random linear incisions which unlike the pinholes do not penetrate the surface. The whorl effect can hardly be said to be realized here. The combination of the saw-tooth and

the flat band would seem to be quintessentially Mamluk, but the fleuron
finds its genesis in an earlier period. Hence, though from a disturbed find-
spot, we tend to think the example fits better into the 13th than the 14th
century.[46]

b. Central pattern of cruciform mesh.

Fig. 166.   The central pattern, though smaller, can be immediately associated with Olmer, pl. XXXVI-B, though it lacks the second saw-tooth of the latter. And
it is of the same class as Pl. XXIII-a. It was found along with Fig. 137, and
for reasons stated in its discussion, we would place this exceptional example in the 12th-13th century, though with hesitation because of the purely
Mamluk surround. A well cut filter with a true whorl effect on the flat
band.

c. Central star pattern.

Fig. 167.   This is almost an exact duplicate of Olmer, pl. XXXVI-A; it lacks only the
pierced central button. It is similar, too, to Fig. 141 herein, which lacks
our developed surround. A surface find; 13th-14th century.

Fig. 168.   The original pattern was a six pointed star whose shield-like center was
pierced with random small holes around a low nodular button. No doubt
it was in the spirit of Olmer, pl. XXXV-C, though the latter's intermediate
flat band was itself star-shaped. The filter was found in a trial trench; 13th-
14th century.

Fig. 169.   The distinctive surround envelopes a rather complex inner pattern. This is
made of an outer twenty pointed star and an inner radiant of nine nail-hole
openings. The former has a diamond motif of nine pinholes on alternate
rays with a small hole punctured in the others. The latter is a combination
of the nail holes of Fig. 125 and the two-hole punctuation of the outer
element of Fig. 132. This finely executed example was found in the *sibakh*;
13th century. The outermost band has forty-seven teeth.

VI. The heraldic. These quintessentially Mamluk motifs are fully surveyed in Olmer,
pls. LXIII-LXXIII. They parallel comparable expression in other metiers (including
architecture), but are not as plentifully represented in the Fustat/ARCE finds as are the
zoomorphic. Nor has the Expedition recovered any filters with epigraphic (Naskhi) motifs,
though a quite splendid recent example has been found at Qusayr al-Qadim on the Red Sea
coast.[47]

---

[46] This filter was found in the fill above the estopment of Pit B (XVI-1'), below which came the cache
of objects, all of the last half of the 8th century, discussed in Fustat-Arts.

[47] Donald S. Whitcomb and Janet H. Johnson, *Qusayr al-Qadim 1978: Preliminary Report* (ARCE/
Cairo: 1979), pl. 43-c. The filter in pl. 44-d is our type B-II-A-1-a, clearly Fatimid: and the fragment in
pl. 38-c is possibly Olmer, pl. XII-C and our type B-II-A-3-b, again Fatimid.

A. THE FLEUR-DE-LYS. There is some argument over whether this is a true heraldic device. In pottery it seems too common to be distinctive, yet it seems to be so in numismatics.[48] As it is rather rare in the world of filters, we will follow Olmer in considering the device apposite.

> Fig. 170. Though our example lacks a surround, it is more finely conceived than Olmer, pl. LXXIII-C but not as fanciful as his pl. LXXIII-B, yet having identical interstitial and surface pinholes. Ours is a surface find; 14th-15th century.

VII. The Zoomorphic. Olmer, pls. LIX-LXI, presents a limited range of examples: the hare, the lion, the eagle, and a singular bird which he opines is a pigeon. The variety of the immediately preceding era is missing; neither the fantastic animal nor the human are represented. And, though the depictions are vivacious and amusing, the sheer beauty of the Ayyubid peacock filter (Olmer, pl. LXIII-A) is not repeated.

A. THE HARE/RABBIT.

> Pl. XIII-c/Fig. 171. This almost exuberant animal moving left has been published (FEPR '64, fig. 2-a). It has a typical saw-tooth surround and all the interstices are pinholes and there is a like decoration on the surface of the hare. The center of the pattern is a low nodular button; as a whole, it resembles Olmer, pls. LIX-B and LX-A. However, it is an oddity in that the vessel is of red, rather than white, clay. A surface find; 14th-15th century.

> Fig. 172. An incomplete filter but clearly related to Olmer, pl. LIX-B in that there is a lozenge-like surface betwixt the left front and right rear legs. The button is more pronounced than that of Fig. 171, and the vessel is of the more usual white-grey clay. A surface find; 14th-15th century.

B. THE BIRD.

> Fig. 173. Just the central part of the filter remains. A bird with lowered head is passant to the right which, as can be seen from the last two filters and from Olmer, is opposite to the motion of the quadrapeds. It seems to have had a radiant surround with each spoke pinholed, but whether this was intermediate or outer cannot be assumed, though in size it matches Fig. 174 below. A surface find; 14th-15th century.

> Fig. 174. Though incomplete, a very beautiful filter with a central motif of a bird, possibly a guinea fowl, passant to the right. However, if the surface above the head be taken for the comb, we might have a peacock with the brush in process of erection. the sickle band to the right of the figure relates the filter to Olmer, pl. LX-C, whose figure he deems "*une pintade.*" The central button has a concave surface. The radiant surround of pinpointed spokes could relate it to Fig. 173. A surface find; 14th-15th century.

---

[48] Paul Balog, *Coinage of the Mamluk Sultans of Egypt and Syria* (American Numismatic Society, New York: 1964), pp. 18-38.

APPENDICES

Appendix A (for Category A)

Certain objects unearthed during the Fustat Expedition's work call for special attention, though they lay outside the broad categorizations offered for the period ca. 700- ca. 1000 A.D. They may be individually "exotic" or different, or may represent fugitive examples, most often incomplete or from less sure chronological loci, of types more adequately represented in Olmer. Thus within terms of our excavations, they are atypical, and will be described separately, with the proviso that later work at Fustat may more intelligently fold them into the broad typology. They will be denominated as a group "XA," i.e., as being chronologically within category A but stylistically distinct from the given range.

XA-1. Glass.

Fig. 175. This object was found in the undisturbed section of the famous cistern which produced the lustre goblet and other objects discussed in our "Fustat and Islamic Arts of Egypt"[49] wherein the chronology is fully discussed. Though incomplete, we may see the original vessel as of two parts: the upper straight neck of manganese tinted glass, the lower bulbous body of a light bluish green tinted glass. There is no handle, and six randomly spaced holes were pierced through the conjoint surface. This latter factor associates this glass filter with the ceramic ones of type A-I-A. A broken glass filter came forth from the same locus.[49a] Second half of the 8th century.

XA-2. Glazed.

Fig. 176. This almost unique filter vessel has been published (FEPR '65-I, fig. 13-b), more for its externally moulded decoration, and its importance as an example of early lead glazed ware, than for the fact that it had a filter at the jointure of neck and shoulder. No doubt that the filter was as rudimentary in pattern as those of group A-I-A, but the speckled green glaze covering the vessel makes it unique within filters of this period. As it was found within the *dakkah* fill of an early foundation, it can be assigned to the 8th-9th century.

---

[49] Fustat-Arts, passim.

[49a] This second filter was of the same dimensions and color combination as those of Fig. 175, but had eleven holes randomly punched. (Reg. No. 65-5-150; Corning Museum)

XA-3. Slip-painted, red clay.

Pl. XXIII-d/Fig. 177.   In 1972, a great number of shards were found in the hard-pressed baulks which represented the remains of the fills of rooms all of whose walls were made of burnt bricks laid in mud mortar, a sure clue to the earliest period of the habitation of Fustat.[50] All were of red-clay, thin-walled, dimple bottomed and sometimes with a convex "button" at the center of the base, and all covered by a pinkish cream slip. Sometimes there was a further linear and epigraphic decoration in a blackish brown slip. One shard carried the word "jizah," permitting us to denominate a Gizah ware.[51] The filters were simply of round punches in rings about the center, a feature which relates the ware to type A-I-A. As no early filter vessels with slipped decoration have been reported for the early period, Gizah ware takes on a different importance. No samples appeared from later dated loci; hence we may assume it did not last beyond the finale of the 9th century.

XA-4. Additional pattern to type A-III-A.

Fig. 178.   As the section of this filter fragment is concave and the object was found in the same undisturbed locus as that of Pl. 1-d, a 9th century dating would not be misleading. The full pattern might have been in the spirit of Olmer, pl. XLIV-D, which he hesitatingly assigns to the Tulunid period. His example is a five-pointed star, whereas ours was probably six-pointed. Nonetheless, the central motif was here poorly executed allowing a certain dubiety to arise.

XA-5. Unglazed, red clay.

Fig. 178-a.   Though the filter of this vessel lacks any interest whatsoever, it is analogous to those of our very earliest datable examples. But it is the shape and the find-spot which lend it an importance greater than categorical propinquity. It has a finely ribbed body, almost imperial in the sharp articulation. It was one-handled and the filter was convex, completing the curve of the shoulder, which means that the straight sided neck was added. Its find-spot (XXI-9 S) is fully described in FEPR '72-II, within the undisturbed hardened baulk fill of which were found more fragments of early lustered glass and a coin of Abd al-Malik ibn Yazid, the first Abbasid governor of Egypt, and dated 133 (751 A.D.). Mid-8th century; unregistered.[52]

---

[50] Reconsideration, passim and Numismatics, pp. 171 f. and pl. 2.

[51] The problem is discussed in FEPR '72-I and n. 54 therein.

[52] The fineness of the potting is reminiscent of the unglazed ribbed wares found in the lowest stretches of the stratigraphical cuts made in the streets and pavement fills throughout the excavations, excellent samples of which may be seen in Numismatics, pl. 5. These are now known to have been of the 7th-8th century, i.e., just prior and just subsequent to the introduction of glazing.

XA-6. Unglazed, white buff ware.

Fig. 178-b.   This is a much squatter vessel than the water bottle shapes we have been discussing. The body is bulbous, the base flat, and the neck flares almost to the width of the body. It is one-handled and the filter is characteristically concave and not at the jointure of neck and shoulder. It might have been used for liquids more precious and more viscuous than water, such as kitchen oil. It was found in canal G in XVI-23/24, whose contents were found to be undisturbed; cf. FEPR '71-1. A glass weight of the Abbasid governor Isa b. Mansur, 831-832 A.D., accompanying the vessel confirms the 9th century dating we have assigned to many of the filter vessels in the middle range of Category A. Unregistered. A variant, also unregistered and from a comparable find-spot can be seen in Fig. 178-c.

Appendix B (for Category B)

The double tradition of "continuing" and "canonical" pattern is so strong during the Fatimid apogee and shortly after, that it tends to overwhelm any subsidiary filter patterns. These latter lack the artistic thrust and variety of the former, but they have an intrinsic interest as being different relative to material, shape and mode of decoration. As most can be placed firmly in Fatimid contexts, they add significantly to our knowledge of the artisinal production of the era, without disturbing our comprehension of the grander line of Fatimid filter art. For dating reasons, we denominate them as group "XB."

XB-1. Brown buff clay, slip painted.

Fig. 179.   The clay, being distinct from the more usual buff-white range, marks this vessel as unusual. A light brown slip covers the entire external surface. The decoration of the upper part of the bulbous body is in red-brown slip: two sets of wavy parallel lines interrupted twice by hatched design within rough half ellipses. There is a light orange red wash on the shoulder. The vessel has an indented base. It was found in the upper portion of a pit whose narrower lower portion had been estopped. In the upper fill was a *fals* fragment of the Caliph al-Muqtadir (908-932, Abbasid) and two glass *jetons* of Al-Hakim (996-1020, Fatimid). Thus it would seem that our example is of the 10th-11th century. The design on the outer side is distinctly Coptic, perhaps a Nubian Christian import.[53] The seven randomly gouged holes are unimportant relative to the dating.

XB-2. Red clay, slip and incised decoration. From many of the indisputably Fatimid contexts shards of a very strongly potted filter vessel type came forward. They were all of a micaceous red clay, and had external decoration in white and black slip, sometimes

---

[53] A finer example of a slip-painted Nubian filter, of a pink-brown clay native to the region, can be seen in fig. 13 in article cited in n. 44 **supra**; found at Kasr al-Wizz.

accompanied by wavy incised lines. All could be assumed to be one-handled and long spouted and ring-based. The filters per se were either ungainly or quite simple, which meant that they did not distract attention from the peasant sturdiness of the vessel shape. Because of the latter fact, they are clearly divided from the artistic range of filter patterns.

a. Random gouging of filter.

Fig. 180.   An almost complete specimen. The filter lacks pattern, per se. The major decoration is on the shoulder: a wavy band between parallel lines, all of white slip. A thick inchoate line appears higher on the shoulder. The find-spot allows us to assign the vessel to the 11th century.

b. Radial pattern of filter.

Fig. 181.   This fine vessel is complete except for the spout, but its placement is identical to that of Fig. 180. The filter is composed of four sickle gougings around a central small hole. The decoration externally is of a white slip band bordered by two black slip narrow bands; the center band has angled double vertical incisings. Though found in a disturbed context, the general shape and decoration allows a Fatimid dating: 11th-12th century.

Fig. 182.   The shape of this filter vessel portion has been published (Pits, pl. XVI-3) and its date therein discussed. A bit of white slip decoration remains external, and the shape of the neck and handle clearly relate it to the foregoing examples. The pattern is a series of narrow radial slits, almost a water-wheel motif, around a central small hole.

Fig. 183.   Though only the neck remains, its shape and external decoration of white and black circles on an incised wavy line, mark it as belonging to this subordinate range of filters. The filter pattern is of radial straight slashes about a very small central hole. A surface find; 11th-12th century.

c. Filter missing.

Fig. 184.   There can be no doubt from the spout, the position of the missing handle, the base and the external slip and incised decoration that this incomplete vessel is analogous to others of this type. The white and dark red-brown slip bands in a double set each contains an incised wavy line. A surface find; 11th-12th century.

Fig. 185.   The shape of this vessel has been published (Pits, pl. XVI-2), and though the neck and filter are missing the spout, the bulbous body, the base and the incised and slip decoration external announce it as being of this category. Its find-spot also helps to corroborate an 11th-12th century dating.

XB-3. Splash glaze decoration.

Pl. XXIVa/Fig. 186.   This particular mode of decoration (alternate daubs, splashes or lines of manganese and turquoise glazes on a transparent colorless glaze) can be seen on lamps and bowls,[54] and in this so far unique example we

---

[54] Cf. *Qusayr al-Qadim* (n. 46 supra), pls. 38-n and 41-a for Sector P7d-3.

have it applied to a filter vessel. Though the filter is missing, the "hook-ons" are clearly apparent and like the other glazed and plain filter examples, within the Fatimid context,[55] it was of the central knitting type, B-I-C. The clay is of the same color as those filters of the mono-glazed and lustered varieties. It was found in a pit whose contents were all of the 11th-12th century.

Appendix C (for Category C)

Whereas, with some caution, we may assume a ceramic security for the 14th century on the basis of the Preliminary Report from Qusayr al-Qadim, nothing remotely assured exists for the 15th century. By an almost stylistic attrition, Olmer and the Fustat Expedition/ARCE simply typologize what is "left over." The mounds at Fustat are generally unstratified and reveal too much disturbance and admixture to be chronologically beneficial.[56] Hence, on the one hand we are unsure exactly how many types were manufactured after 1200, and, on the other, how long certain ones were made, perhaps into the Ottoman period. In sum, our types in Category C have a relative motival validity with a concurrent fragility of dating. Even so, the following types seem *beside* our professed typology for the Mamluk period, though archaeologically related. They will be referred to as group "XC."

XC-1. Splash glaze.

Pl. XXIV-b/Fig. 187. Though it might be thought at first that this glazed filter with additional glaze daubing external might be related to our XB-3 (Fig. 186 and Pl. XXIV-a) and thus be construed as Fatimid, neither the pattern of the filter nor its placement will permit this. The former makes it akin to types C-I and C-III, and the latter to the filters in Figs. 132 and 136. The basic glaze is similar to that on Fig. 127. Another departure is that whereas the elements of the pattern (four triangular and four elliptical outlines) are obvious, the holes do not conform to the shapes. A surface find, most tentatively assigned to the 14th-15th century.

XC-2. Red clay, slip painted external.

Fig. 188. Red clay filters are exceptional in all periods, the only ones for Category C being those of Fig. 171 (and Pl. XXIII-c) and Fig. 189 below. The shape of the neck is also exceptional, while the filter pattern is unexceptional. Only the external surface of the neck is decorated: circles, lines in various directions, and ellipses in reserve, all in dark brown slip on a beige pink slip base.

---

[55] Olmer, pl. A of introduction; Fig. 56 and Pl. IX-c and d herein; and a filter in the collection of the University of Pennsylvania Museum (no. 29-140-597), which is covered by a manganese/aubergine siliceous glaze.

[56] Shard Count '68, passim, but with the reservation relating to the mound investigated in 1973 (n. 40 supra).

The decoration is Coptic in feeling, or perhaps Nubian of the very latest
Christian period, hence an import. A surface find, quite possibly of the
13th-14th century.

XC-3. Red clay.

Fig. 189.   An interesting filter in that it is made of red clay, but the central cruciform
motif contains a wavy zig-zag line element which echoes the Fatimid
stylistic.[57] It may have been meant for decorative slipping. It is a surface
find; as it is too crudely executed to be Fatimid canonical, we reluctantly
assign it to the 13th-14th century.

Appendix D (Finds from 1980 Season)

The third part of the Fustat Expedition concession (denominated Fustat-C) had not been
worked until 1980, because, as it was beyond the remains of the wall of Salah ad-Din, it
did not seem as vulnerable to development schemes as either Fustat-A or B. However, late
in 1979, the Governorate of Cairo decided to use this particular area (more particularly that
lying between the Saladinian wall and the pools of Ayn al-Sira) as the new rubbish heap of
Cairo. A huge moving mass of debris appeared due south of Sh. Salah Salim, its contents
burned day and night, the remains to be solidified by the addition of an asbestos-like coagu-
lent. This, then, would become a suitable foundation for yet another building project. By
September of 1980, the new mound was within 35 m of the heretofore high mound which
represented Fustat-C and loomed ten meters above it. The Governorate could assure no
surcease of dumpage, so an emergency season was dictated before Fustat-C was entirely lost
to scientific enquiry.

Once more, and for the last time, the Smithsonian Institution provided funds through its
Soft Currency Program. Additional hard currency support was provided by the American
University in Cairo, the Corning Museum of Glass and the American Numismatic Society.
Intensive excavation proceeded for nine weeks with quite unexpected results. Most of these
are recounted in the appropriate Preliminary Report, but for our purposes the following
data are most pertinent:

a. With very few "sportive" exceptions, nothing on or within the mound could be
dated after 1050 A.D. The numismatic evidence corroborated this, and a survey of
the surrounding mounds proved the absence of any post-1200 ceramic evidence,
which abounded throughout the mounds of Fustat-A and B.[58] Finally, when the
Antiquities Service undertook to investigate the mound between ours and the
moving rubbish heap of the Governorate, the results were in every way comparable.

b. The extensive architectural remains within the mound proved to be built not upon
the *gabal* as had obtained throughout Fustat-A and B, but upon the heightened fill
of the previous occupation. As no foundation rested upon the *gabal*, the remains

---

[57] The finer Fatimid model can be seen in *Qusayr al-Qadim*, pl. 46-a.
[58] Cf. Shard Count and FEPR '72-I, n. 1.

of the secondary occupation gave all appearances of being jerry-built and of a quite different planning, e.g., there was not a trace of a courtyard, of stone paving, or of the Samarra-*bayt* module, or of the usual complex entry-way to the domicile.

c. Careful investigation of these upper remains lead to the conclusion that there were two periods of occupation between ca. 900 and ca. 1000, and a third almost squatter-like which terminates ca. 1050.

d. The water table was very high in this area and made it almost impossible to find the architectural traces of the very earliest settlement, i.e., the one reared on the *gabal*. Various sondages throughout the site (abutting or within the upper domicile remains) however established the presence of the *gabal* (app. 6.5 m below the upper traces) and proof of an occupation ca. 700-800.

It is against these facts that we interpret the fifteen filters found during the 1980 season. Some are novel, but all may be fitted into the typological survey already discussed and with one exception they justify the periodization we have posited. Each will be noted by its appropriate numbering and placed in the Table at the rear of the volume.

A-II.   "Simple/mechanical" with imposed decoration.

Fig. 190. A bit more than half of the filter survives, but the shape and design are ascertainable. It is rather large and seems to echo the candelabra motif of Fig. 7-d, supra. Unlike the latter, the design is not cruciform, but rather radial: five lines of pinpointing ending in a candelabra, five alternating lines reaching the border of the filter which is a binding circlet of pinholes. The clay is buff-brown and the surface is rather discolored. Its find-spot was amid the rubbe at the base of the mound. On archaeological grounds we can only say it was made before 1050. But the style of decoration, the placement and curvature of the filter, and the distinctive color of the clay point to the earliest period of our study. Finally, its stylistic affinity with the filter in Fig. 7-d allow us to place its manufacture as some time around 800 A.D. Nothing, even motivally, comparable in Olmer's list.

A-III-B.   Early "decorative" with V-shaped latticing.

Fig. 191. Like the filters in Figs. 11 and 192, the legs of the V have scratched lines. But the internal design is rather an unsuccessful attempt toward latticing, leaving something rather like large, heavy wavy lines. However, this *incipient* lattice motif can be connected to that in Olmer's pl. XLVIII-C which he dates to the Tulunid period. Our filter is of buff-white clay, is concave in profile and placed along the neck of the vessel, which argues for a date before 950, as do the other artifacts found with it in an undisturbed pit related to a 10th century habitation.

Fig. 192. It is the V which dictates putting this filter in this category, for the latticing, as such, lacks any symmetry. Indeed, it is interrupted by an internal triangle whose sides have the same scratched lines as the V. The side panels are somewhat novel: a V-shaped opening enclosing a tiny hole, with two triangular openings on either side of the V, each pair interrupted by a comma-like motif, which can also be seen at the base of the inner triangle. The clay is buff-white, the profile concave, and the placement along the neck. Both this filter and that in Fig. 193 were found in an undisturbed pit associated with architectural remnants of the early to mid-10th century. We would date both filters to the early 10th century. Nothing exactly comparable in Olmer.

A-III-C.   Early "decorative" with triangle latticing.

Fig. 193.   This quite elegant and unique filter is difficult to categorize as the true latticing is external to the triangle, which does have a circlet of triangular openings. Only two sides of the triangle have the familiar scratched lines. These are also present on the three flat circles which subtend the triangle and divide the latticing. Although the surface is highly discolored, the clay was originally white-buff. Other characteristics and find-spot parallel those of Fig. 192 with which it was found. Additional support for the early 10th century dating comes from the external scratched design on the neck.

A-III-D.   Early "decorative" with quadrant latticing.

Fig. 194.   The vessel is complete except for its handle and parts of the rim. The design is simplicity itself: the interesting flat bands have incised lines and end in largish triangular openings and there are two more of these at the crossing. The four interstitial areas are lattices of small triangular openings. It can be compared with Fig. 6-d of Ancillary where two opposing triangular spaces have latticing; but ours is a finer and more symmetrical example of the cruciform pattern. The incised decoration on the neck as well as the white-buff clay, concave curvature of the filter and its placement along the neck point definitely to the pre-Fatimid period. The find-spot was a pit associated with building traces of the late 9th-early 10th century. All the artifactual data from undisturbed loci attendant to the delicate foundations of the domicile were of the 10th century, and more particularly, from its earlier moiety. Hence we would date this vessel and its unique filter to the first half of the 10th century.

A-III-E.   Early "decorative" with lattice in parallel registers.

Fig. 195.   This filter may be compared with that in Fig. 14 supra in that both have three panels with slash openings acting as dividers. It shares with Figs. 10, 13 and 14 buff-white clay, the elegant ribbing of the neck, the high placement along the neck and the incised external design. The central register has at least one lyre-like shape, but overall must be seen as a failure relative to the beveled effect. All these would seem to echo the central panel of Olmer's pl. XLVIII-A. The find-spot was again an undisturbed pit associated with a 10th century occupancy. However, its parallel characteristics and/or motifs to those in Figs. 10, 13 and 14 point to a dating in the late 9th-early 10th century.

Fig. 196.   The intended design of this filter was to have three or four fleurons in each of the two central panels and a variation of the same in the outer two. The fleuron effect was achieved by the barrette motif and/or four triangular openings radiating from a central hole. However, the barrette was used only on each of the five fleurons, while the sixth was formed of unsymmetrical triangular openings. The panels are separated by three narrow flat bands having random incisions or openings. The filter is of white-buff clay and flat in profile but the hinging to the neck was concave and it is placed along the neck and not at the jointure with the shoulder. The precise ribbing below the rim and the incised pseudo-epigraphic decor external give additional reason for a dating before 950. However, the undisturbed find-spot also yielded the base of an early lead glazed bowl and an inset plaque of carved bone, both of the 8th-9th century. This *sibakh* level lay low in the mound where the dating sequence tends to be wider than in the lower strata. Hence it would seem wiser to assign this filter to the late 9th century.[59]

A-IV-A. Early "decorative" hatchwork surfaces/flat geometrical.

Fig. 197.   This whitish buff filter has a cruciform design with an odd polygonal opening at the crossing. Each arm has its surface scratched with a hatchwork design and bordered by slash openings. Three of the four interstitial triangles each contains a curlicue opening with either one or two triangular openings at the rim of the entire design; the fourth has these latter openings only and lacks any hatchwork. These poorly executed motifs are definitely pre-Fatimid in origin, the convex profile and the placement at the junction of neck and shoulder anticipates the period. Its find-spot (within some surface rubble and adjacent to some exposed masonry) provides little help except to say it comes from before 1050. Considering the hatchwork and the curlicue slash motif, we would place the filter's manufacture as late 10th century, just before the onset of the canonical Fatimid filters. Once again there is nothing comparable in Olmer's list.

A-V-A. Early "decorative" filigreed effect/filigree geometrical.

Fig. 198.   This filter is simply a lesser rendering of that in Pl. V-a and Fig. 26. The curving vertical of the stenographic "baraka" sign, also repeated thrice here, is elegantly toothed, but the filigree arc-panels are not so elegantly planned or executed. The profile is flat and the filter placed at the junction of neck and shoulder; this must remain the strongest clue as to dating for from its find-spot (the *dakkah* fill around some exposed foundations) all we can aver is that it must have been made before 1050. The clay is buffish

---

[59] There is a certain motival similarity to Olmer's pl. LXXIX-A which he is disinclined to date, but it is obvious from the photo that the filter was placed along the neck and that it was concave in profile. Thus we would place it in the late 9th-early 10th century.

white. As both ours and Fig. 26 are of the same general type as Olmer's
pls. LXXVIII-D and E we find it to be equally a transition piece wherein
the filigree points to a time before the imposition of the Fatimid canonical
filters, i.e., before 1000 A.D.

A-V-B.   Early "decorative" filigreed effect/zoomorphic motifs.

Fig. 199.   A nicely articulated fish with hatchwork scratched on its body faces right
in the central panel of this filter. There is an attempted filigree surrounding
it and two small circlets attach the panel at the tail to the rim of the whole
design. The outer panels contained meshed triangular openings, and the
upper one has a zig-zag ruching which the lower lacks; both must be seen
as attempts at filigree effect. The fish motif parallels those of Olmer's pls.
LVI and LVII, but these lack our filigree effect. However, the one line of
zig-zag ruching is canonical, a hint of the later stereotype. Thus we would
place this buff-white filter as slightly before 1000. Its find-spot (rubble fill
of the mound above the masonry remnants mentioned in the introductory
remarks of this Appendix) is of no help in achieving a more acute dating.
Again the profile is convex and the placement at the junction of neck and
shoulder.

B-I-B-1.   "Continuing" patterns/dominant slash/central triangle.

Fig. 200.   The central triangle is pierced at random by seven curlicue or hook-like
slashes, comparable to those in Fig. 197. There are also five straight slash
openings, two of which help to establish the bottom of the triangle. Two
side panels each contain two lines of zig-zag ruching, which are a pronounced motif in the canonical list. (Compare this to the single line of
zig-zagging in Fig. 199.) When this fact is added to the resemblance to
Fig. 44 with its filigree-like slashes, the quandary deepens. Its find-spot
(again surface rubble attendant to exposed masonry traces) simply tells us
that it was made before 1050. Its convex profile and placement at the
juncture of neck and shoulder must also be considered. Thus, if Fig. 199
is placed slightly before 1000, this one should be placed slightly after.

**B-II-A-1-d.   "Canonical" patterns/geometrical/circular inclusive without border/flower
designs.**

Fig. 201.   Despite its being incomplete, the remaining petals of the flower can be
deduced. It is a unique filter and its eight-petalled pattern may have
been an attempt to copy the chrysanthemum motif of S'ung ceramics
which were being imported and imitated in the Fatimid period.[60] It is an

---

[60] Cf. Bo Gyllensvard, "Recent Finds of Chinese Ceramics at Fostat. II," *Bull. of the Museum of Far
Eastern Antiquities*, Number 47 (Stockholm: 1975), pp. 93-117 and George T. Scanlon, "Egypt and
China: Trade and Imitation," *Islam and the Trade of Asia*, ed. D. S. Richards (Oxford and Philadelphia:
1971), pp. 81-95.

interesting animad-version for the 11th century in that it returns to adding a scratched design to the surface; there are very few openings for a canonical filter and they are very simply distributed so as to call attention to the scratched outline of the flower. Each petal had three small circular openings as did the spaces between the petals. The center had eight tear-drop openings. The filter is of buff-white clay, its profile is convex and the placement is at the jointure of neck and shoulder. This object was found in the *sibakh* layer beneath the covering rubble of the mound and above the *dakkah* stratum. No doubt it belongs to the latest period of occupancy of the structures connoted by the *dakkah*, hence before 1050. The elements of its design are unique to our series and to Olmer's; nevertheless it can be placed sometime in the period 1000-1050 A.D.

B-II-A-2-c. "Canonical" patterns/geometrical/circular inclusive with border/flower designs.

Fig. 202. Here we have nothing but the beautiful center piece of what must have been a buff-white filter with serrated petal-leaves comparable to Figs. 77 and 90 which can be related to Olmer's pl. XLV-A and D. We will never know whether our filter had a zig-zag circular border (hence the only problem in the typological placement), but it would certainly have had more leaves than either of our other examples. The center is a splendid example of deft cutting; the inner portion a delicate filigree mesh, the outer a rather advanced form of the barrette. The upward pull at the edge of the fragment might mean that the profile was concave, which would be untypical of the canonical filters. As the find-spot says little more than it cannot have been made after 1050, and that the filters of Figs. 77 and 90 were both found in undisturbed loci of the 11th century, we would assign this fragment to the first half of that century.

C-V-B. Surround(s) of triangular cuts/double band surround.

Fig. 203. This filter is unlike anything in Olmer, and represents the "sport" in our 1980 finds. The central motif's mock-radial pattern can be fitted into the Fatimid canonical typology, but the double band of triangular openings has been seen by us and Olmer as operative in the Ayyubid-Mamluk sequence. Either this object is a chronological anamoly relative to Fustat-C, or indicates that what we have considered Ayyubid-Mamluk motifs were being used in the 11th century. Until contrary evidence comes in from the other mounds in this particular area of Fustat, we cannot disallow this latter factor; hence we will sustain a dating of 11th-12th century.

XA-3. Slip-painted, red clay.

Fig. 204. This oddity can only be fitted into Appendix A which surveys objects obviously used as filters and found within loci clearly of pre-Fatimid dating, but which lack other characteristics of the category. This neck of a vessel contains a primitive filter composed of three large punched, rather than cut, holes and the clay is of a distinct brownish-red hue. Externally the surface is covered by a creamy-brown slip, on which a human face is painted in reddish-brown slip. The flange handle serves as a nose and there is a necklace of red-brown dots on the shoulder. About a third of the neck is missing; this part contained the other flange handle which might also have served as the nose of another Picasso-like visage. It was discovered in the sondage through the fill on which our top domiciles were reared. The sondage ran into a somewhat high water-table; nonetheless we were able to establish the *gabal* level and in the process prove the presence of an 8th century habitation. Our object was found associated with a fragment of a thick-walled glass weight carrying the names of the Finance Directors Muhammad b. Sa'id and Umar b. Yahya, who served during 152-7/762-6. Thus our oddity can be assigned to the 8th century.*

*Since reading the proof copy of this manuscript a number of filters from Italy and Sicily have been brought to the attention of the author. Since these published items do not include profiles, it is difficult to determine their place in our typology, or if they represent imports from Egypt or exemplify indigenous traditions: cf. Francesco Gabrieli and Umberto Scerrato, *Gli Arabi in Italia* (Milano 1979), figs. 185, 280, 286, 287, 288, 364, 365 and 366.

TYPOLOGICAL TABLES OF REGISTERED FILTERS

Key to Typological Tables

A.   Pre-Fatimid Period: ca. 700–ca. 1000 A.D.

    I.   The "simple/mechanical"

       A.   The unribbed neck
       B.   The ribbed neck

    II.   The "simple/mechanical" with imposed decoration

    III.   Early "decorative" filter

       A.   Open-work with surface scratching
       B.   V-shaped latticing
       C.   Triangle lattice
       D.   Quadrant lattice
       E.   Lattice in parallel registers
       F.   Parallel line latticing

    IV.   Hatchwork surfaces

       A.   Flat geometrical
       B.   Lattice geometrical
       C.   Zoomorphic hatchwork

    V.   Filigreed effect

       A.   Filigree geometrical
       B.   Zoomorphic motifs with filigree elements

B.   The Fatimid Period: ca. 1000–ca. 1200 A.D.

    I.   "Continuing" patterns

       A.   Filigree radial
       B.   Dominant slash
          1.   Central triangle
          2.   Central quadrangle
          3.   Central pentagon
          4.   Miscellaneous

       C.   Central "knitting" pattern

II. "Canonical" patterns

    A. Geometrical

        1. Circular inclusive patterns without border
            a. Mesh
            b. Mesh with intermediate dividers
            c. Star and star-and-knot patterns
            d. Flower designs

        2. Circular inclusive patterns with border
            a. Mesh
            b. Star and star-and-knot patterns
            c. Flower designs

        3. Triangular patterns
            a. Central lattice and triplet circlets
            b. Central lattice and ruching in the arcs
            c. Divided central triangle and circlets
            d. Central Fleuron/flower

        4. Rectangular patterns
            a. Straight-sided rectangle
            b. Curve-sided rectangle
            c. Bent-sided rectangle

        5. Diamond and fleuron patterns
            a. Fleuron accessory
            b. Fleuron equal

        6. Pentagonal patterns

        7. Radial patterns
            a. Four-spoked
            b. Five-spoked
            c. Six-spoked
            d. Seven-spoked
            e. Eight-spoked

        8. Parallel vertical panels
            a. Central lattice
            b. Central lattice and dividers
                1. Double and joint, perpendicular to vertical dividers
                2. Double and spaced, angled to vertical dividers
                3. Triple and joint, perpendicular to vertical dividers
                4. Triple and spaced, angled to vertical dividers
            c. Flat diamond lattice
            d. Triple division into rectangles
            e. Cross bands
            f. Miscellaneous

    B. Zoomorphic

        1. Human approximations

        2. Animals

            a. Elephant

            b. Gazelle

            c. Lion

            d. Hare/rabbit

            e. Peacock

    C. Inscriptional/epigraphical

C.   The Ayyubid and Mamluk Era: ca. 1200–ca. 1500 A.D.

    I. Radial central patterns without an obvious surround

      A. Two-element single band

      B. Two-element double band

         1. Single small hole punctuating outer band

         2. Single small hole punctuating both bands

         3. Double small hole punctuating outer band

         4. Quadruple small-hole motif punctuating outer band

         5. Pyramidal small-hole motif

         6. Two-element triple band

    II. Cruciform motif without a surround

    III. Star patterns without a surround

      A. No extra decoration

      B. Trefoil spokes with added decoration; no central pattern

      C. Trefoil spokes around central pattern

      D. Central star dominant

      E. Star and round shield

    IV. Spoke-radial surround

      A. Incipient

      B. With radial central pattern

      C. Cruciform mesh central pattern

      D. Central star pattern

         1. Six-spoked

         2. Ten-spoked

         3. Three trefoils and interstitial pin-point mesh

         4. Four trefoils and interstitial pin-point mesh

         5. Three quatrefoils and interstitial pin-point mesh

TYPOLOGICAL TABLES

TYPE	ILLUS. HEREIN	REG. NO.	FIND-SPOT	COMP. EXAMPLE	PUBL.	DATE	DISPOSITION
A-I-A	Fig. 1	68-10-25	XXI-6 Pit Q, 4.7 m; FEPR '68-II, Plan I	—	Pits, Fig. 7	8th-early 9th century	Kelsey
	Pl. I-a Fig. 2	66-4-28	XI-12 Pit A, 3.0 m; FEPR '66, Plan II	—	—	9th century	I.M.
	Fig. 3	64-6-26	VIII-1 Fnd.; FEPR '64, Plan II	—	—	9th-10th century	Akron
A-I-B	Fig. 4	66-3-45	XI-20 Pit A, 1.5-2.O m; FEPR '66, Plan II	—	—	8th-early 9th century	I.M.
	Fig. 5	71-10-13	XVI-23 Pit K, 6.0 m; FEPR '71-I, Plan I	—	FEPR '71-I, Fig. 20	9th century	I.M.
	Fig. 6	68-10-8	XXI-6 Pit K, 1.3-1.8 m; FEPR '68-II, Plan I	—	Pits, pls. XV-6 and 7	8th century	Kelsey
A-II	Fig. 7a	68-12-77	XXI-8 Pit U, 5.8 m; FEPR '68-II, Plan I	—	Pits, pl. XVII-1, R.G., Fig. 4-a	8th-9th century	Kelsey
	Fig. 7b	68-12-76	XXI-8 Pit U, 5.8 m; FEPR '68-II, Plan I	—	Pits, pl. XVII-2, R.G., Fig. 4-b	8th-9th century	Kelsey
	Fig. 7c	68-12-78	XXI-8 Pit U, 5.8 m; FEPR '68-II, Plan I	—	Pits, pl. XVII-3, R.G., Fig. 5	8th-9th century	Kelsey
	Fig. 7d	68-11-54	XI'-7 Pit D, 4.0 m; FEPR '68-I, Plan I	—	Pits, pl. XXI-1, R.G., Fig. 4-c	8th-9th century	Kelsey
	Fig. 190	80-10-34	C-III-5 rubble	—	—	ca. 800	AUC

TYPE	ILLUS. HEREIN	REG. NO.	FIND-SPOT	COMP. EXAMPLE	PUBL.	DATE	DISPOSITION
A-III-A	Pl. I-b	65-4-100	XVI-I′cist. B, 1-1.5 m; FEPR '65-I, Plan II	—	FEPR '65-I, Fig. 11-c	8th century	I.M.
	Pl. I-c	65-3-105	XVI-10 cist. 0′ sieve of base fill; FEPR '65-I, Plan	Olmer, pl. LXXIX-A	FEPR '65-II, Fig. 2-b	8th century	Akron
	Fig. 9	71-5-7	VI-18 Pit C, 5.0 m; FEPR '71-I, Plan	—	FEPR '71-I, Pl. XI-3	9th century	I.M.
	Fig. 10	71-5-15	XI-3 Pit R, 3.0-3.5 m; FEPR '71-I, Plan	—	FEPR '71-I, Fig. 3	9th century	Kelsey
A-III-B	Pl. I-d	65-3-114	XVI-18 Pit V, 1.5 m; FEPR '65-I, Plan II	—	Anc., Fig. 7-b,	ca. 850	Princeton
	Fig. 11	66-5-14	XI-18 garbage Pit P′-0′; FEPR '66, Plan II	—	Anc., pl. 3, Fig. 3-c	ca. 850-900	I.M.
	Pl. II-a	68-12-71	XXI-8 Pit U, 4.7 m; FEPR '68, Plan I	Olmer, pl. XLVIII-c, lattice only	Pits, Fig. 9	early 10th century	Kelsey
	Fig. 191	80-10-76	C-IV-6 Pit D′, 2.8 m	Olmer, pl. XLVIII-c	—	early 10th century	AUC
	Fig. 192	80-10-71	C-IV-24 Pit N, 1.7-2.7 m	—	—	early 10th century	AUC
A-III-C	Pl. II-b	65-2-36	XVI-21 Surface; FEPR '65-I, Plan II	—	Anc., Fig. 4-a	ca. 900	Princeton
	Fig. 12	65-5-167	XXXI-13, canal M′; FEPR '65-II, Plan II	Olmer, pls. XLVIII-b and LXXVIII-A	FEPR 65-II, Fig. 6-c, and Anc., Fig. 4-b	ca. 900	Princeton
	Fig. 193	80-10-72	C-IV-24 Pit N, 1.7-2.7 m	—	—	early 10th century	AUC

TYPE	ILLUS. HEREIN	REG. NO.	FIND-SPOT	COMP. EXAMPLE	PUBL.	DATE	DISPOSITION
A-III-D	Pl. II-c	68-11-76	XXVI-13 Pit X′, 2.0 m; FEPR '68-II, Plan I	—	FEPR '68-II, Fig. 8	ca. 900	Kelsey
	Pl. II-d	65-4-6	XVI-6 F, find level; FEPR '65-I, Plan II	—	Anc., Fig. 6-d	ca. 900	I.M.
	Fig. 194	80-10-66	C-IV-12 Pit F′, 3.5 m	Anc., Fig. 6-d	—	early 10th century	I.M.
A-III-E	Pl. III-a Fig. 13	68-12-80	XI-2 Pit B, 3.0 m; FEPR '68-I, Plan I	—	FEPR '68-I, Fig. 16	9th-10th century	Kelsey
	Fig. 14	72-10-23	XXI-6 A middle level; FEPR '72-I, Plan	Olmer, pl. XLVIII-A, central register only	—	early 10th century	Ashmolean
	Pl. III-b	65-5-154	XVI-II Pit R′, 2.5 m; FEPR '65-I, Plan II	—	FEPR '65-I, Fig. 3-a	before 950	I.M.
	Pl. III-c Fig. 15	65-4-127	XVI-I L, below; FEPR '65-I, Plan II	— —	FEPR '65-I, Fig. 3-d	before 950	Or. Inst.
	Fig. 195	80-10-68	C-IV-7 Pit F, 1.40 m	Figs. 10, 13, 14 herein	—	ca. 900	AUC
	Fig. 196	80-10-60	C-III-10 U, *sibakh* inside walls	—	—	late 9th century	AUC
A-III-F	Fig. 16	71-6-12	VI-18 Pit C, 4.0 m; FEPR '71-I, Plan	—	—	ca. 900	Kelsey
A-IV-A	Pl. III-d Fig. 17	71-6-31	XXVI-10/XXVII-6 canal W; FEPR '71-II, Plan	—	FEPR '71-II, Fig. 22	10th century	Kelsey
	Fig. 197	80-10-61	C-IV-24 rubble south of walls	—	—	late 10th century	AUC
A-IV-B	Fig. 18	68-11-29	XXVI-4 Pit P′, 3.8 m; FEPR '68-II, Plan I	Olmer, pl. LVIII-13	—	10th century	Kelsey

TYPE	ILLUS. HEREIN	REG. NO.	FIND-SPOT	COMP. EXAMPLE	PUBL.	DATE	DISPOSITION
A-IV-C	Pl. IV-a Fig. 19	68-10-31	XXI-7/8 canal U-V; FEPR '68-I, Plan I	Olmer, pl. LVIII-13	Pits, Fig. 8	9th-10th century	Kelsey
	Fig. 20	78-10-46	XXVII-3 Pit P; FEPR '78, Plan	Olmer, pl. LVIII-13	—	10th century	AUC
	Pl. IV-b Fig. 21	65-3-23	XVI-7 Cistern F'; FEPR '65-I, Plan II	—	FEPR '65-I, Fig. 3-b	10th century	Princeton
A-V-A	Pl. IV-c Fig. 22	64-6-24	VII-5, below pavement; FEPR '64, Plan II	—	FEPR '64, Fig. 3-f	10th century	Princeton
	Fig. 23	71-6-26	XXVI-10/XXVII-6 canal W; FEPR '71-II, Plan	—	—	10th century	Kelsey
	Pl. IV-d Fig. 24	65-3-29	XVI-4 Pit B' FEPR 65-I, Plan II	—	Anc., text Fig. 6-b	late 10th century	Princeton
	Fig. 25	72-10-19	XXI'-10 surface; FEPR '72-I, Plan	similar to Olmer, pl. LXXVIII-E	—	late 10th century	Missouri
	Pl. V-a Fig. 26	66-5-56	XI'-3 Pit B, 5.0 m; FEPR '66, Plan II	Composite of Olmer, pls. LXVIII-D, -E	Anc., text Fig. 5-b	late 10th century	Princeton
	Fig. 198	80-10-31	C-III-10, below dakkah	Pl. V-A and Fig. 26 herein	—	late 10th century	AUC
A-V-B	Fig. 27	78-10-44	XXVII-13 X; FEPR '78, Plan	—	—	late 10th century	AUC
	Fig. 28	73-9-15	Fustat A, XXI-8 E' fill above and around rim of Pit; FEPR '78, Plan	—	—	10th century	I.M.

TYPE	ILLUS. HEREIN	REG. NO.	FIND-SPOT	COMP. EXAMPLE	PUBL.	DATE	DISPOSITION
A-V-B	Fig. 199	80-10-2	C-IV-13 Level 17, rubble	Olmer pls. LVI and LVII	—	before 1000	AUC
B-I-A	Pl. V-b	65-2-15	XVI-II cistern R′; FEPR 65-I, Plan II	—	Anc., text Fig. 4-d	late 10th-11th century	Princeton
	Pl. V-c	65-2-16	XVI-II cistern R′; FEPR 65-I, Plan II	—	Anc., text Fig. 4-c	late 10th-11th century	Princeton
	Fig. 30	65-5-55	XI′-3 Pit B, 5.0 m; FEPR ʼ66, Plan II	—	Anc., Fig. 3-b	late 10th-11th century	Princeton
	Fig. 31	71-10-9	XXII-16 surface; FEPR ʼ71-II, Plan	Central motif of Olmer, pl. LXXIX-c	—	late 10th-11th century	Kelsey
	Fig. 32	78-11-4	XXVII-14 X deep fill; FEPR ʼ78, Plan	—	—	early 11th century	AUC
B-I-B-1	Fig. 33	68-11-16	XI′-6 Pit A, 4-4.6 m; FEPR ʼ71-I, Plan I	—	—	11th century	Kelsey
	Pl. V-d Fig. 34	65-5-156	XXXI-18 canal to latrine U; FEPR ʼ65-II, Plan II	—	F.F., Fig. 1-e	early 11th century	Or. Inst.
	Fig. 35	66-4-17	XI′-8 Pit Z, 2-3.0 m; FEPR ʼ66, Plan II	F.F., Fig. 1-e	—	11th century	Princeton
	Pl. VI-a Fig. 36	65-3-46	XVI-14 cistern C′ at base; FEPR ʼ65-I, Plan II	—	F.F., Fig. 1-d	early 11th century	Princeton
	Pl. VI-b	65-3-156	XVI-6 canal C; FEPR ʼ65-I, Plan II	—	F.F., Fig. 2	11th century	Akron
	Pl. VI-c Fig. 37	65-4-9	XVI-6′ surface; FEPR ʼ65-I, Plan II	—	F.F., Fig. 1-b	11th century	Princeton

TYPE	ILLUS. HEREIN	REG. NO.	FIND-SPOT	COMP. EXAMPLE	PUBL.	DATE	DISPOSITION
B-I-B-1	—	64-4-76	VII-4 later period level; FEPR '64, Plan II	Pl. VI-C, Fig. 37	—	11th century	Akron
	Fig. 38	66-4-16	XI'-8 Pit Z, 2-3.0 m; FEPR '66, Plan II	—	—	11th century	Princeton
	Fig. 39	66-5-105	II-8 exposed Pit, 2.0-2.5 m; FEPR '66, Plan II	—	—	11th century	Princeton
	Pl. VI-d Fig. 40	65-4-112	XVI-6 cistern K, 6.3 m; FEPR '65-I, Plan II	—	FEPR '65-I, Fig. 3-c	11th century	Princeton
	Pl. VII-a Fig. 41	65-4-115	Idem.	—	F.F., Fig. 1-a	11th century	Princeton
	Pl. VII-b Fig. 42	64-5-64	VIII-13 surface; FEPR '64, Plan II	—	F.F., Fig. 1-f	11th century	Princeton
	Fig. 43	66-5-57	XXVI-7 D fill of basin; FEPR '66, Plan III	—	—	11th century	Princeton
	Fig. 44	78-10-43	XXVII-13 X lower fill under fallen vault; FEPR '78, Plan	—	—	end of 10th century	AUC
	Fig. 45	68-10-29	XXI-7/8, canal U-V; FEPR '68-I, Plan I	—	—	end of 10th century	Kelsey
	Pl. VII-c Fig. 46	64-5-79	VII-19 below pavement of secondary construction; FEPR '64, Plan II	—	—	end of 10th century	Akron
	Pl. VII-d	65-3-20	XVI-7 G-F' cistern; FEPR '65-I, Plan II	—	Anc., text Fig. 6-a	late 10th-early 11th century	I.M.
	Pl. VIII-a Fig. 47	64-5-20	VIII-12 gutter; Fustat '64, Plan II	—	F.F., Fig. 3-b	early 11th century	Akron
	Fig. 200	80-10-75	C-IV-12 C, rubble	—	—	after 1000	AUC

TYPE	ILLUS. HEREIN	REG. NO.	FIND-SPOT	COMP. EXAMPLE	PUBL.	DATE	DISPOSITION
B-I-B-2	Fig. 48	68-10-14	XXI-11 L′, fnd. fill; FEPR '68-II, Plan I	–	–	late 10th century	Kelsey
	Fig. 49	71-11-10	XXVII-6 canal Y′; FEPR '71-II, Plan	–	–	end of 10th century	Kelsey
	Fig. 50	68-10-32	XXI-7/8 canal U-V; FEPR '68-II, Plan I	–	–	end of 10th century	Kelsey
	Fig. 51	68-10-30	XXI-7/8 canal U-V; FEPR '68-II, Plan I	–	–	end of 10th century	Kelsey
	Fig. 52	68-10-36	XXI-3 Z *sibakh*; FEPR '68-II, Plan I	–	–	end of 10th century	Kelsey
	Pl. VIII-b Fig. 53	66-5-54	XI-12 shallow Pit in *dakkah*; FEPR '66, Plan II	–	Anc., text Fig. 6-b	end of 10th century	Princeton
	Fig. 54	72-10-32	XXI′-5 Pit B-D, 2.1-2.5 m; FEPR '72-I, Plan	–	–	late 10th-early 11th century	Missouri
B-I-B-3	Fig. 55	64-4-44	VII-15 south of cistern under fallen niche; FEPR '64, Plan II	Olmer, pl. LXXVIII-c	–	late 10th-early 11th century	Akron
B-I-B-4	Pl. VIII-c	68-10-48	XXVI-4 Pit W, 3.5 m; FEPR '68-II, Plan I	Olmer, pl. LXXVIII-d	FEPR '68-II, Fig. 17-a	after 950 (?)	Kelsey
	Pl. VIII-d	65-3-41	XI-24 cistern V, 1.0 m; FEPR '65-I, Plan II	Olmer, pl. LXXIX-d	Anc., text Fig. 4-c	late 10th century	Princeton
	Pl. IX-a	65-2-13	XVI-II cistern R, 0.8 m; FEPR '65-I, Plan	leaf and spine form like Olmer, pl. LXVII-c	Anc., text Fig. 5-a	late 10th century	Princeton

TYPE	ILLUS. HEREIN	REG. No.	FIND-SPOT	COMP. EXAMPLE	PUBL.	DATE	DISPOSITION
B-I-C	Fig. 56	65-3-82	XVI-10 cistern 0′, 3.0 m; FEPR '65-I, Plan II	Olmer, pl. XLIV-a	—	11th century	I.M.
	Fig. 57	65-4-79	XII-21 cistern M, 0.5 m; FEPR '65-I, Plan II	Olmer, pl. XLIV-a	—	11th century	Or. Inst.
	Pl. IX-b Fig. 58	65-5-41	XXI-I Y above fnd.; FEPR '65-I, Plan I	—	F.F., Fig. 3-c	11th century	Princeton
	Fig. 59	78-9-11	XXVI-17 *sibakh*; FEPR '78, Plan	F.F., Fig. 3-c	—	11th century	AUC
	Pl. IX-c Fig. 60	71-10-31	XXVII-16 surface; FEPR '71-II, Plan	F.F., Fig. 3-c	—	11th century	I.M.
	Pl. IX-d Fig. 61	66-5-68	XXVI-18 *sibakh*; FEPR '66, Plan II	—	F.F., Fig. 3-d	11th century	Princeton
	Pl. X-a Fig. 62	66-5-103	II-8 exposed Pit, 2.5 m; FEPR '66, Plan II	—	F.F., Fig. 3-e	11th century	Princeton
	Pl. X-b Fig. 63	66-4-62	XI′-25 fnd. level; FEPR '66, Plan II	—	F.F., Fig. 3-f	11th century	I.M.
B-II-A-I-a	Pl. X-c Fig. 64	65-2-96	XVI-21 H cistern, 3.0 m; FEPR '65-I, Plan II	Olmer, pl. XXI-b	F.F., Fig. 10-f	11th-12th century	Princeton
	Pl. X-d Fig. 65	65-3-126	XI-15 surface; FEPR '65-I, Plan II	Olmer, pl. XXI-f and center of XXII-e	F.F., Fig. 11-a	12th century	Princeton
	Pl. XI-a Fig. 66	65-5-84	XXX-14 surface; FEPR '65-II, Plan II	—	F.F., Fig. 11-b	12th century	Princeton
B-II-A-I-b	Pl. XI-b Fig. 67	65-1-9	XVI-II fill between walls near B-N; FEPR '65-I, Plan	Olmer, pl. XXII-c	F.F., Fig. 11-d	11th-12th century	Princeton

TYPE	ILLUS. HEREIN	REG. NO.	FIND-SPOT	COMP. EXAMPLE	PUBL.	DATE	DISPOSITION
B-II-A-I-b	Pl. XI-c Fig. 68	64-5-19	VIII-3 surface; FEPR '64, Plan II	—	FEPR '64, Fig. 2-f	12th century	Princeton
B-II-A-I-c	Pl. XI-d Fig. 69	66-3-25	XI'-10 surface; FEPR '66, Plan II	—	F.F., Fig. 5-e	11th century	I.M.
	Pl. XII-a Fig. 70	64-4-62	VII-15 cistern P'; FEPR '64, Plan II	—	F.F., Fig. 6-b	11th-12th century	Akron
	Pl. XII-b Fig. 71	65-3-11	XVI-5 cistern P', 1.2 m; FEPR '65-I, Plan	—	F.F., Fig. 5-d	11th century	Princeton
	Pl. XII-c	64-4-33	VIII-3 surface; FEPR '64, Plan II	—	F.F., Fig. 6-c	11th-12th century	Akron
	Pl. XII-d Fig. 72	65-3-28 red clay	XVI-5 cistern P', 4.0 m; FEPR '65-I, Plan II	—	F.F., Fig. 5-c (profile only)	11th century	I.M.
	Fig. 73	65-4-11	XVI-23 surface; FEPR '65-I, Plan II	—	—	11th-12th century	Princeton
	Pl. XIII-a Fig. 74	65-3-76 red clay	XVI-10 cistern 0', 3.0 m; FEPR '65-I, Plan II	—	F.F., Fig. 5-a	11th century	Or. Inst.
	Fig. 75	66-5-51	XXVI-7 surface; FEPR '66, Plan III	—	—	11th-12th century	Princeton
	Pl. XIII-b	66-5-104	II-8 exposed pit, 2.5 m; FEPR '66, Plan II	—	FEPR '66, Fig. 1	11th century	Princeton
	Pl. XIII-c	65-3-71	XVI-10 cistern 0', 2.5 m; FEPR '65-I, Plan II	—	F.F., Fig. 5-b	11th century	I.M.
B-II-A-1-d	Pl. XIII-d Fig. 76	66-5-100	VI-17 exposed pit, 3.5 m; FEPR '66, Plan II	—	—	11th century	I.M.
	Pl. XIV-a	66-5-77	XXVI-12 gutter T; FEPR '66, Plan III	—	F.F., Fig. 6-a	11th-12th century	I.M.

TYPE	ILLUS. HEREIN	REG. NO.	FIND-SPOT	COMP. EXAMPLE	PUBL.	DATE	DISPOSITION
B-II-A-1-d	Fig. 77	68-10-49	XXVI-4 pit W, 3.0 m; FEPR '68-II, Plan I	Olmer, pl. XLV-D	—	early 11th century	Kelsey
	Fig. 201	80-10-28	C-IV-6 A, *sibakh*	—	—	1000-1050	AUC
B-II-A-2-a	Pl. XIV-b	66-3-16	XI'-10 surface; FEPR '66, Plan II	—	F.F., Fig. 13-c	11th century	Princetion
	Pl. XIV-C Fig. 78	66-5-60	VI'-18 pit A, 7.25 m; FEPR '66, Plan II	like Olmer, pl. XXII-c	F.F., Fig. 12	11th century	I.M.
	Pl. XIV-d	66-3-17	XI-10 surface; FEPR '66, Plan II	like Olmer, pl. XXII-c	F.F., Fig. 11-e	11th century	Princeton
	Pl. XV-a	66-5-79	XX-22 R; FEPR '66, Plan III	central pattern like Olmer, pl. XXII-c	F.F., Fig. 11-f	before 1170	Princeton
	Fig. 79	72-11-20	XXI'-14 *sibakh*; FEPR '72-I, Plan	in the spirit of Olmer, pl. XXII-d	—	before 1170	Missouri
	Pl. XV-b	66-5-2	VI'-7 fill of long gutter; FEPR '66, Plan II	—	F.F., Fig. 13-a	before 1170	Princeton
	Pl. XV-c	66-4-12	XVI'-5 pit A, 2.0-2.5 m; FEPR '66, Plan II	—	F.F., Fig. 13-b	11th-12th century	Princeton
	Fig. 80	72-10-42	XXI-14 *sibakh*; FEPR '72-I, Plan	—	—	1150-1200	Ashmolean
B-II-A-2-b	Fig. 81	68-12-70	XI'-1 surface; FEPR '68-I, Plan II	border like Olmer, pl. XXII-A	—	11th-12th century	Kelsey
	Fig. 82	72-10-18	XXVI-6 surface; FEPR '72-II, Plan	like Olmer, pl. XXX-A	—	11th-12th century	Ashmolean
	Fig. 83	78-10-10	XXI-23 L fill below paving; FEPR '72-II, Plan	—	—	11th century	AUC

TYPE	ILLUS. HEREIN	REG. NO.	FIND-SPOT	COMP. EXAMPLE	PUBL.	DATE	DISPOSITION
B-II-A-2-b	Fig. 84	65-4-113	XVI-6 cistern K, 5.0 m; FEPR '65-I, Plan II	Olmer, pl. XLIII-A	—	11th century	Princeton
	Fig. 85	65-5-38	XXXI-14 surface; FEPR '65-II, Plan II	Olmer, pl. XLIII-A	—	11th century	Kelsey
	Pl. XV-d	65-4-81	XVI-6 cistern K, 5.80 m; FEPR '65-I, Plan II	Olmer, pl. XLIII-A	F.F., Fig. 4-a	11th century	Princeton
	Pl. XVI-a	65-2-47	XVI-17 I', base of N. wall; FEPR '65-I, Plan II	Olmer, pl. XLIII-E	F.F., Fig. 4-c	11th century	Princeton
	Pl. XVI-b	66-4-21	VI-7 trench on the *gabal*; FEPR '66, Plan II	Olmer, pl. XLIII-E	F.F., Fig. 4-e	11th century	Princeton
	Pl. XVI-c	66-3-8	XVI'-5 pit A, 0.5-1.0 m; FEPR '66, Plan II	—	F.F., Fig. 4-f	11th century	Princeton
	Fig. 86	72-11-29	XXI'-13 E, *sibakh*; FEPR '72-I, Plan	—	—	11th-12th century	Ashmolean
	Pl. XVI-d	66-5-102	II-8 exposed pit, 2.5 m; FEPR '66, Plan II	—	F.F., Fig. 4-d	11th century	Princeton
B-II-A-2-c	Pl. XVII-a	65-5-61	XXXI-13 surface; FEPR '65-II, Plan II	—	F.F., Fig. 4-b	11th-12th century	Princeton
	Pl. XVII-b Fig. 87	64-4-38	VII-15 cistern beneath niche; FEPR '64, Plan II	Olmer, pl. IX-b	FEPR '64, Fig. 2-c	11th-12th century	Princeton
	Fig. 88	68-9-9	XXI-7 surface; FEPR '68-I, Plan I	—	—	11th-12th century	Kelsey
	Fig. 89	64-6-29	VIII-12, N.E. corner at fnd; FEPR '64, Plan II	like Olmer, pl. XLVI-b	—	11th-12th century	Akron
	Fig. 90	78-9-39	XXVI-22 pit C, 1.2 m; FEPR '78, Plan	like Olmer, pl. XLV-a	—	11th century	AUC

TYPE	ILLUS. HEREIN	REG. NO.	FIND-SPOT	COMP. EXAMPLE	PUBL.	DATE	DISPOSITION
B-II-A-2-c	Fig. 202	80-9-5	C-IV-7 Level 5	—	—	1000-1050	AUC
B-II-A-3-a	—	65-3-79	XVI-10 cistern 0′, 3.0 m; FEPR '65-I, Plan II	—	F.F., Fig. 7-a	11th century	Princeton
	Fig. 91	65-5-62	XI-22 surface; FEPR '65-I, Plan II	F.F., Fig. 7-a	—	11th-12th century	Princeton
	Fig. 92	65-3-132	XVI-I surface; FEPR '65-I, Plan II	F.F., Fig. 7-a	—	11th-12th century	Or. Inst.
	Fig. 93	68-11-73	XI′-5 surface; FEPR '68-I, Plan I	F.F., Fig. 7-a	—	11th-12th century	Kelsey
	Pl. XVII-c	66-3-7	XVI′-5 surface; FEPR '66, Plan II	—	F.F., Fig. 7-d	11th-12th century	Princeton
B-II-A-3-b	Pl. XVII-d Fig. 94	65-4-82	XII-21 cistern M, 0.5 m; FEPR '65-I, Plan II	—	F.F., Fig. 7-b	11th century	Or. Inst.
	Pl. XVIII-a	65-5-105	XXXI-13 surface; FEPR '65-II, Plan II	—	F.F., Fig. 7-c	11th-12th century	Akron
B-II-A-3-c	Pl. XVIII-b	64-6-6	VII-5 pit below secondary structure; FEPR '64, Plan II	—	F.F., Fig. 7-e and FEPR '64, Fig. 3-e	11th century	Akron
B-II-A-3-d	Fig. 95	72-10-12	XXI-1 M, street fill; FEPR '72-I, Plan	like Olmer pl. XII-A	—	11th-12th century	Missouri
	Pl. XVIII-c Fig. 96	65-4-95	XVI-6 cistern K, 7.0 m; FEPR '65-I, Plan II	Olmer, pl. X-B	F.F., Fig. 7-f	11th century	Princeton

TYPE	ILLUS. HEREIN	REG. NO.	FIND-SPOT	COMP. EXAMPLE	PUBL.	DATE	DISPOSITION
B-II-A-4-a	Fig. 97	68-11-98	VI'-24/25 pit T, 2.1 m; FEPR '68-I, Plan I	like Olmer, pl. VI-d	—	11th century	Kelsey
	Pl. XVIII-d	66-5-7	XXVI-3 surface; FEPR '66, Plan III	like Olmer, pl. XIV-d	F.F., Fig. 8-d	11th-12th century	Princeton
	Fig. 98	71-11-16	XXVII-12 pit C, 1.5 m; FEPR '71-II, Plan	like Olmer, pl. XIV-d	FEPR '71-II, Fig. 21	11th century	Kelsey
	Fig. 99	78-9-6	XXVI-17/23, surface; FEPR '78, Plan	like Olmer, pl. VI-a	—	11th-12th century	AUC
B-II-A-4-b	Pl. XIX-a	66-4-58	VII-12 trench fnd. level; FEPR '66, Plan II	—	F.F., Fig. 8-c	11th-12th century	Princeton
	Fig. 100	68-10-10	XXI-16/17, surface; FEPR '68-II, Plan I	—	—	11th-12th century	Kelsey
B-II-A-4-c	Pl. XIX-b	65-4-73	XII-21 cistern M, 0.5 m; FEPR '65-I, Plan II	—	F.F., Fig. 8-b	11th century	Or. Inst.
B-II-A-5-a	Fig. 101	72-11-25	XXI'-8 surface; FEPR '72-I, Plan	like Olmer, pl. XVIII-c	—	11th-12th century	Missouri
B-II-A-5-b	Pl. XIX-c Fig. 102	65-3-81	XVI-10 cistern 0', 3.0 m; FEPR '65-I, Plan II	—	F.F., Fig. 8-a	11th century	Princeton
B-II-A-6	Pl. XIX-d	64-6-5	Fustat A VII-5 N. part, below secondary paving; FEPR '64, Plan	like Olmer, pl. IX-c	FEPR '64, Fig. 3-d and F.F., Fig. 8-e	11th-12th century	Akron
B-II-A-7-a	Pl. XX-a	64-3-34	VIII-2 fill; FEPR '64, Plan II	—	F.F., Fig. 10-b	11th-12th century	Akron

TYPE	ILLUS. HEREIN	REG. NO.	FIND-SPOT	COMP. EXAMPLE	PUBL.	DATE	DISPOSITION
B-II-A-7-a	—	66-5-78	XX-22 R fnd. fill; FEPR '66, Plan III	—	F.F., Fig. 10-a	before 1170	Princeton
	Pl. XX-b Fig. 103	68-12-14	VI'-8, pit K, 2.6 m; FEPR '68-I, Plan I	like Olmer, pl. XVIII-f	—	11th-12th century	Kelsey
B-II-A-7-b	Fig. 104	68-10-15	XXI-11/12 M, fnd. fill; FEPR '68-I, Plan I	Olmer, pl. III-b	—	11th-12th century	Kelsey
B-II-A-7-c	Fig. 105	65-4-53	XVI-b cistern K, 5.5 m; FEPR '65-I, Plan II	like Olmer, pl. III-c	—	11th century	Or. Inst.
	—	65-4-71	XVI-6 cistern K, 5.5-5.8 m; FEPR '65-I, Plan II	like Olmer, pl. III-c	F.F., Fig. 10-c	11th century	Kelsey
	Fig. 106	65-3-73	XVI-10 cistern 0', 1.5 m; FEPR '65-5, Plan II	like Olmer, pl. III-c,	F.F., Fig. 10-c	11th century	I.M.
	—	65-5-5	XI-13 surface; FEPR '65-I, Plan II	like Olmer, pl. III-c	F.F., Fig. 10-c	11th century	Kelsey
B-II-A-7-d	Fig. 107	68-12-32	VI-17 pit G, 4.2 m; FEPR '68-I, Plan I	like Olmer, pl. V-C	—	11th-12th century	Kelsey
B-II-A-7-e	Pl. XX-c Fig. 108	65-2-73	XVI-21 cistern F, 2.25m; FEPR '65-I, Plan II	F.F., Fig. 10-d	—	11th century	Princeton
	—	65-3-78	XVI-10 cistern 0', 3 m; FEPR '65-I, Plan II	—	F.F., Fig. 10-d	11th century	Princeton
	—	65-3-77	XVI-10 cistern 0', 3 m; FEPR '65-I, Plan II	F.F., Fig. 10-d	—	11th century	I.M.

TYPE	ILLUS. HEREIN	REG. NO.	FIND-SPOT	COMP. EXAMPLE	PUBL.	DATE	DISPOSITION
BA-II-A-8-a	Fig. 109	65-5-155	XXXI-18 canal U from latrine; FEPR '65-II, Plan II	F.F., Fig. 8-f	—	11th century	Princeton
	—	65-4-72	XVI-6 cistern K, 5.5-5.8 m; FEPR '65-I, Plan II	—	F.F., Fig. 8-f	11th century	Princeton
	—	65-3-72	XVI-10 cistern 0′, 1.5 m; FEPR '65-I, Plan II	F.F., Fig. 8-f	—	11th century	Princeton
	—	65-3-84	XVI-10 cistern 0′, 3.0 m; FEPR '65-I, Plan II	F.F., Fig. 8-f	—	11th century	Princeton
	—	65-5-96	XXI-19 surface; FEPR '65-I, Plan II	—	F.F., Fig. 9-b	11th century	Kelsey
	Pl. XX-d	64-5-31	VIII-12 surface; FEPR '64, Plan II	—	FEPR '64, Fig. 3-a	11th century	Princeton
B-II-A-8-b-1	Fig. 110	65-2-101	XVI-21 cistern H, 3.0 m; FEPR '65-I, Plan II	F.F., Fig. 9-d	—	11th-12th century	Princeton
	—	65-3-80	XVI-10 cistern 0′, 3.0 m; FEPR '65-I, Plan II	—	F.F., Fig. 9-d	11th century	Kelsey
	—	65-2-70 (fragment)	XVI-8 E, fill; FEPR '65-I, Plan II	F.F., Fig. 9-d	—	11th century	Princeton
	—	68-12-10	VI′-8 pit K, 2.1 m; FEPR '68-I, Plan I	F.F., Fig. 9-d	Pits; Fig. 12-e	11th century	Kelsey
	—	78-9-28	XXVI-11/16 surface; FEPR '78, Plan	F.F., Fig. 9-d	—	11th-12th century	AUC
B-II-A-8-b-2	—	64-5-77	VII-19 fill of vaulted cistern; FEPR '64, Plan II	—	FEPR '64, Fig. 3-b	11th century	Akron

TYPE	ILLUS. HEREIN	REG. NO.	FIND-SPOT	COMP. EXAMPLE	PUBL.	DATE	DISPOSITION
B-II-A-8-b-2	Fig. 111	68-11-19	XI'-2 surface; FEPR '68-I, Plan I	like FEPR '64, Fig. 3-b	—	11th-12th century	Kelsey
B-II-A-8-b-3	—	65-3-74	XVI-10 cistern 0', 1.5 m; FEPR '65-I, Plan II	—	F.F., Fig. 9-e	11th century	Or. Inst.
	Fig. 112	65-4-27	XXI-2 surface; FEPR '65-I, Plan II	like F.F., Fig. 9-e	—	11th-12th century	Kelsey
B-II-A-8-b-4	Pl. XXI-a	65-4-61	XVI-6 cistern K, 5.0 m; FEPR '65-I, Plan II	—	F.F., Fig. 9-f	11th century	Princeton
B-II-A-8-c	—	65-4-60	XVI-6 cistern K, 5.5 m; FEPR '65-I, Plan II	—	F.F., Fig. 9-a	11th century	Princeton
	—	65-3-106	XI-20 H surface; FEPR '65-I, Plan II	— —	FEPR '65-II, Fig. 2-a	11th-12th century	Princeton
	Fig. 113	68-12-51	VI'-8 pit K, 3.0 m; FEPR '68-I, Plan I	—	Pits, Fig. 12-d	11th century	Kelsey
	—	78-10-36	XXVII-8/13 surface; FEPR '78, Plan	Pits, Fig. 12-d	—	11th-12th century	AUC
B-II-A-8-d	—	65-2-99	XVI-21 cistern H, 3.0 m; FEPR '65-I, Plan II	—	F.F., Fig. 9-c	11th-12th century	Kelsey
	Fig. 114	65-3-36	XVI-22 C fill; FEPR '65-I, Plan II	Olmer, pl. XVII-D	—	11th century	Princeton
B-II-A-8-e	Fig. 115	68-11-85	XI'-5 surface; FEPR '68-I, Plan I	—	—	11th-12th century	Kelsey
	Fig. 116	68-12-11	VI'-8 pit K, 2.6 m; FEPR '68-I, Plan I	Olmer, pl. XVIII-A	Pits, Fig. 12-f	11th century	Kelsey

TYPE	ILLUS. HEREIN	REG. NO.	FIND-SPOT	COMP. EXAMPLE	PUBL.	DATE	DISPOSITION
B-11-A-8-f	Pl. XXI-b	64-4-20	VII-10 east of pave-mented room; FEPR '65, Plan II	Olmer, pl. VI-A	FEPR '64, Fig. 2-b	11th-12th century	Akron
	Fig. 117	65-2-97	XVI-8 J surface; FEPR '65-I, Plan II	Olmer, pl. XV-D	—	11th-12th century	Kelsey
	Fig. 118	72-11-48	XXVI-25 pit J, 0.5-1.8 m; FEPR '72-II, Plan	—	—	11th century	Missouri
	Fig. 119	72-11-9	XXVI-I pit M$'$, 1.0-2.8 m; FEPR '72, Plan	—	—	11th-12th century	Missouri
B-II-B-1	Fig. 120	68-12-7	VI$'$-8 pit K, 2.6 m; FEPR '68-I, Plan I	like Olmer, pl. LXIV-A	Pits, Fig. 12-a	11th century	Kelsey
BII-B-2-a	Fig. 121	72-11-50	XXVI-25 pit J, 0.5-1.8 m; FEPR '72-II, Plan	like Olmer, pls. LV-A and C	—	11th century	I.M.
	Fig. 122	65-3-148	XII-19 surface; FEPR '65-I, Plan II	like Olmer, pls. LV-A and C	—	11th-12th century	I.M.
B-II-B-2-b	Pl. XXI-c	65-3-83	XVI-6 surface; FEPR '65-I, Plan II	like Olmer, pl. LVIII-c	F.F., Fig. 6-e	11th-12th century	Princeton
	Pl. XXI-d	66-5-99	VI-17 pit in trench, 4.0-4.5 m; FEPR '66, Plan II	like Olmer, pl. LVIII-c	F.F., Fig. 6-f	11th century	Princeton
	Fig. 123	68-12-13	VI$'$-8 pit K, 2.1 m; FEPR '68-I, Plan I	like Olmer, pl. LVIII-c	Pits, Fig. 12-c	11th century	Kelsey
B-II-B-2-c	Pl. XXII-a	65-5-39	XVI-6 pit K, sieve; FEPR '65-I, Plan II	like Olmer, pl. LIV-c	F.F., Fig. 6-d	11th century	Princeton

TYPE	ILLUS. HEREIN	REG. NO.	FIND-SPOT	COMP. EXAMPLE	PUBL.	DATE	DISPOSITION
B-II-B-2-d	Pl. XXII-b	65-3-22	XVI-7 F′ cistern; FEPR '65-I, Plan II	—	Anc., Fig. 5-d	before 1050	Akron
B-II-B-2-e	Fig. 124	68-12-12	VI′-8 pit K, 2.6 m; FEPR '68-I, Plan I	like Olmer, pl. LIII	Pits, Fig. 12-b	11th century	Kelsey
B-II-c	Pl. XXII-c	64-5-9	III-23 surface; FEPR '64, Plan II	Olmer, pl. LXXVII-B	FEPR '64, Fig. 2-e	11th-12th century	Princeton
	Pl. XXII-d	66-4-61	XI-16 gutter A; FEPR '66, Plan II	Olmer, pl. LXXV-C	F.F., Fig. 13-d	11th-12th century	Princeton
C-I-A	Fig. 125	65-4-167	XI-18 surface; FEPR '65-I, Plan II	—	—	13th-14th century	Kelsey
C-I-B-1	Fig. 126	65-3-107	XVI-6 surface; FEPR '65-I, Plan II	—	—	13th-14th century	Princeton
C-I-B-2	Fig. 127	65-4-164	XXI-3 surface; FEPR '65-I, Plan II	—	—	14th century	Princeton
	Fig. 128	64-3-26	VIII-8 surface; FEPR '64, Plan II	—	—	14th century	Akron
C-I-B-3	Fig. 129	64-4-61	VIII-8 surface; FEPR '64, Plan II	—	—	14th-15th century	Akron
C-I-B-4	Fig. 130	64-4-32	VIII-12 surface; FEPR '64, Plan II	—	—	14th-15th century	Akron
C-I-B-5	Fig. 131	65-3-45	XI-24 cistern V, sieve; FEPR '65-I, Plan II	—	—	ca. 1200	Princeton

TYPE	ILLUS. HEREIN	REG. NO.	FIND-SPOT	COMP. EXAMPLE	PUBL.	DATE	DISPOSITION
C-I-B-5	Fig. 132	65-3-112	XI-20 I surface; FEPR '65-I, Plan II	—	—	13th-14th century	Princeton
C-I-B-6	Fig. 133	65-4-171	XI-18 surface; FEPR '65-I, Plan II	—	—	13th-14th century	Princeton
C-II	Pl. XXIII-a Fig. 134	64-5-40	VIII-II at level of wall; FEPR '64, Plan II	—	F.F., Fig. 11-c	1160-1200	Princeton
C-III-A	Fig. 135	66-4-18	VI-13 trench; FEPR '66, Plan II	—	FEPR '66, Fig. 3 left	before 1200	Princeton
C-III-B	Fig. 136	65-5-88	XI-22/23 surface; FEPR '65-I, Plan II	—	—	13th-14th century	Or. Inst.
	Fig. 137	66-4-44	XI'-20 sibakh level; FEPR '66, Plan II	—	—	12th-13th century	Princeton
	Fig. 138	66-4-19	VI-23 trench; FEPR '66, Plan II	—	FEPR '66, Fig. 3 right	before 1200	I.M.
	Fig. 139	71-10-38	XXVII-21 surface; FEPR '71-II, Plan	—	—	before 1200	Kelsey
C-III-C	Pl XXIII-b	64-4-77	VII-3 surface; FEPR '64, Plan II	—	FEPR '64, Fig. 2-d	13th-14th century	Akron
C-III-D	Fig. 140	65-4-126	XII-11 surface; FEPR '65-I, Plan II	—	—	before 1200	Princeton
	Fig. 141	72-10-5	XXI'-5 middle sibakh; FEPR '72-I, Plan	Olmer, pl. XXXVI-A	—	13th-14th century	Ashmolean

TYPE	ILLUS. HEREIN	REG. NO.	FIND-SPOT	COMP. EXAMPLE	PUBL.	DATE	DISPOSITION
C-III-E	Fig. 142	66-3-15	XI'-10 surface; FEPR '66, Plan II	Olmer, pl. XXXIV-C	—	14th-15th century	I.M.
C-IV-A	Fig. 143	65-4-59	XXI-1 surface; FEPR '65-I, Plan II	—	—	13th-15th century	Princeton
	Fig. 144	64-3-27	VIII surface; FEPR '64, Plan II	—	—	13th-15th century	Princeton
C-IV-B	Fig. 145	65-5-15	XI-23 fill above pavement; FEPR '65-I, Plan II	similar to pl. XV-c herein	—	before 1200	Princeton
	Fig. 146	65-3-13	XVI-21 cistern K; FEPR '65-I, Plan II	Pl. XV-c and Fig. 145 herein	—	before 1200	Princeton
C-IV-C	Fig. 147	64-4-21	II-III near pottery grid; FEPR '64, Plan I	Pls. XI-c and XXIII-a herein	—	before 1200	Akron
C-IV-D-1	Fig. 148	65-4-29	XXI-2 surface; FEPR '65-I, Plan II	—	—	13th-15th century	Princeton
	Fig. 149	65-2-62	XVI-21 surface; FEPR '65-I, Plan II	—	—	13th-15th century	Princeton
	Fig. 151	65-1-14	XVI-16 surface; FEPR '65-I, Plan II	—	—	13th-15th century	Princeton
C-IV-D-2	Fig. 152	68-9-26	XXI-13 surface; FEPR '68-II, Plan I	—	—	14th-15th century	Kelsey
C-IV-D-3	Fig. 153	71-10-5	XXII-16 surface; FEPR '71-II, Plan	—	—	14th-15th century	I.M.

TYPE	ILLUS. HEREIN	REG. NO.	FIND-SPOT	COMP. EXAMPLE	PUBL.	DATE	DISPOSITION
C-IV-D-3	Fig. 154	72-10-16	XXV-1/2 surface; FEPR '72-II, Plan	—	—	15th century	Missouri
C-IV-D-4	Fig. 155	78-10-22	XXI-3 pit Y; FEPR '78, Plan	—	—	14th-15th century	AUC
C-IV-D-5	Fig. 156	65-5-89	XI-19 pit U'; FEPR '65-I, Plan II	similar to Olmer, pl. XXXVIII-A	—	13th-14th century	Princeton
C-IV-E	Fig. 157	72-11-49	XXVI-25 pit G', 2.0 m; FEPR '72-II, Plan	similar to Olmer, pl. XLII-B	—	13th-14th century	Ashmolean
C-IV-F	Fig. 158	65-2-24	XVI-22 surface; FEPR '65-I, Plan II	—	—	14th-15th century	Princeton
C-IV-G	Fig. 159	64-5-81	VIII-13 surface; FEPR '64, Plan II	—	—	1200	Princeton
C-V-A	Fig. 160	64-6-33	VIII-12, fnd. level; FEPR '64, Plan II	Olmer, pl. XXXV-B	—	13th-14th century	Akron
C-V-B	Fig. 161	64-6-32	VII-12 trench; FEPR '64, Plan II	—	—	13th-15th century	Akron
	Fig. 162	65-3-119	XI-23 surface; FEPR '65-I, Plan II	—	—	13th-14th century	Princeton
	Fig. 203	80-10-54	C-IV-11 S, *sibakh*	—	—	11th-12th century	AUC

TYPE	ILLUS. HEREIN	REG. NO.	FIND-SPOT	COMP. EXAMPLE	PUBL.	DATE	DISPOSITION
C-V-C-1	Fig. 163	65-2-26	XVI-22 surface; FEPR '65-I, Plan II	—	—	14th-15th century	Princeton
	Fig. 164	68-11-20	XI'-2 surface; FEPR '68-I, Plan I	—	—	13th-14th century	Kelsey
C-V-C-2-a	Fig. 165	65-4-87	XVI-11B cistern, 0.5-1.0 m; FEPR '65-I, Plan II	—	—	13th century	Or. Inst.
C-V-C-2-b	Fig. 166	66-4-43	XI'-20 *sibakh*; FEPR '66, Plan II	center similar to Olmer, pl. XXXVI-**B**	—	12th-13th century	Princeton
C-V-C-2-c	Fig. 167	65-1-24	XVI-16 surface; FEPR '65-I, Plan II	Olmer, pl. XXXVI-A and Fig. 141 herein	—	13th-14th century	Or. Inst.
	Fig. 168	64-6-1	VII-2 second level of trench; FEPR '64, Plan II	similar to Olmer, pl. XXXV-C	—	13th-14th century	Akron
	Fig. 169	66-4-67	XI-16 *sibakh*; FEPR '66, Plan II	—	—	13th century	I.M.
C-VI-A	Fig. 170	65-5-7	XI-18 surface; FEPR '65-I, Plan II	similar to Olmer, pl. LXXIII-C	—	14th-15th century	Kelsey
C-VII-A	Pl. XXIII-c Fig. 171	64-3-39	VII-5 surface; FEPR '64, Plan II	similar to Olmer, pls. LIX-B, LX-A	FEPR '64, Fig. 2-a	14th-15th century	Princeton
	Fig. 172	71-11-2	XVI-23 surface; FEPR '71-I, Plan	similar to Olmer, pl. LIX-**B**	—	14th-15th century	I.M.
C-VII-B	Fig. 173	65-3-122	XVI-I surface; FEPR '65-I, Plan II	—	—	14th-15th century	I.M.

TYPE	ILLUS. HEREIN	REG. NO.	FIND-SPOT	COMP. EXAMPLE	PUBL.	DATE	DISPOSITION
C-VII-B	Fig. 174	66-5-114	XI'-8 surface; FEPR '66, Plan II	—	—	14th-15th century	Princeton
APPENDICES							
XA-1	Fig. 175	65-5-25	XVI-I' cistern B, 4-4.8 m; FEPR '65-I, Plan II	—	—	ca. 750-800	I.M.
XA-2	Fig. 176	65-4-175	XI-15 N.W. corner below *dakkah* fill; FEPR '65, Plan II	—	FEPR '65-I, Fig. 13-b	8th-9th century	I.M.
XA-3	Fig. 177	bottle, unregistered	XXI'-5/10/15; FEPR '72-I, Plan	—	FEPR 72-I, Fig. 32	8th-9th century	ARCE
	Fig. 204	80-10-55	C-IV-7 J, sondage	—	—	8th century	I.M.
XA-4	Fig. 178	65-4-34	XVI-18 cistern V; FEPR '65-I, Plan II	similar to outer design of Olmer, pl. XLIV-D	—	9th century	Princeton
XB-1	Fig. 179	72-10-33	XXI'-5 Pit B-D, 1.8-2.3 m; FEPR '72-I, Plan	—	—	10th-11th century	Ashmolean
XB-2-a	Fig. 180	65-2-44	XVI-11 cistern X', 0.8 m; FEPR '65-I, Plan II	—	—	11th century	I.M.
XB-2-b	Fig. 181	65-5-116	XI-18 cistern Z, 0-1.5 m; FEPR '65-I, Plan II	—	—	11th-12th century	Kelsey
	Fig. 182	68-12-40	VI'-8 Pit K, 2.1 m; FEPR '68-I, Plan I	—	Pits, pl. XVI-3	11th century	Kelsey

TYPE	ILLUS. HEREIN	REG. NO.	FIND-SPOT	COMP. EXAMPLE	PUBL.	DATE	DISPOSITION
APPENDICES							
XB-2-b	Fig. 183	64-6-31	XXI-8 surface, really XXVI-8 of Fustat B; FEPR '66, Plan III	–	–	11th-12th century	Princeton
XB-2-c	Fig. 184	64-4-3	VII-10 surface; FEPR '64, Plan II	–	–	11th-12th century	Princeton
	Fig. 185	68-11-52	XXI-7 Pit V; FEPR '68-I, Plan I	–	–	11th-12th century	Kelsey
XB-3	Pl. XXIV-a Fig. 186	68-12-50	VI'-19/20/24/25 Pit T, 1.5 m; FEPR '68-I, Plan I	–	FEPR '68-I, Fig. 10	11th-12th century	Kelsey
XC-1	Pl. XXIV-b Fig. 187	68-11-72	VI-16 surface; FEPR '68-I, Plan II	–	–	14th-15th century	Kelsey
XC-2	Fig. 188	65-4-168	XI-9 surface; FEPR '65-I, Plan II	–	–	13th-14th century	Kelsey
XC-3	Fig. 189	65-4-162	XI-21 F surface; FEPR '65-I, Plan II	–	–	13th-14th century	Princeton

Figures have all been reduced to 68%.
Figures with * are reduced to 68% + 75%.
Figures with ** are reduced to 68% + 68% + 75%.

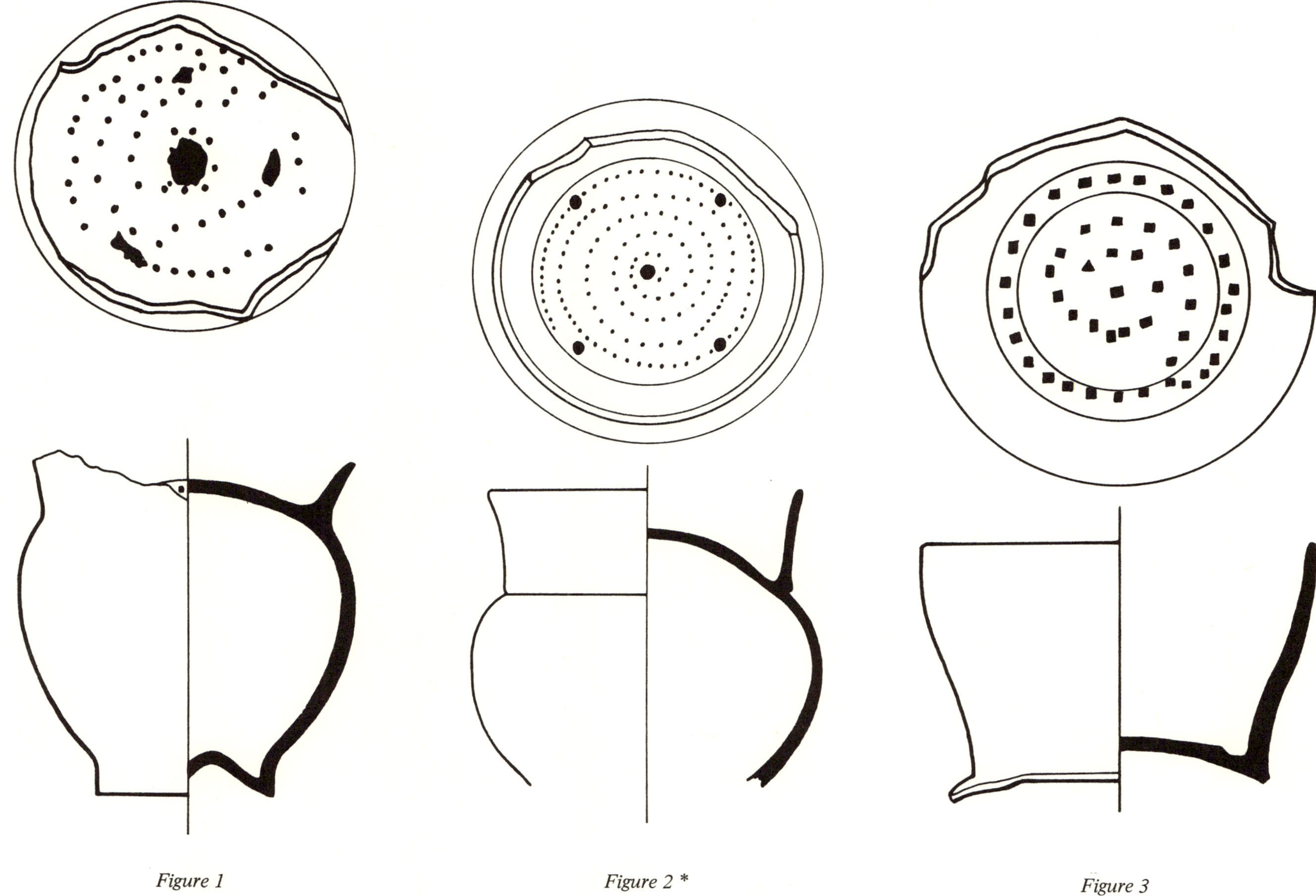

Figure 1

Figure 2 *

Figure 3

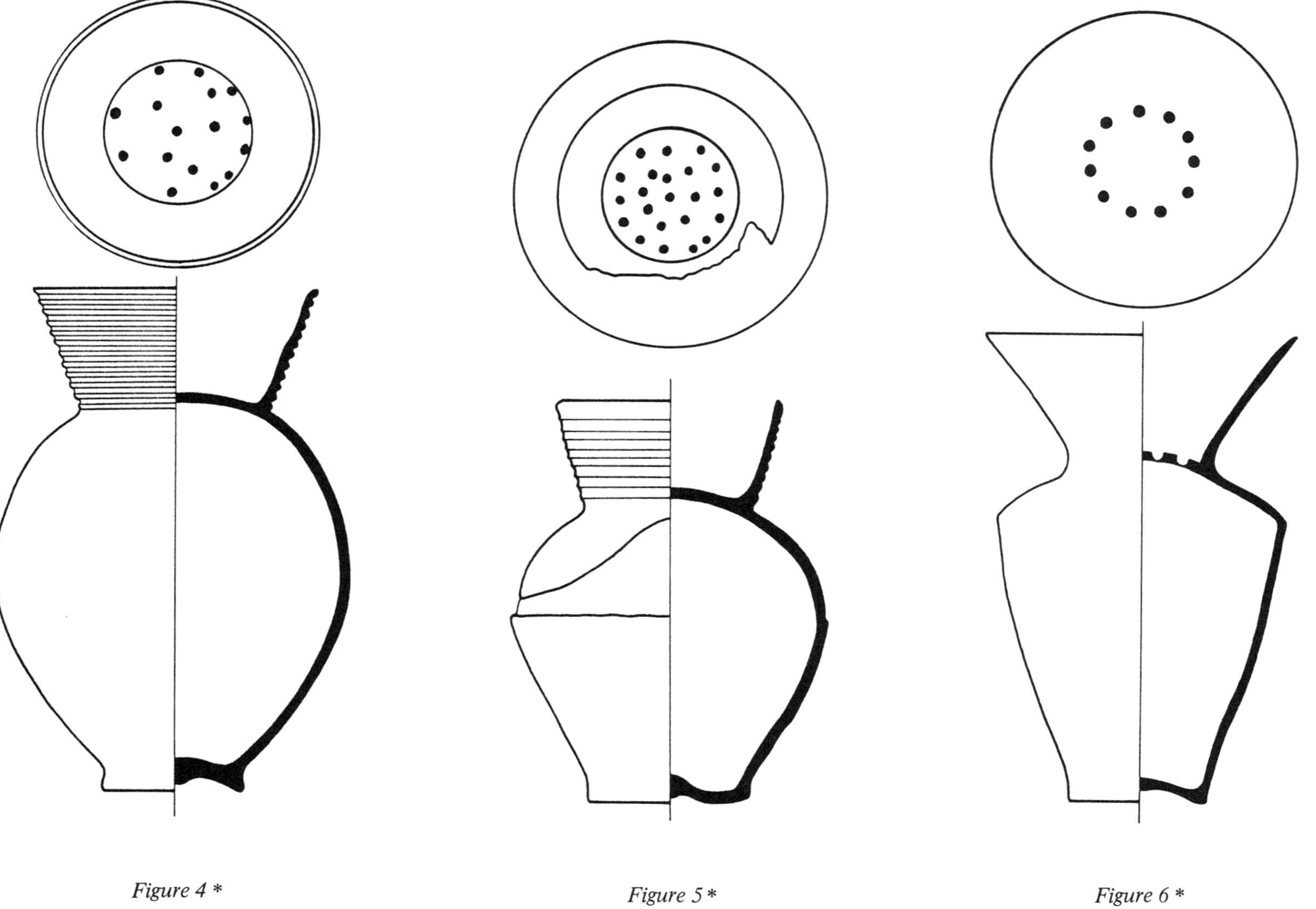

Figure 4 *

Figure 5 *

Figure 6 *

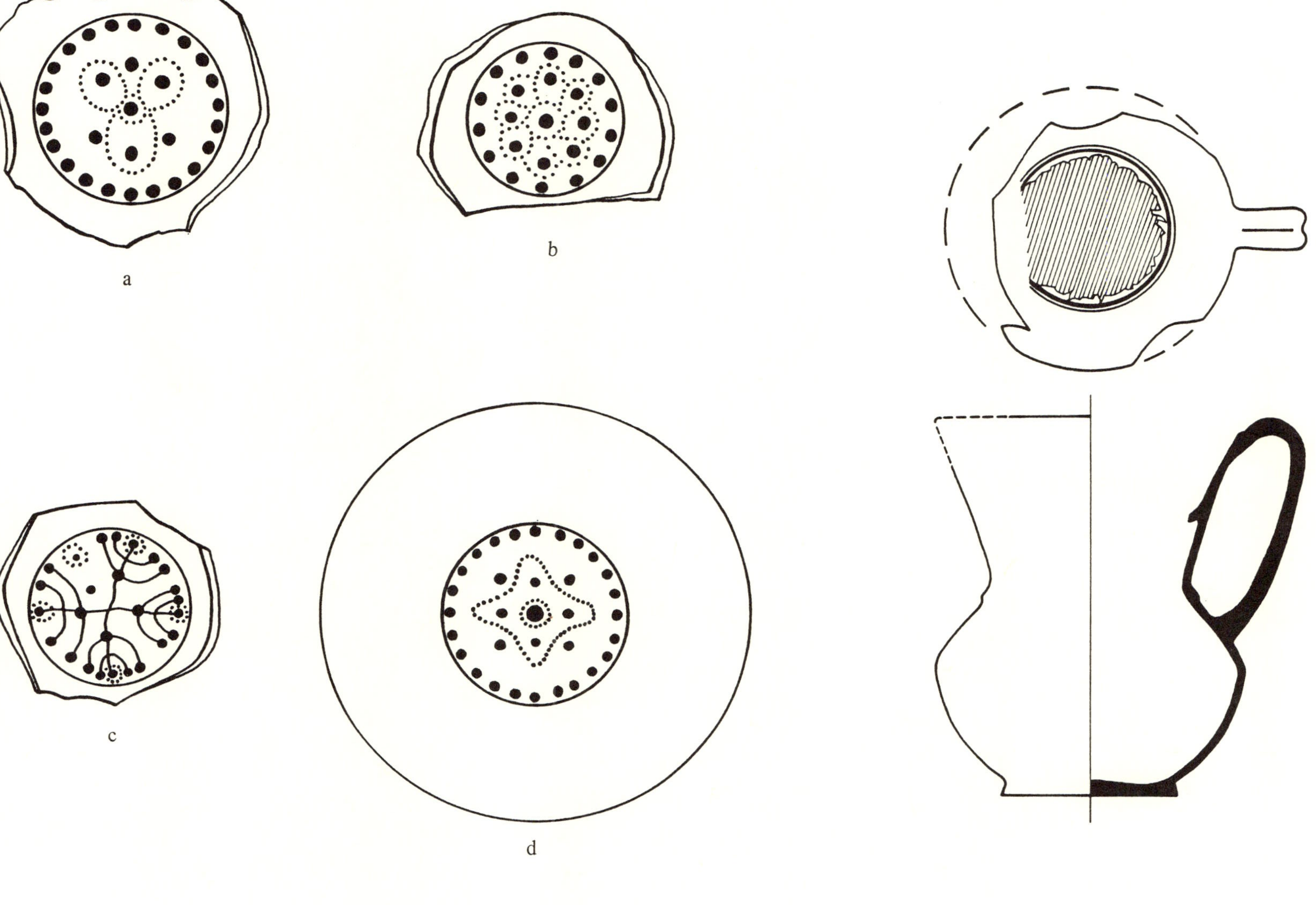

Figure 7

Figure 8 *

Figure 11

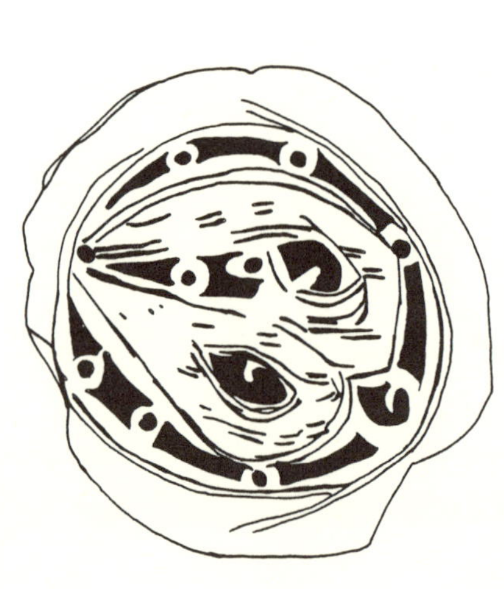

Figure 9

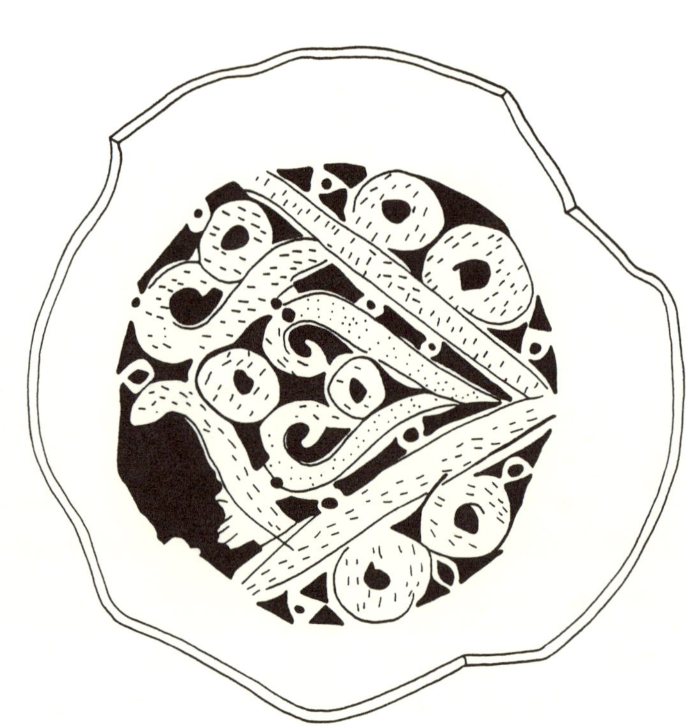

Figure 10

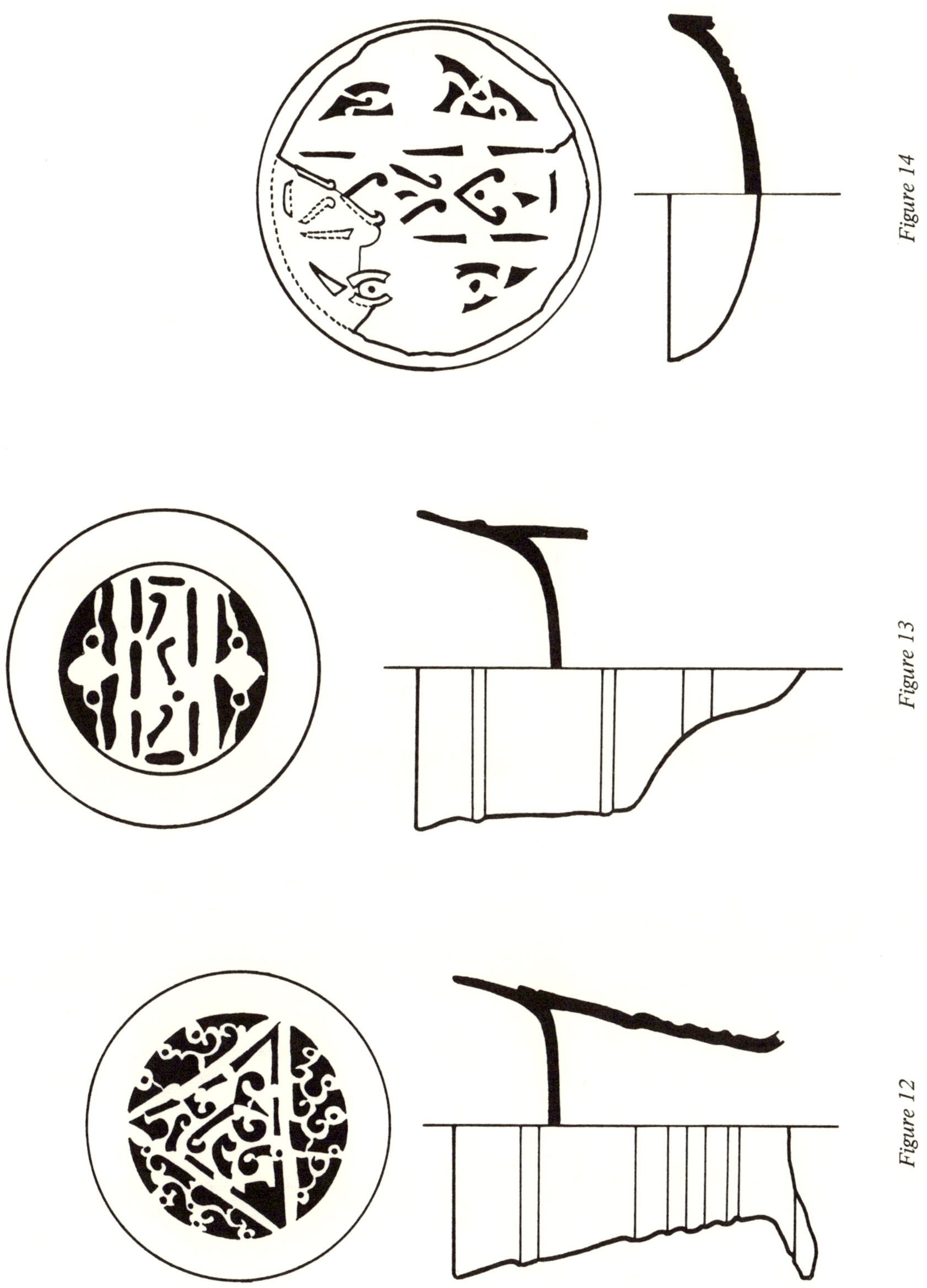

Figure 14

Figure 13

Figure 12

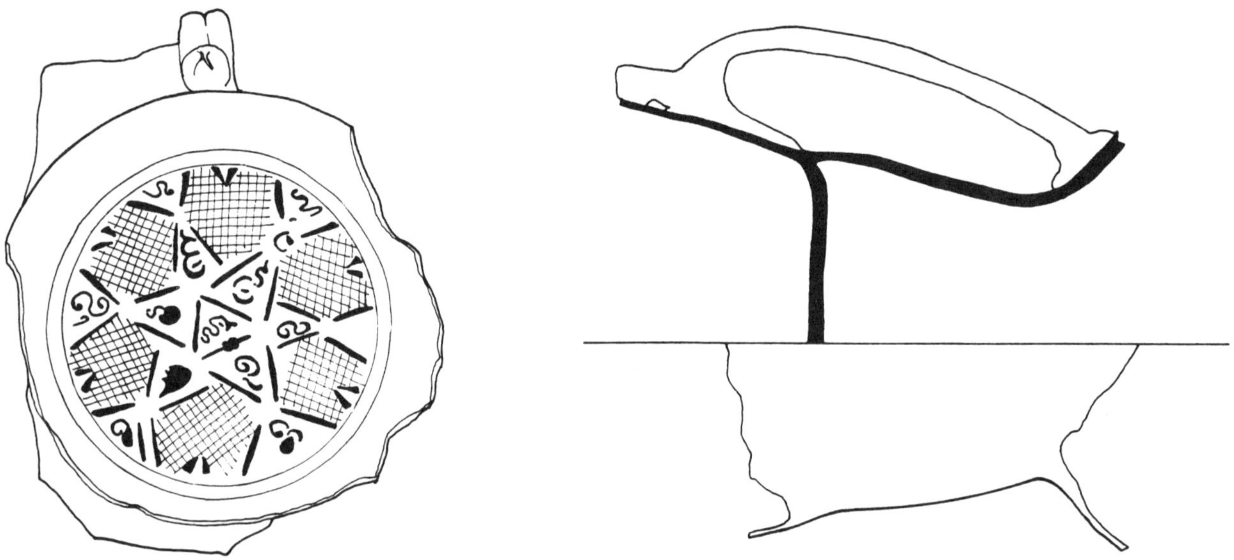

Figure 17

Figure 16

Figure 15

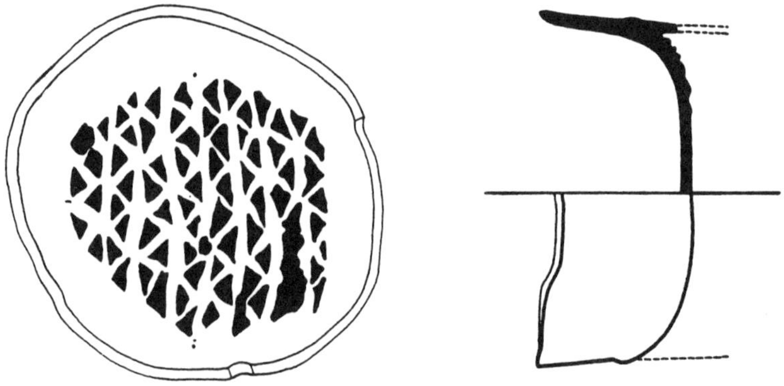

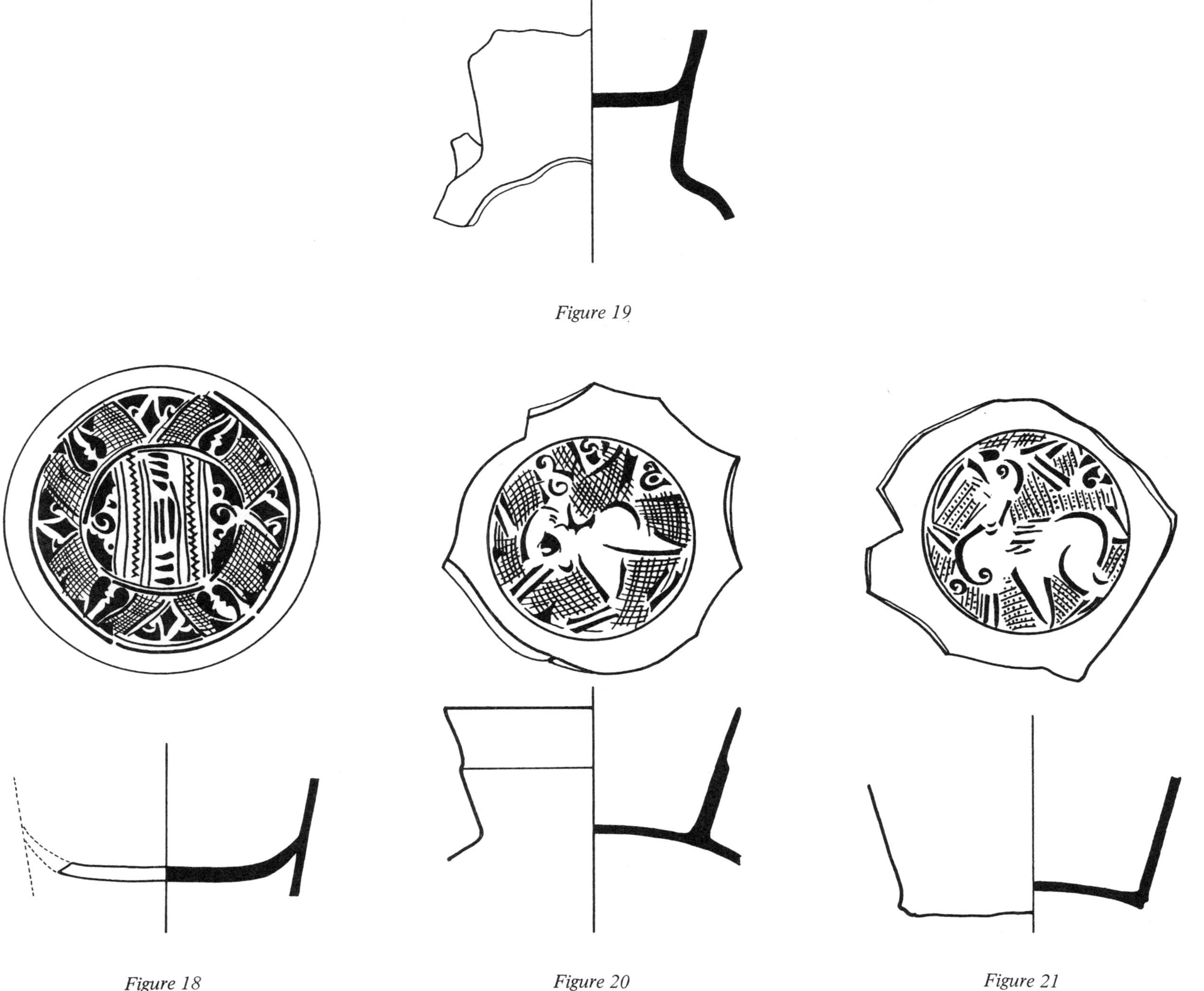

Figure 19

Figure 18

Figure 20

Figure 21

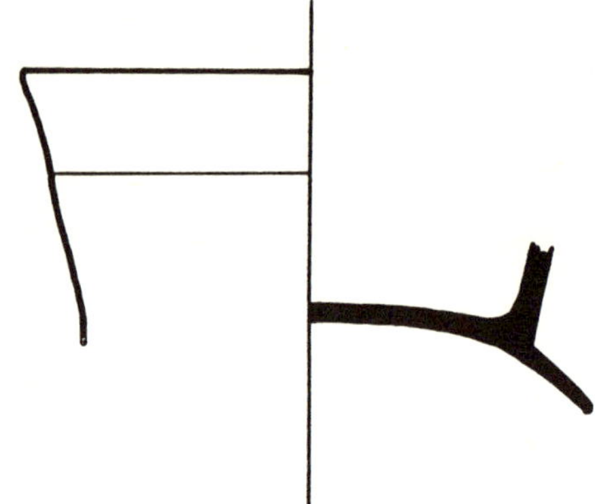

Figure 22

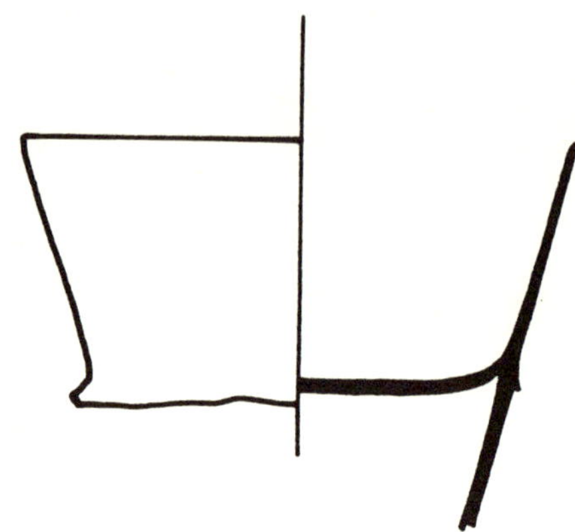

Figure 24

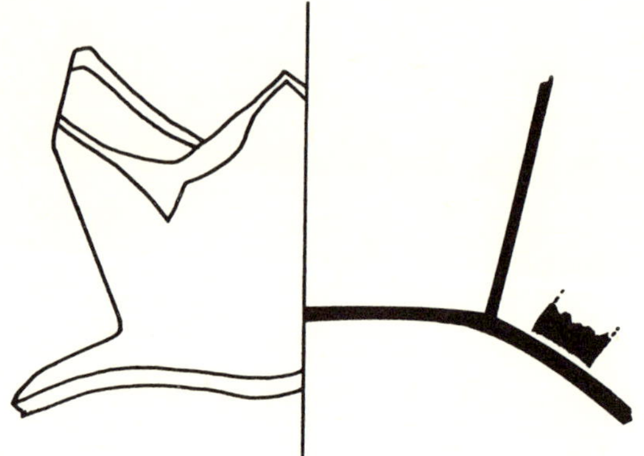

Figure 25

Figure 23

Figure 26

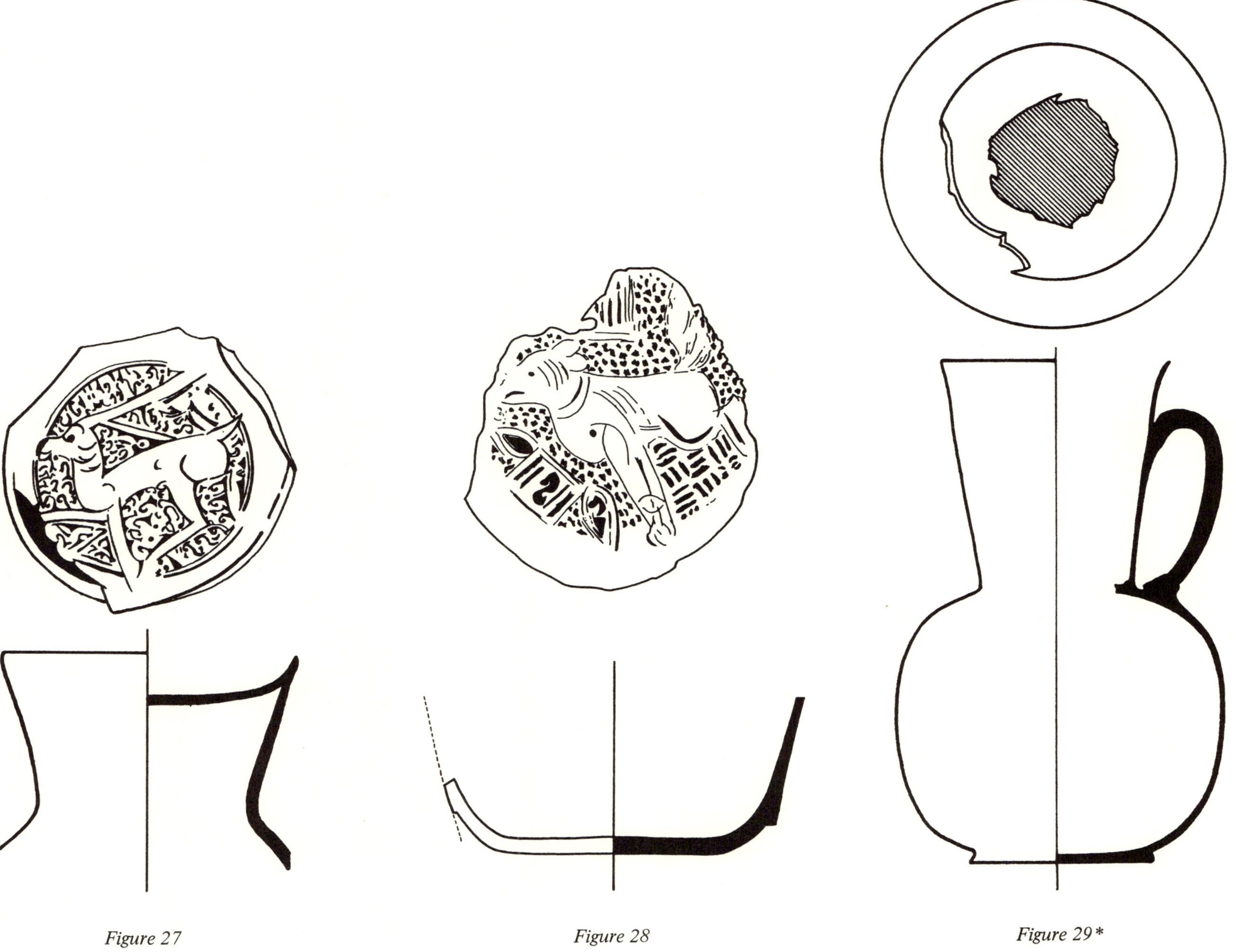

Figure 27

Figure 28

*Figure 29**

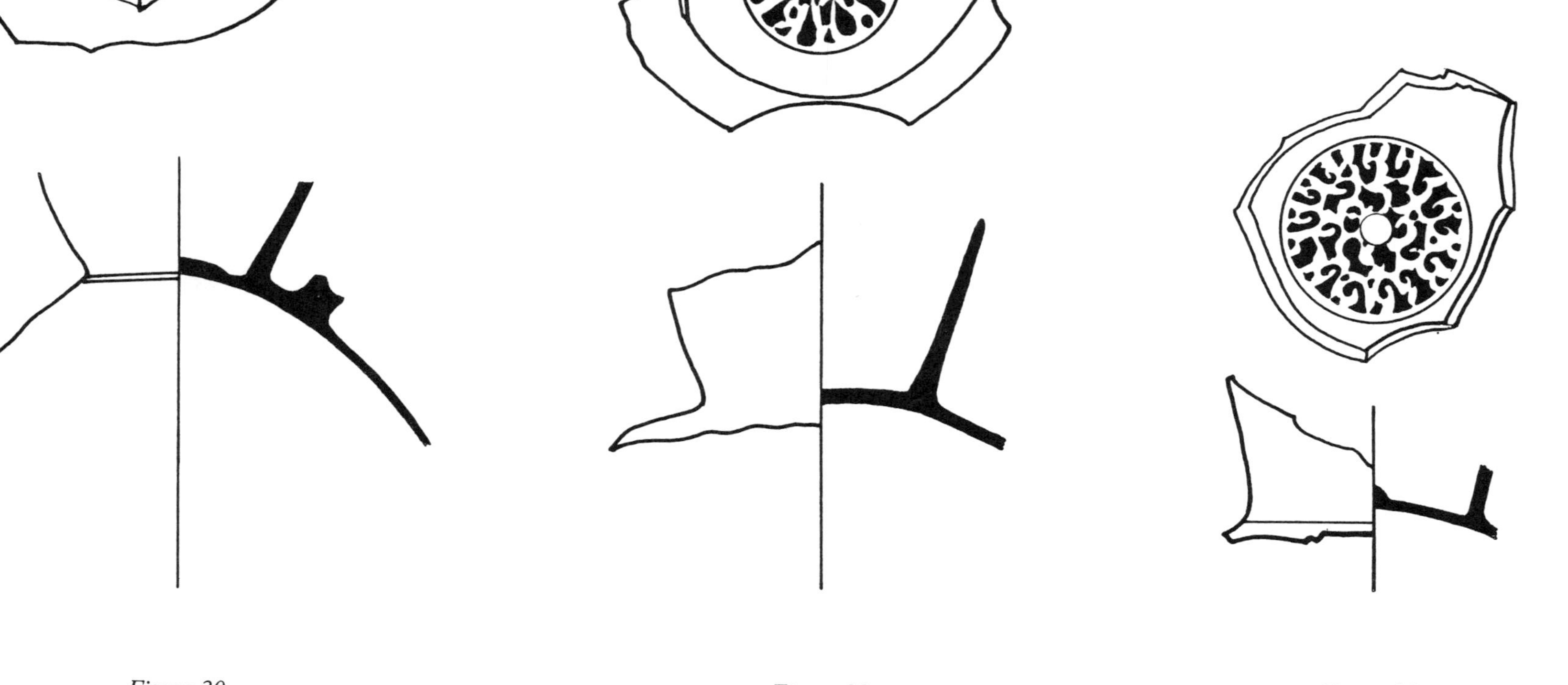

Figure 30

Figure 31

Figure 32

Figure 33

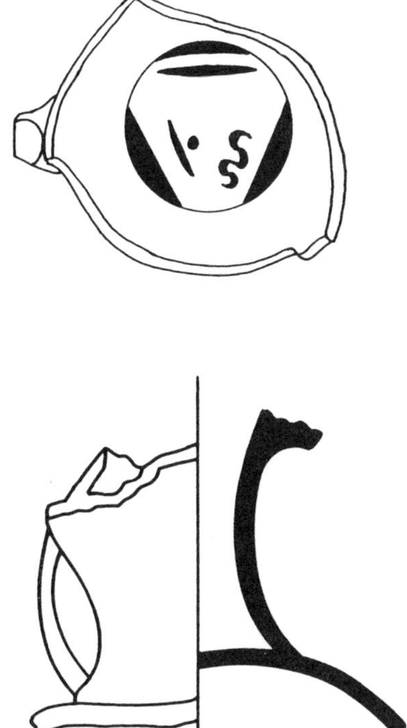

Figure 35

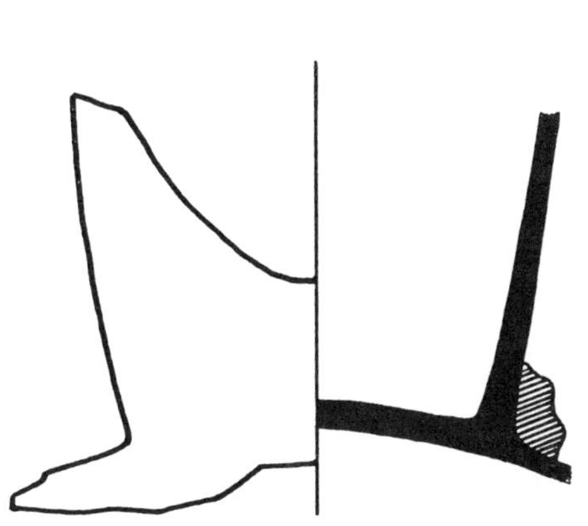

Figure 34

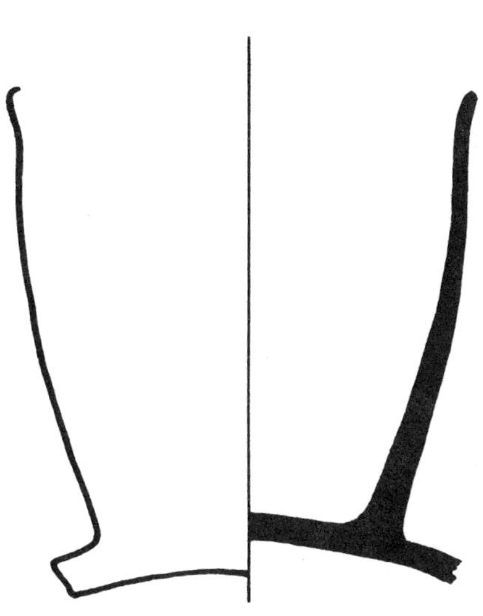

Figure 36

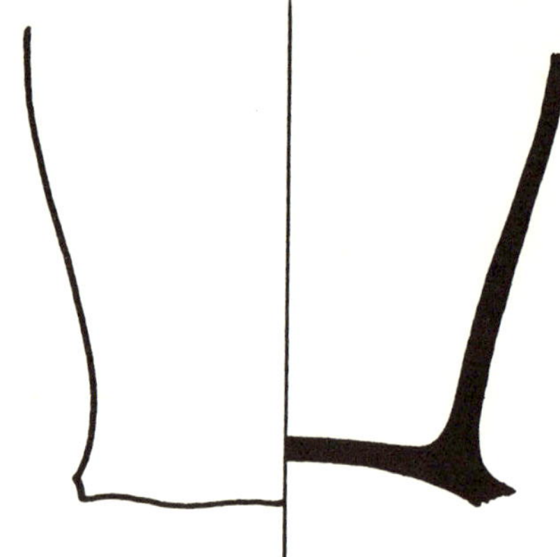

Figure 37

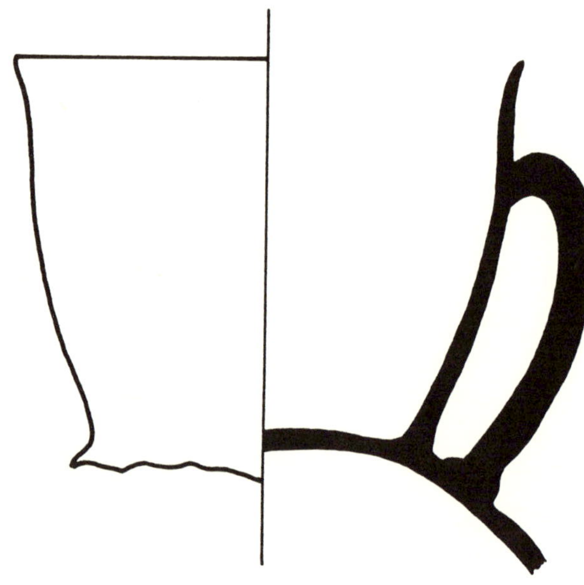

Figure 39

Figure 38

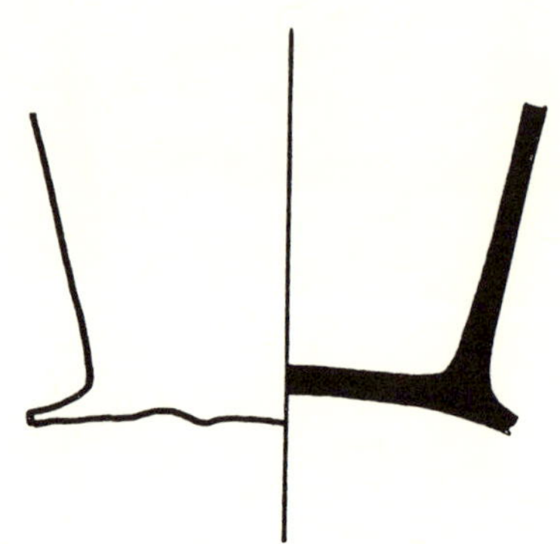

Figure 40

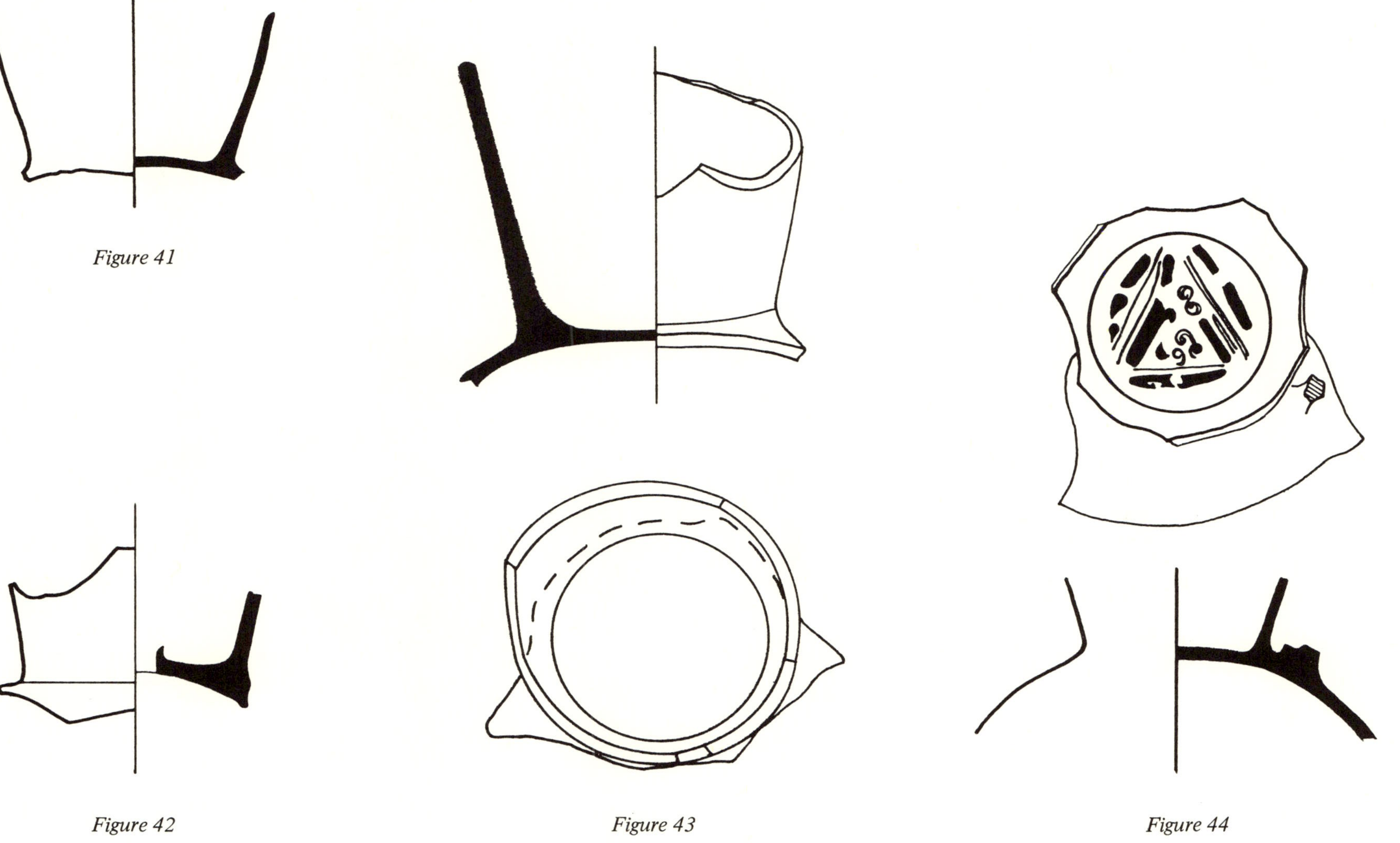

Figure 41

Figure 42

Figure 43

Figure 44

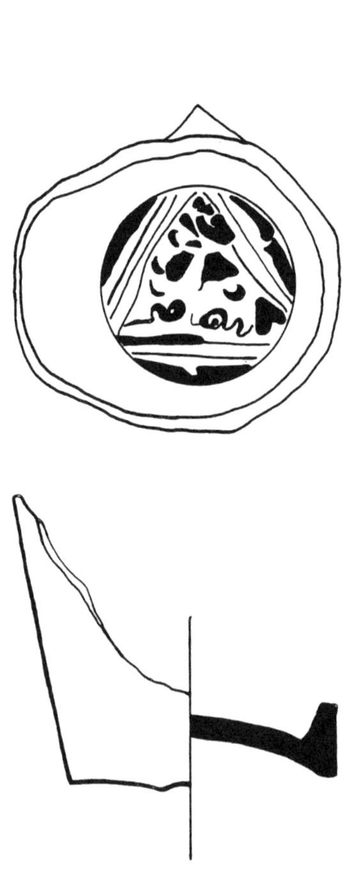

Figure 45

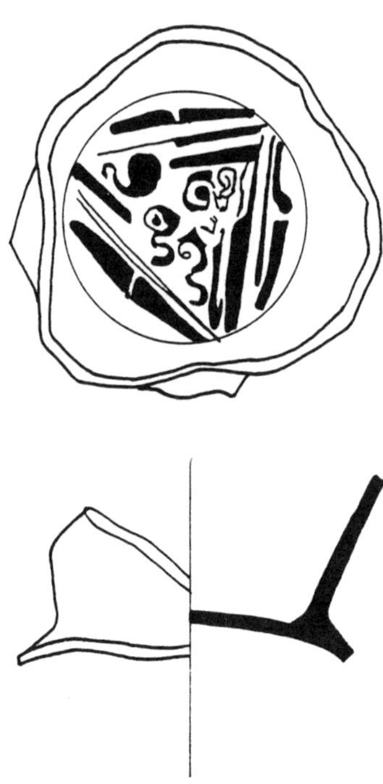

Figure 46

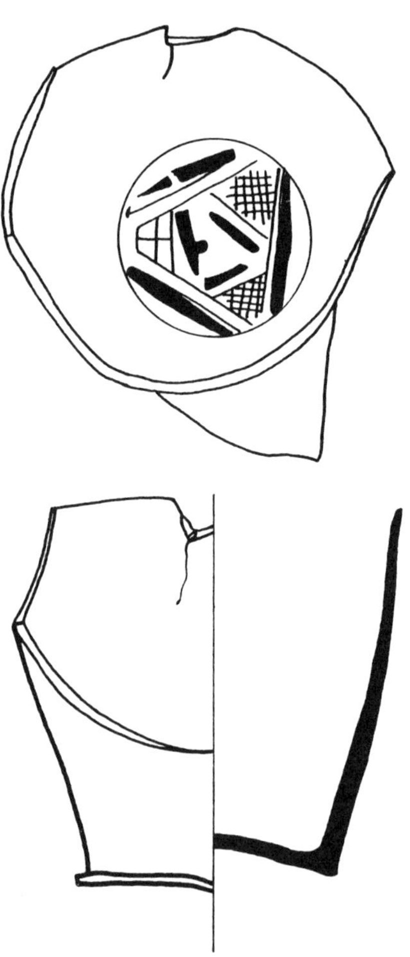

Figure 47

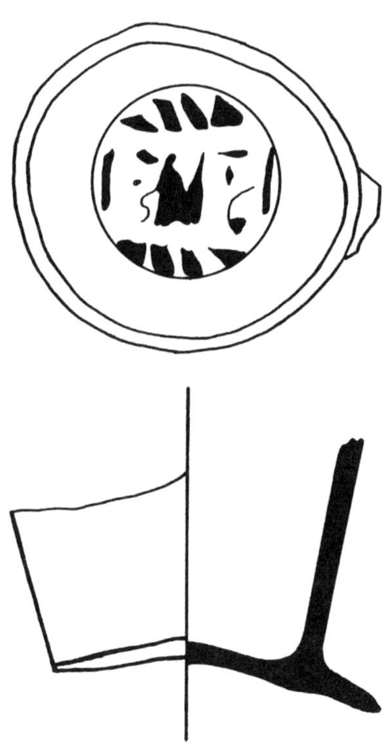

Figure 48

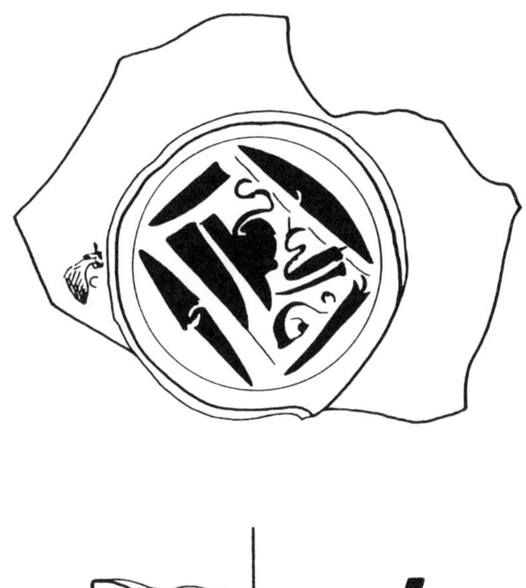
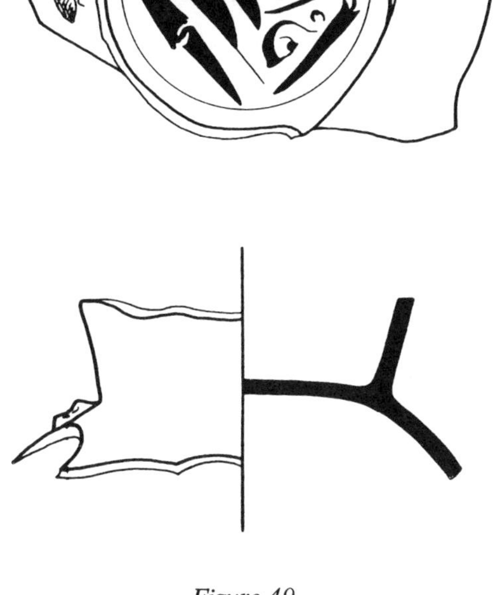

Figure 49

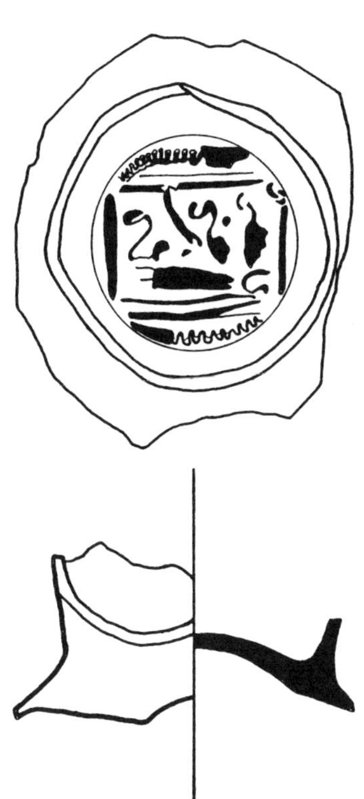

Figure 51

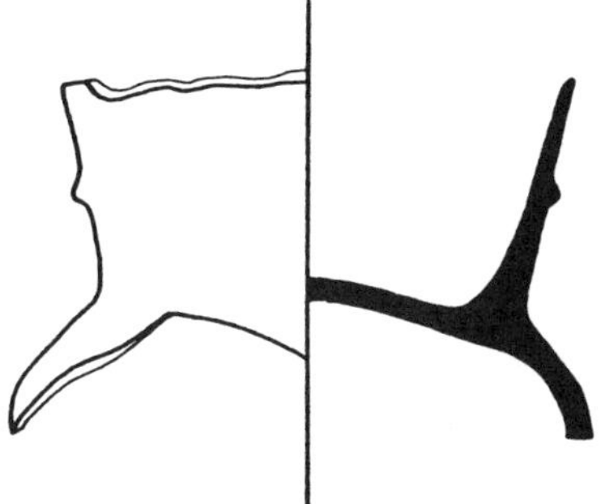

Figure 50

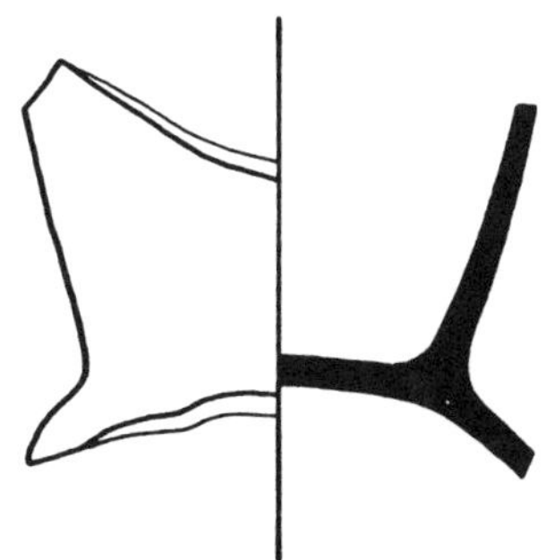

Figure 52

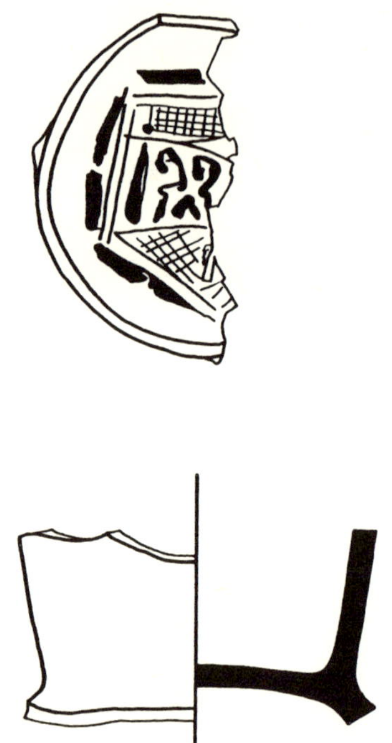

Figure 53

Figure 55

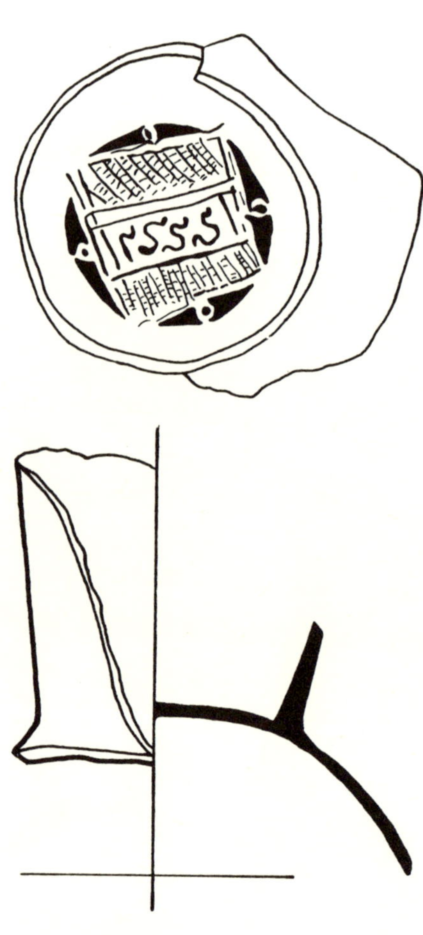

Figure 54

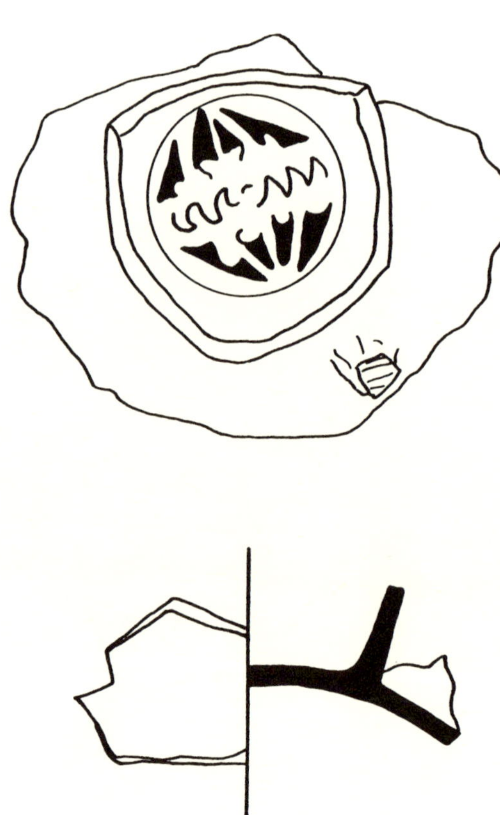

Figure 56

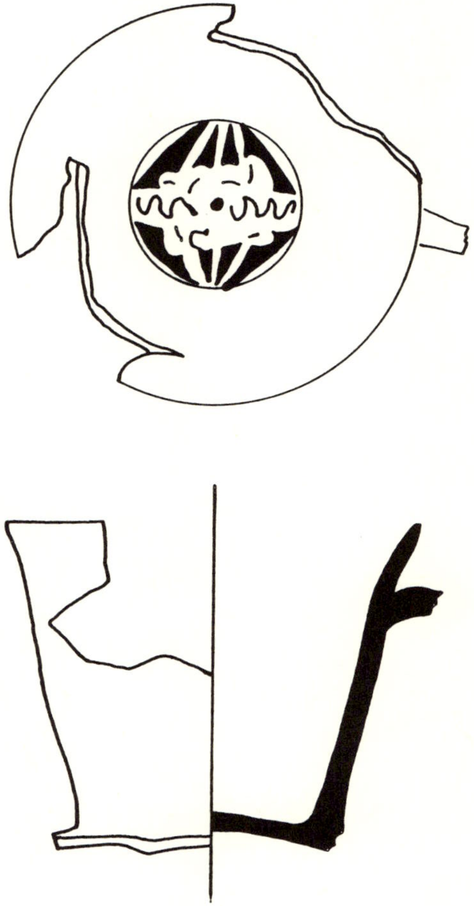

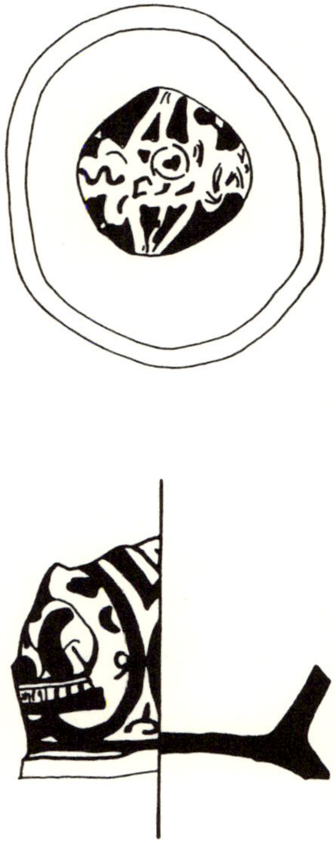

Figure 60

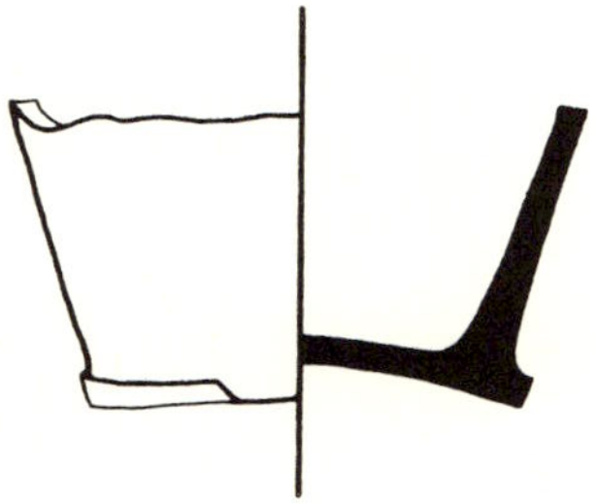

Figure 58

Figure 59

Figure 57

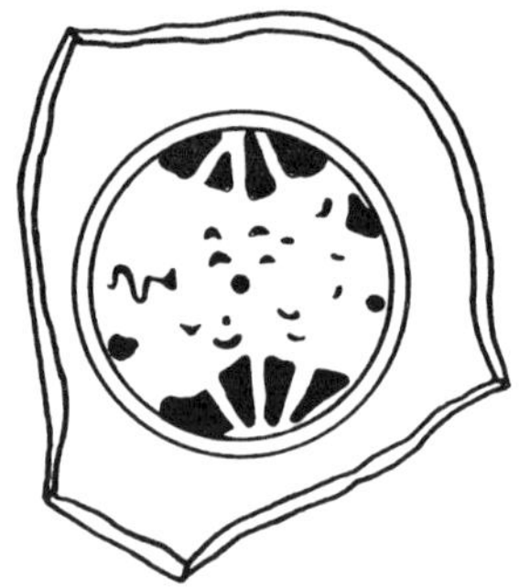

Figure 61

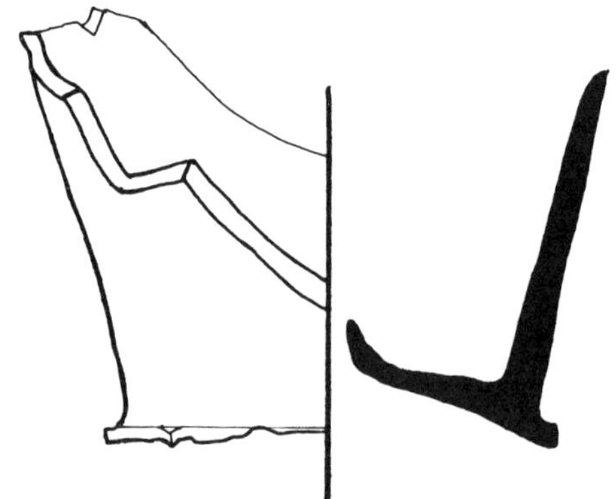

Figure 63

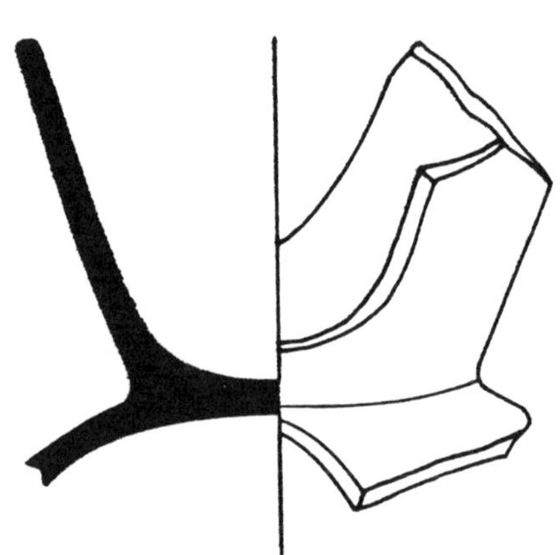

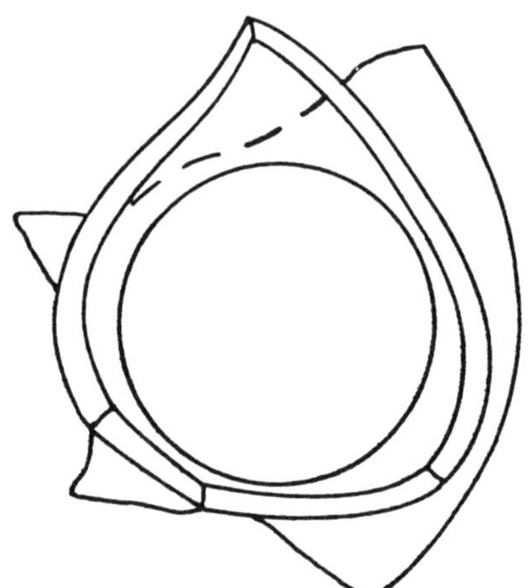

Figure 62

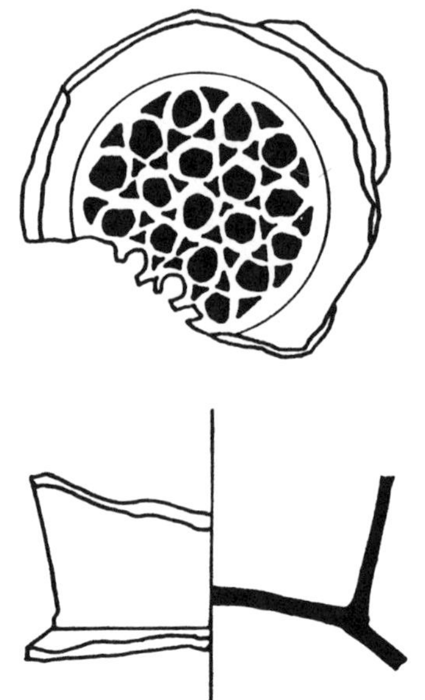

Figure 64

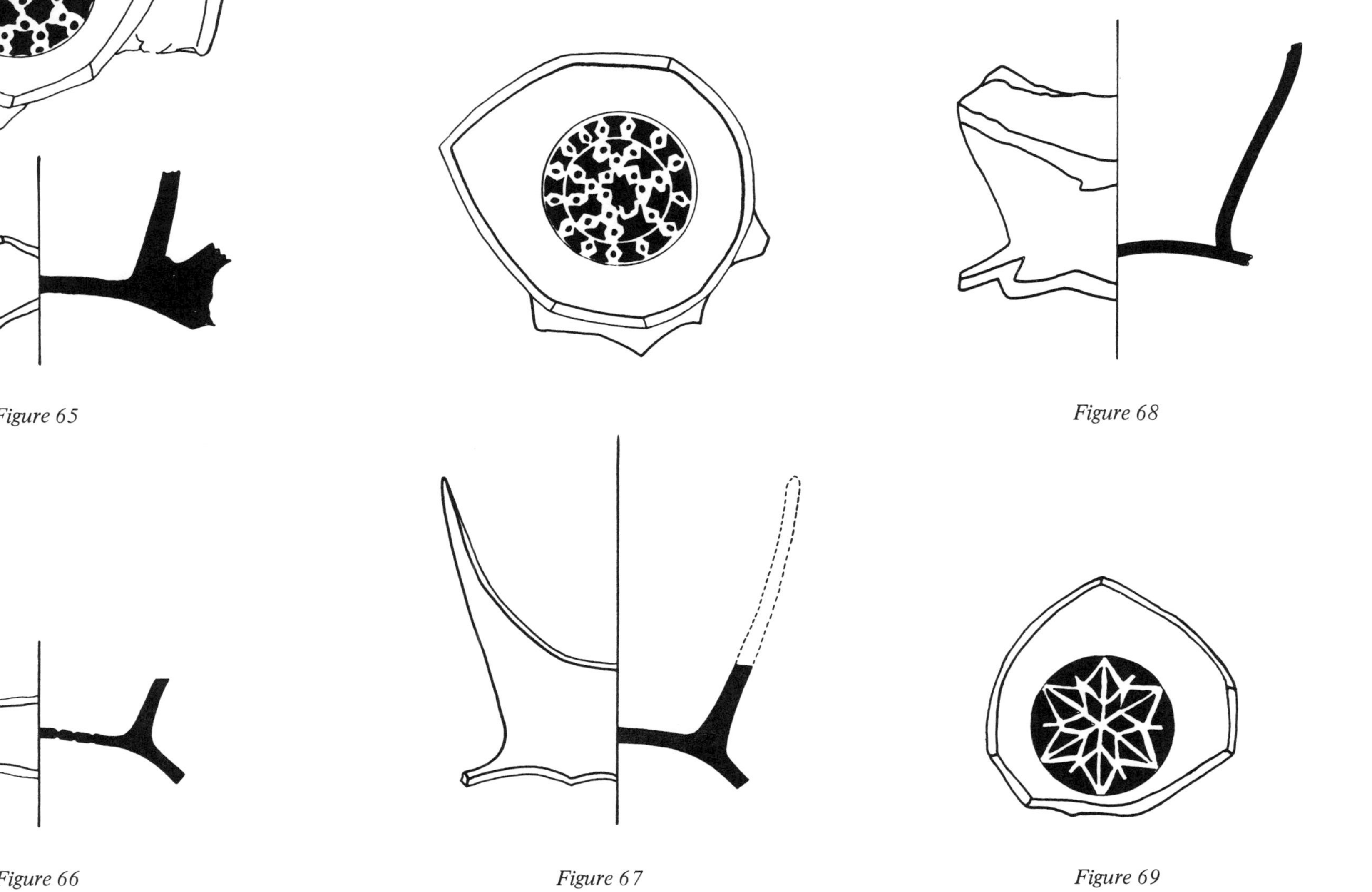

Figure 65

Figure 66

Figure 68

Figure 67

Figure 69

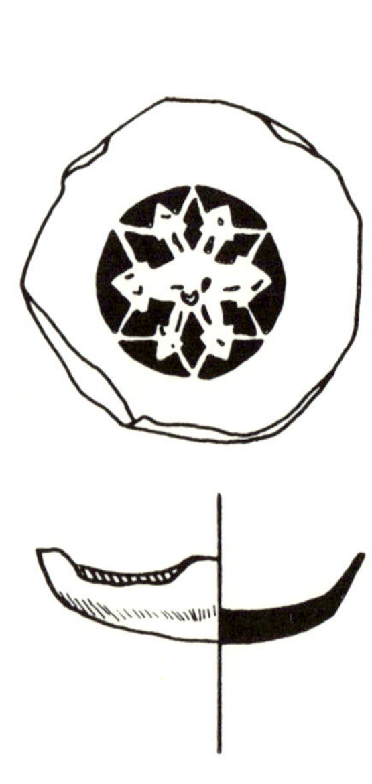

Figure 70

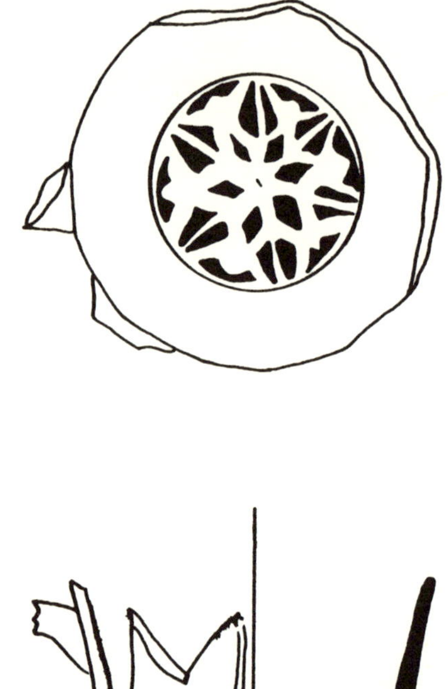

Figure 72

Figure 71

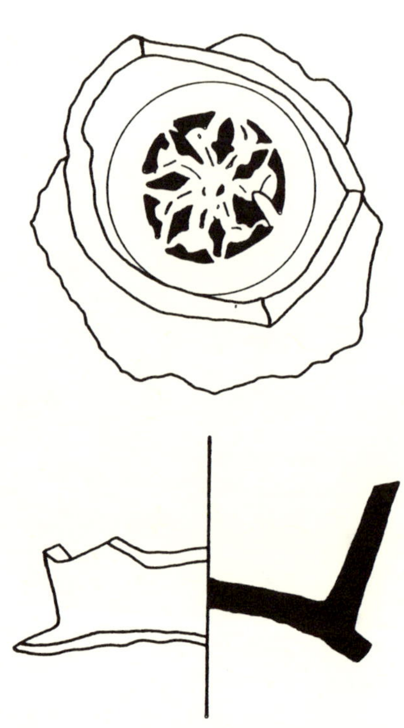

Figure 73

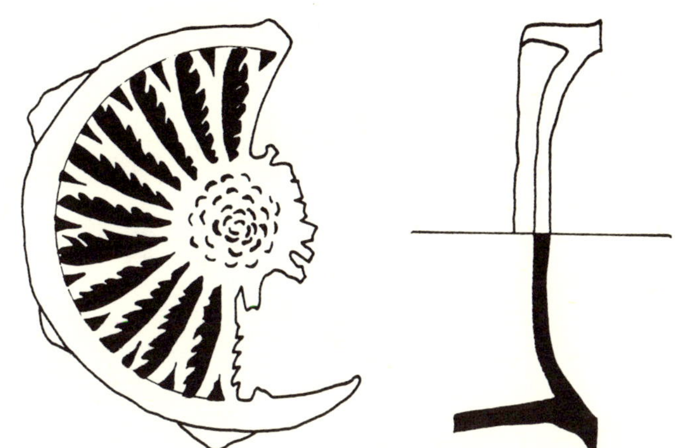

Figure 77

Figure 76

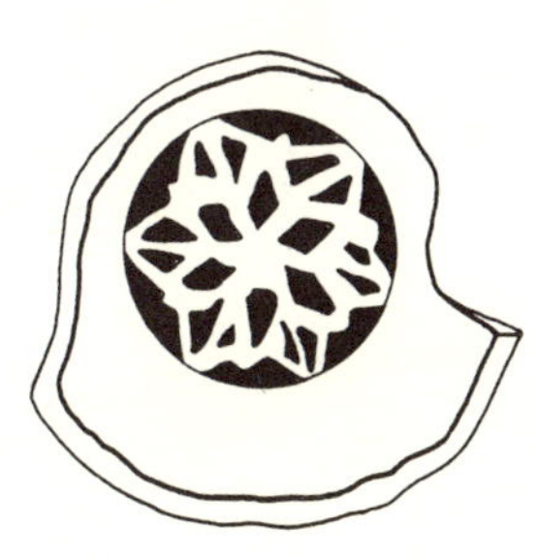

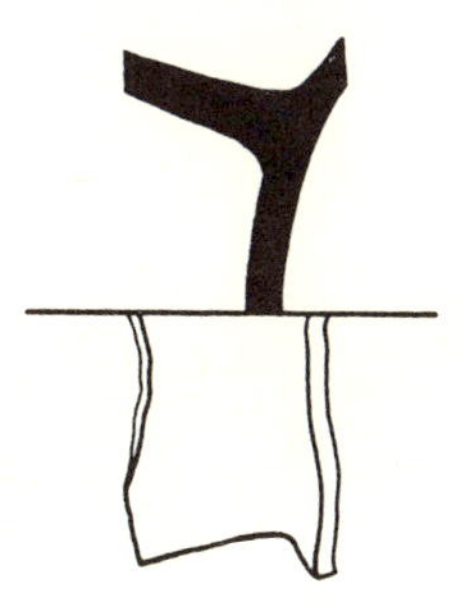

Figure 74

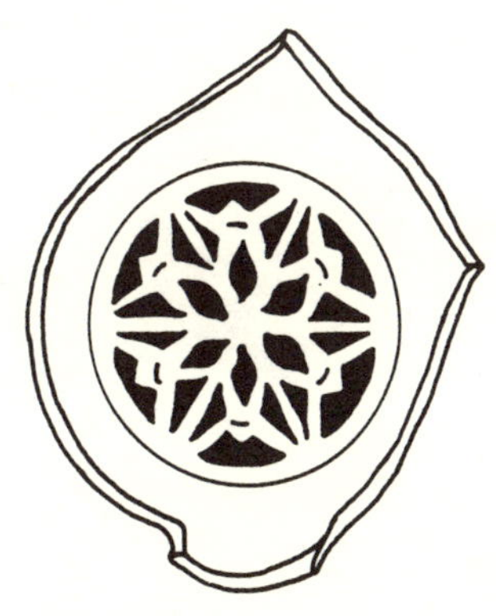

Figure 75

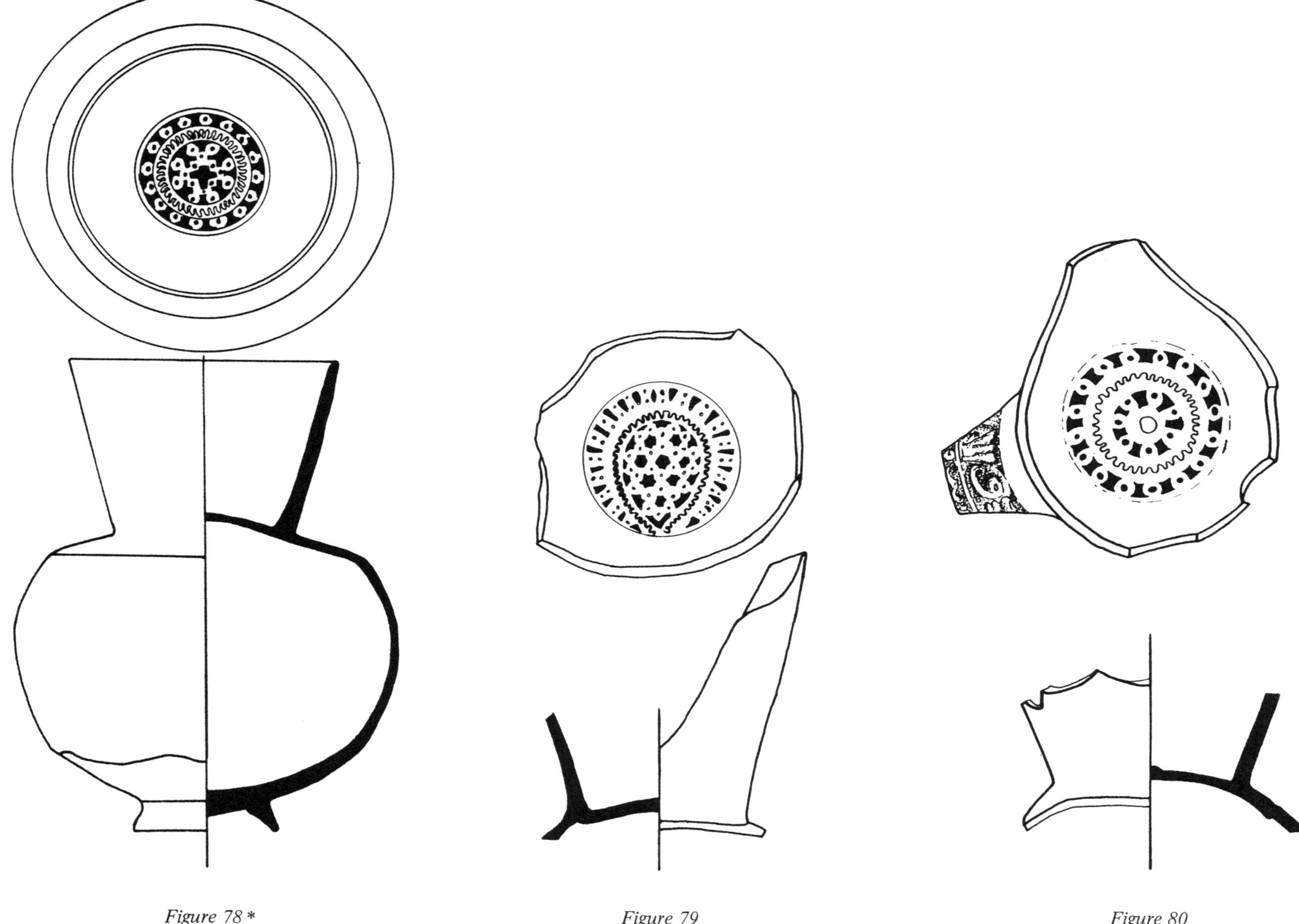

Figure 78 *

Figure 79

Figure 80

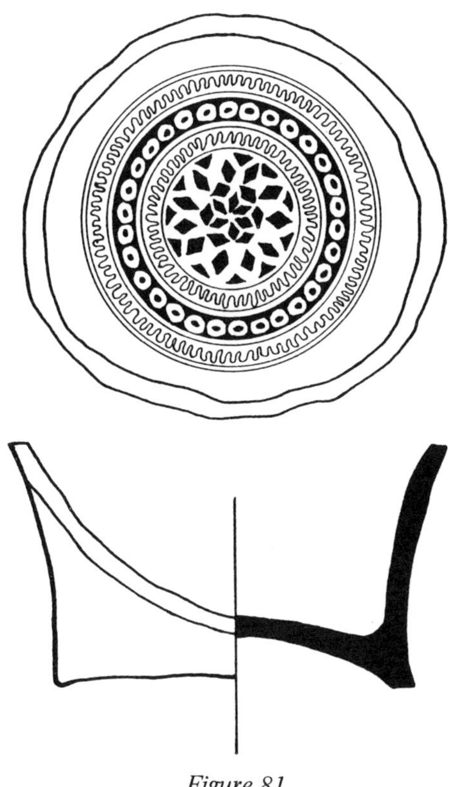

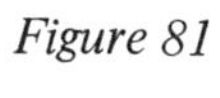

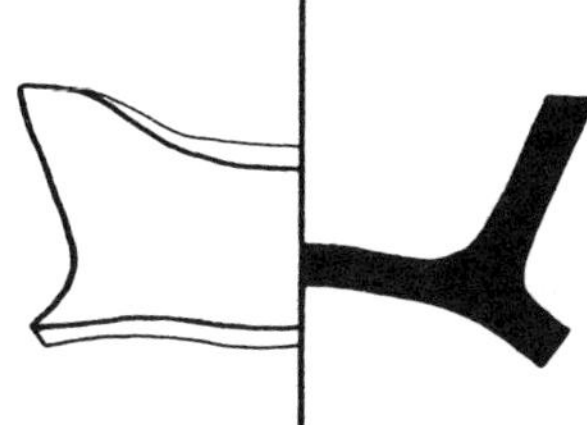

Figure 83

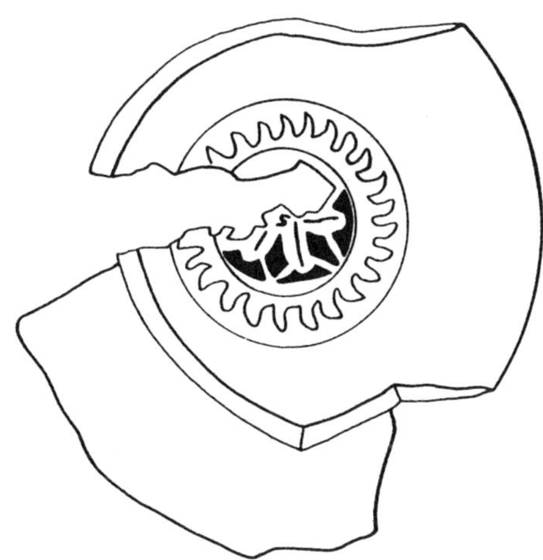

Figure 81

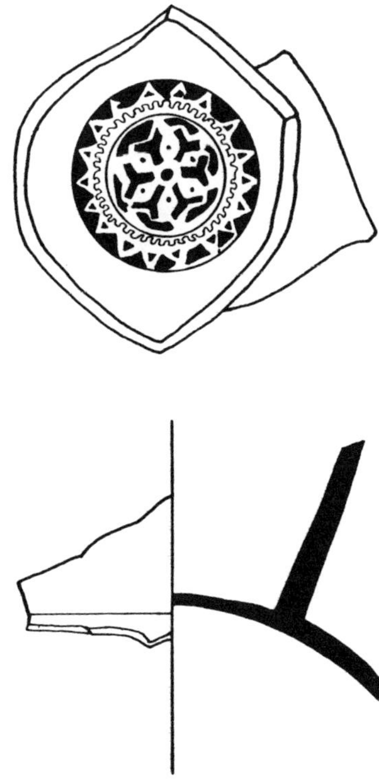

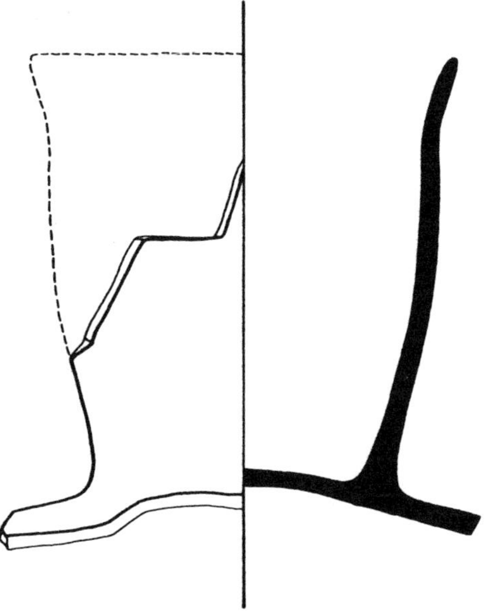

Figure 82

Figure 84

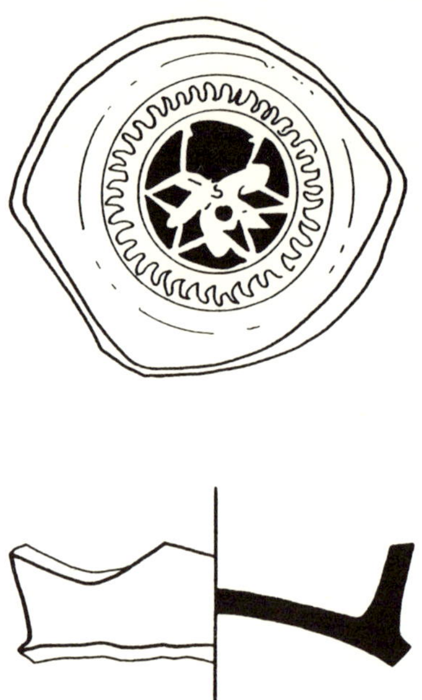

Figure 85

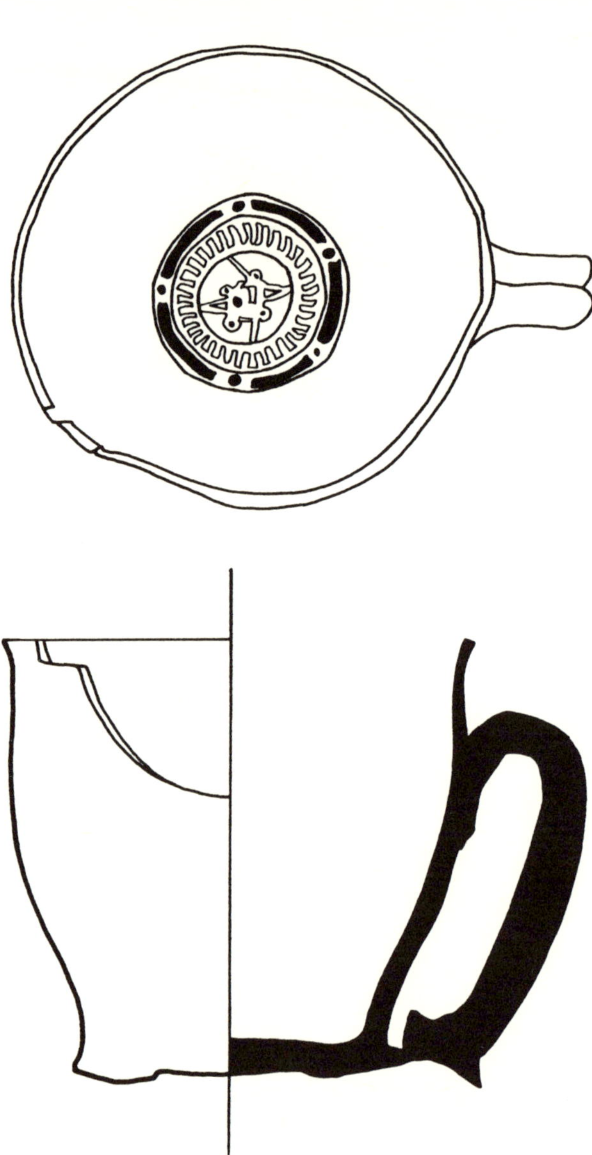

Figure 87

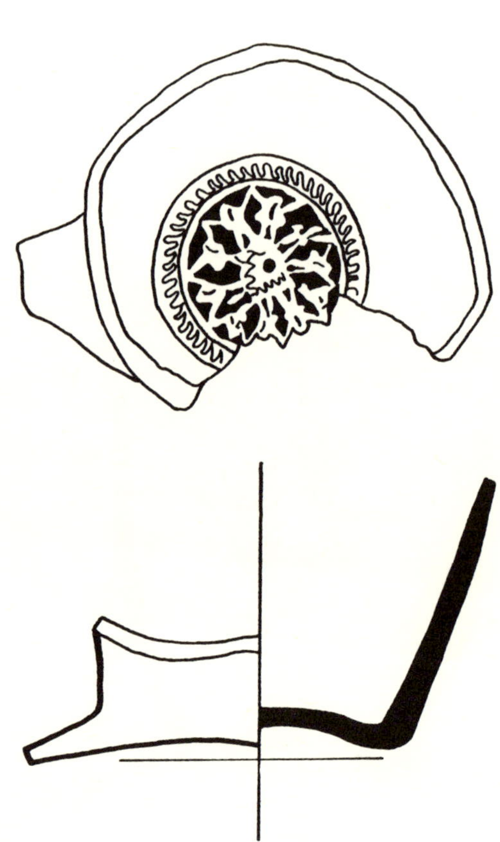

Figure 86

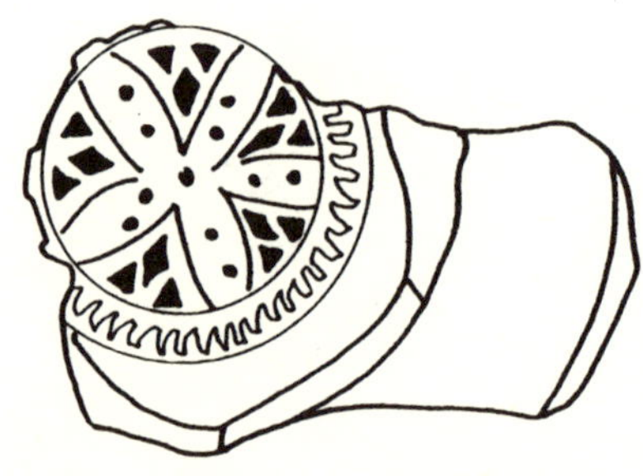
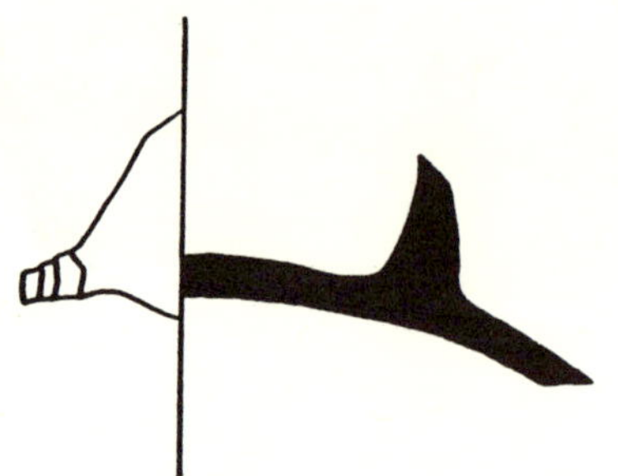

Figure 88

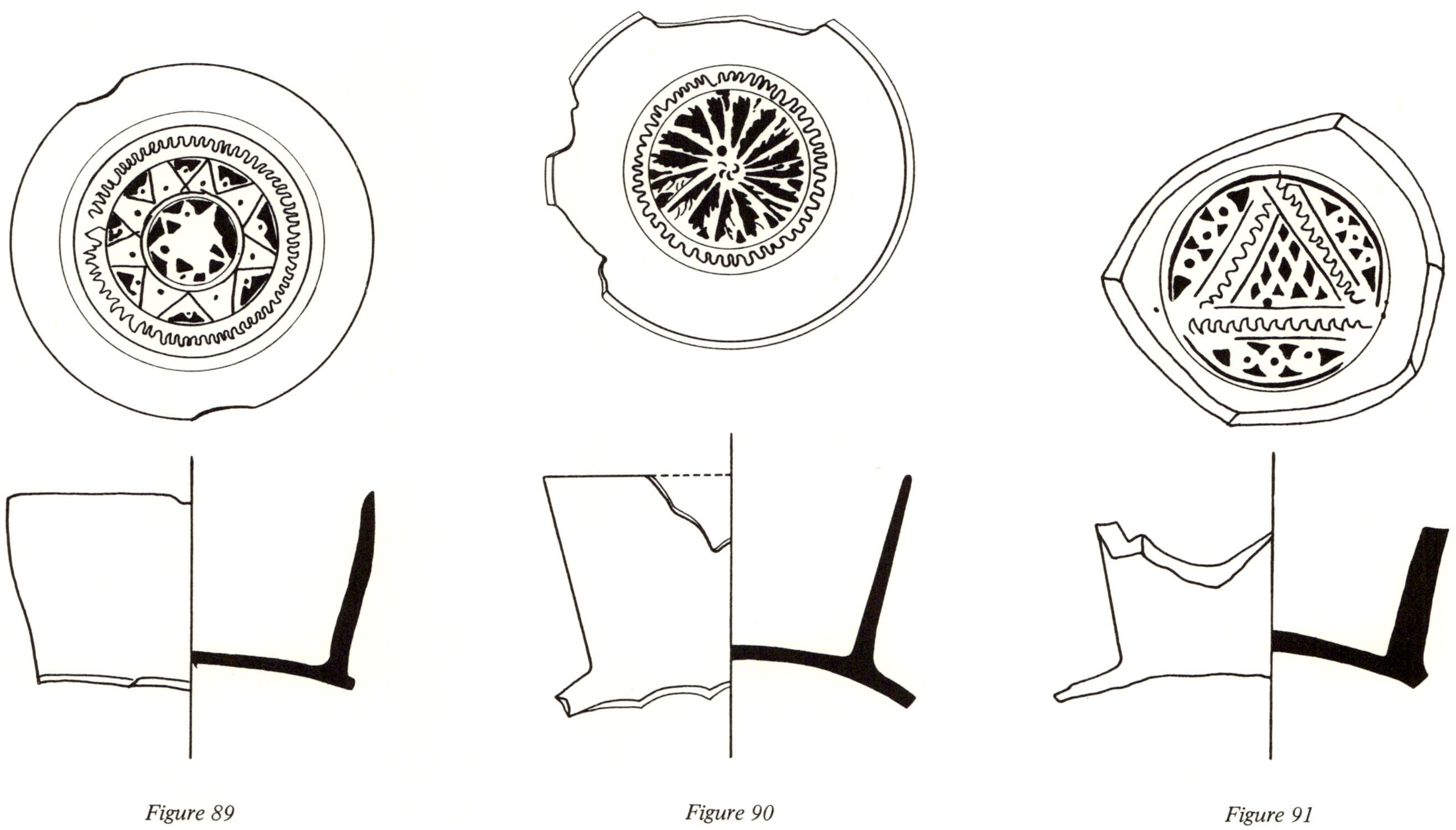

Figure 89   Figure 90   Figure 91

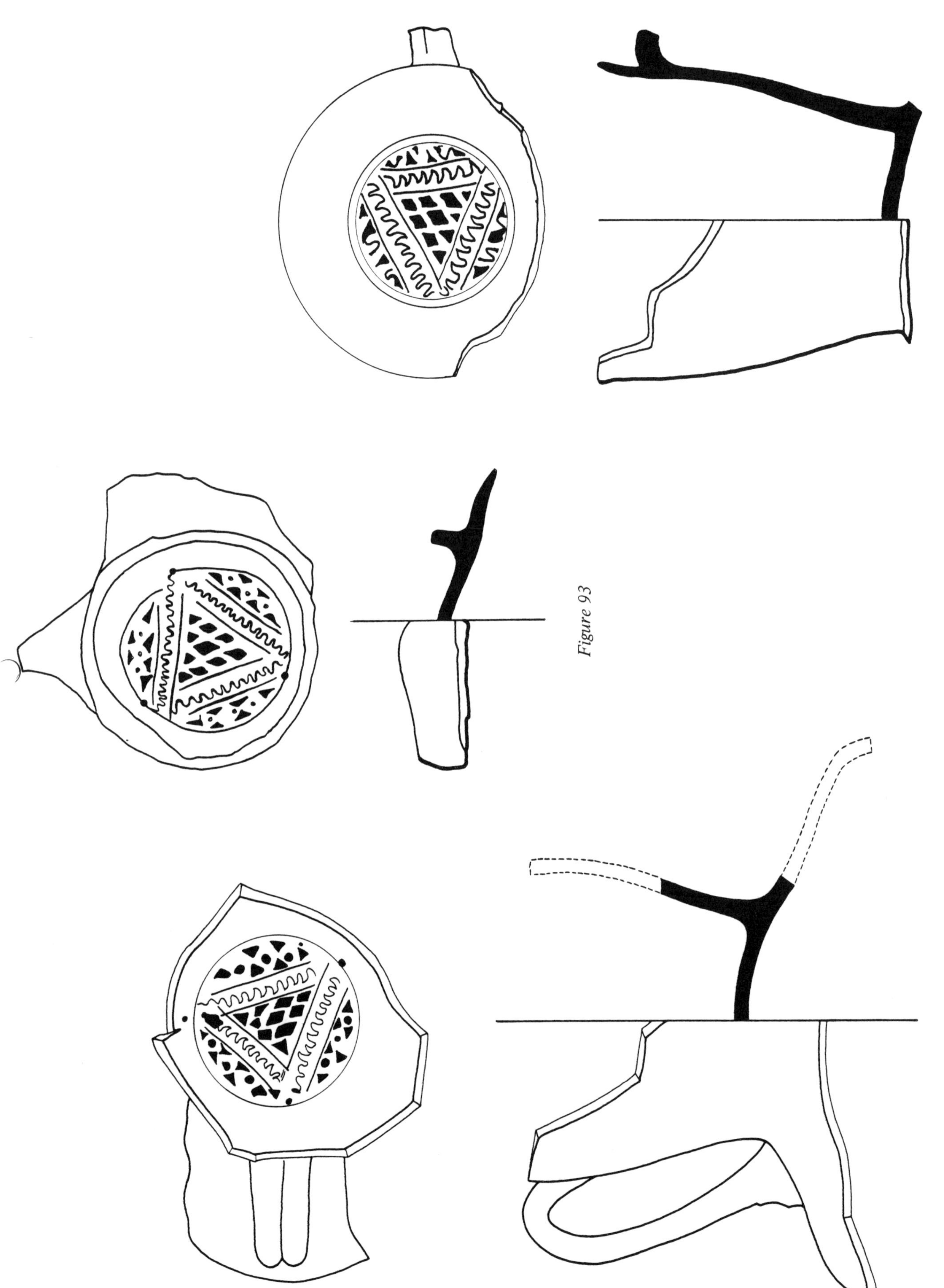

Figure 94
Figure 93
Figure 92

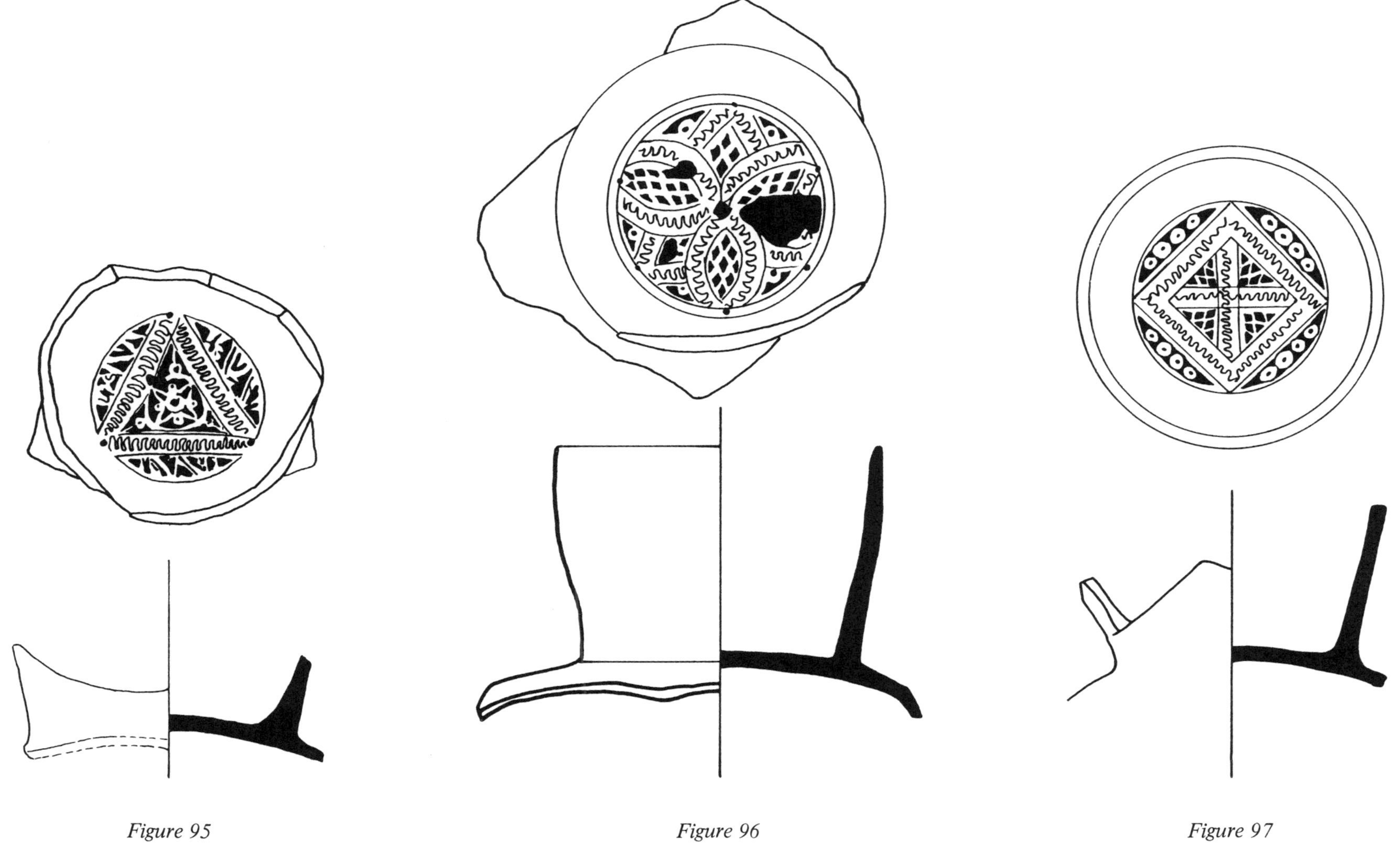

Figure 95

Figure 96

Figure 97

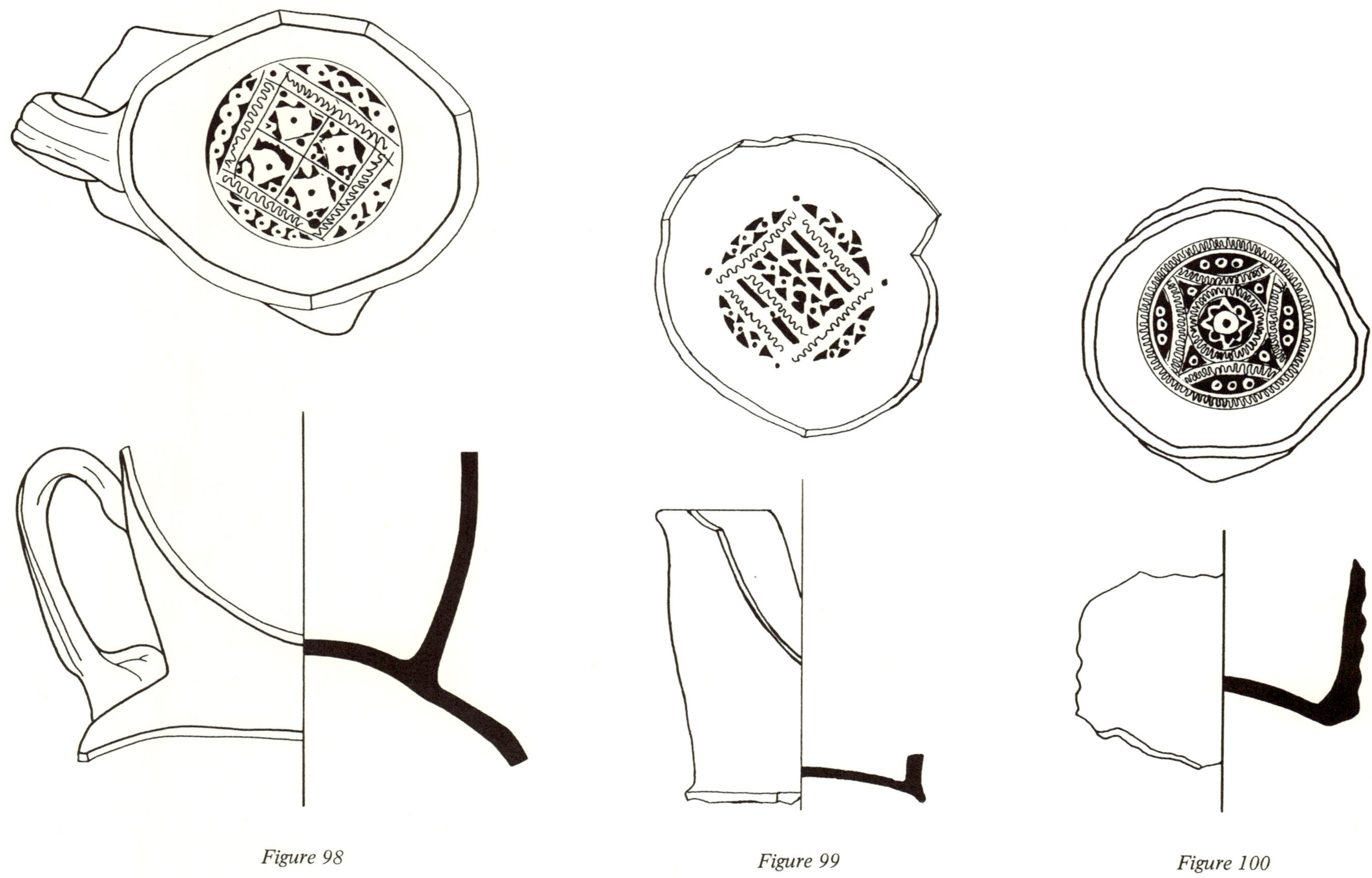

Figure 98

Figure 99

Figure 100

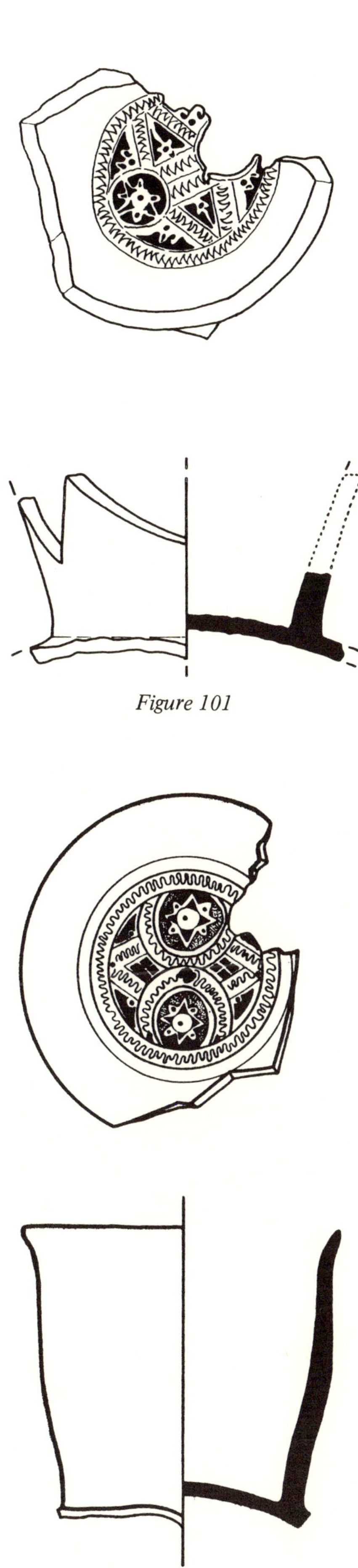

Figure 101

*Figure 102 **

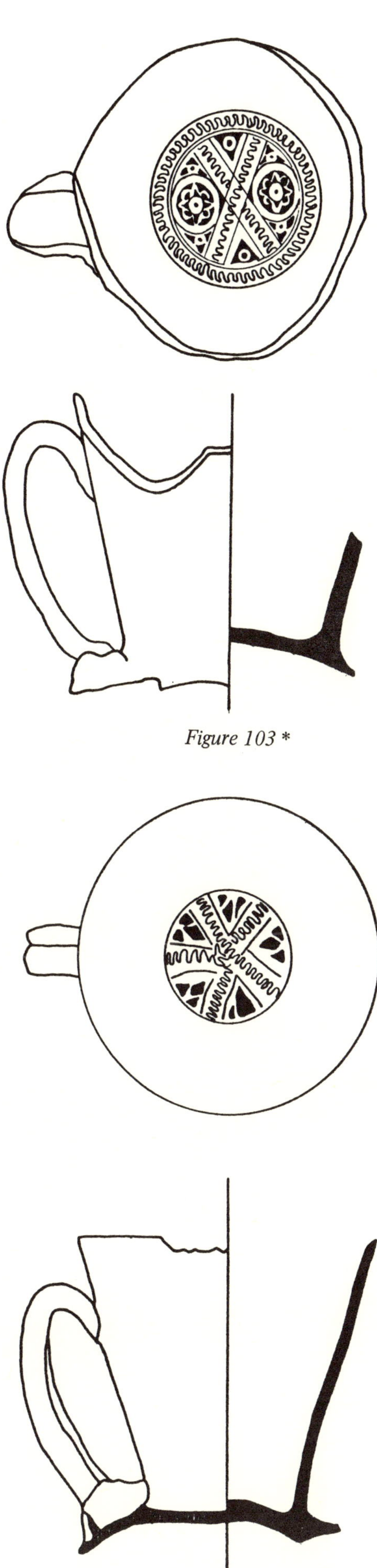

*Figure 103 **

*Figure 104 **

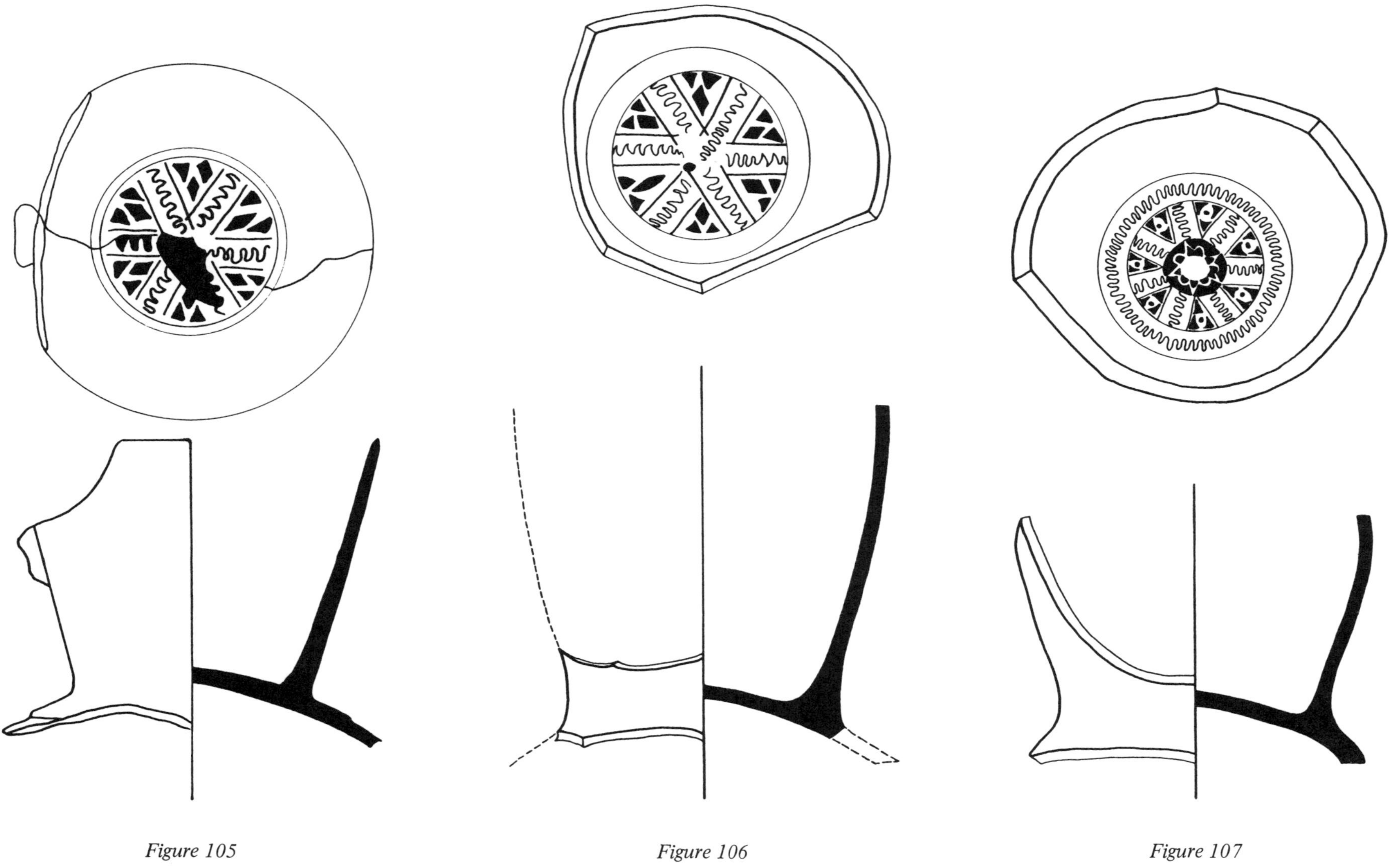

Figure 105

Figure 106

Figure 107

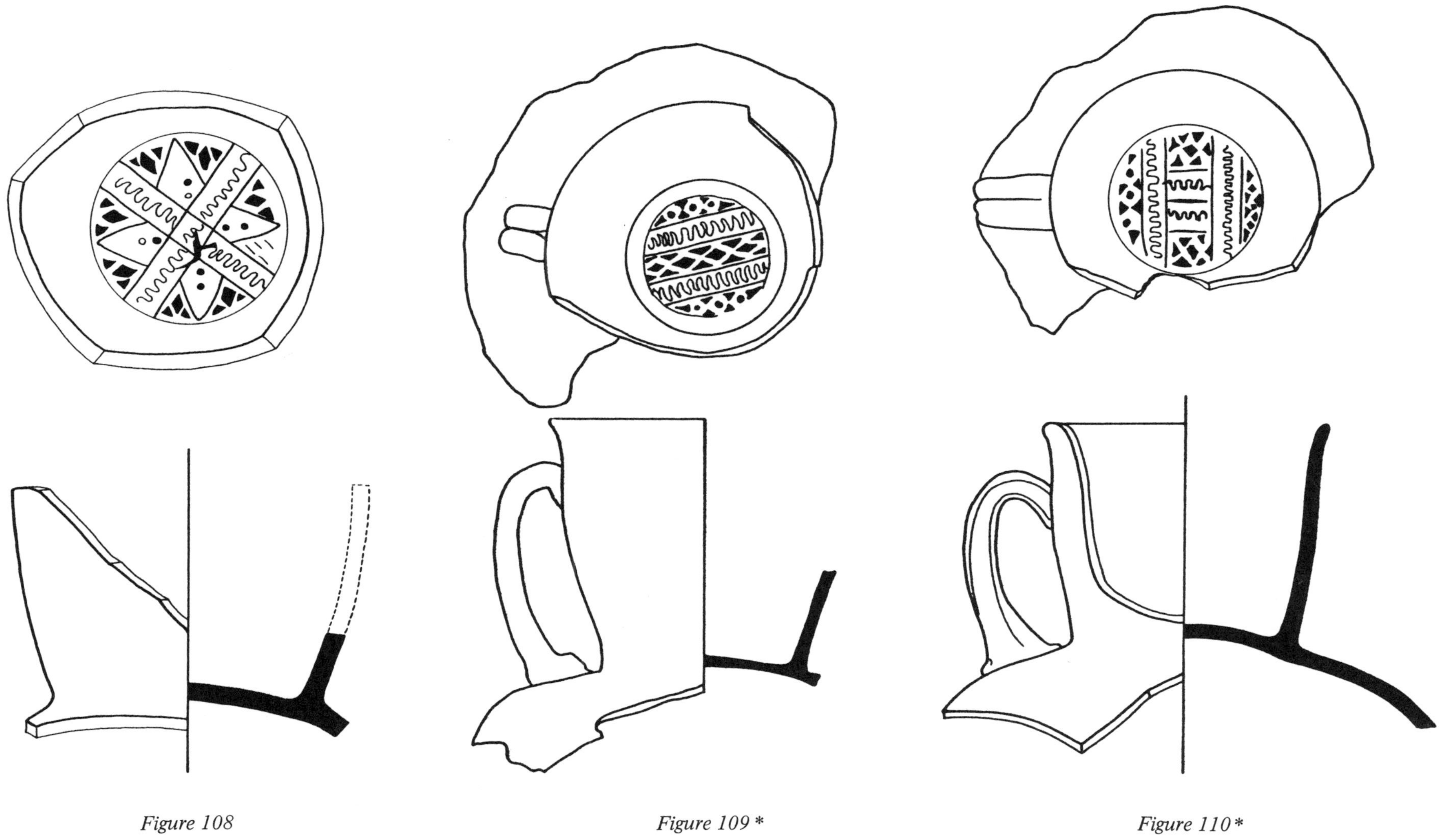

Figure 108

Figure 109 *

Figure 110 *

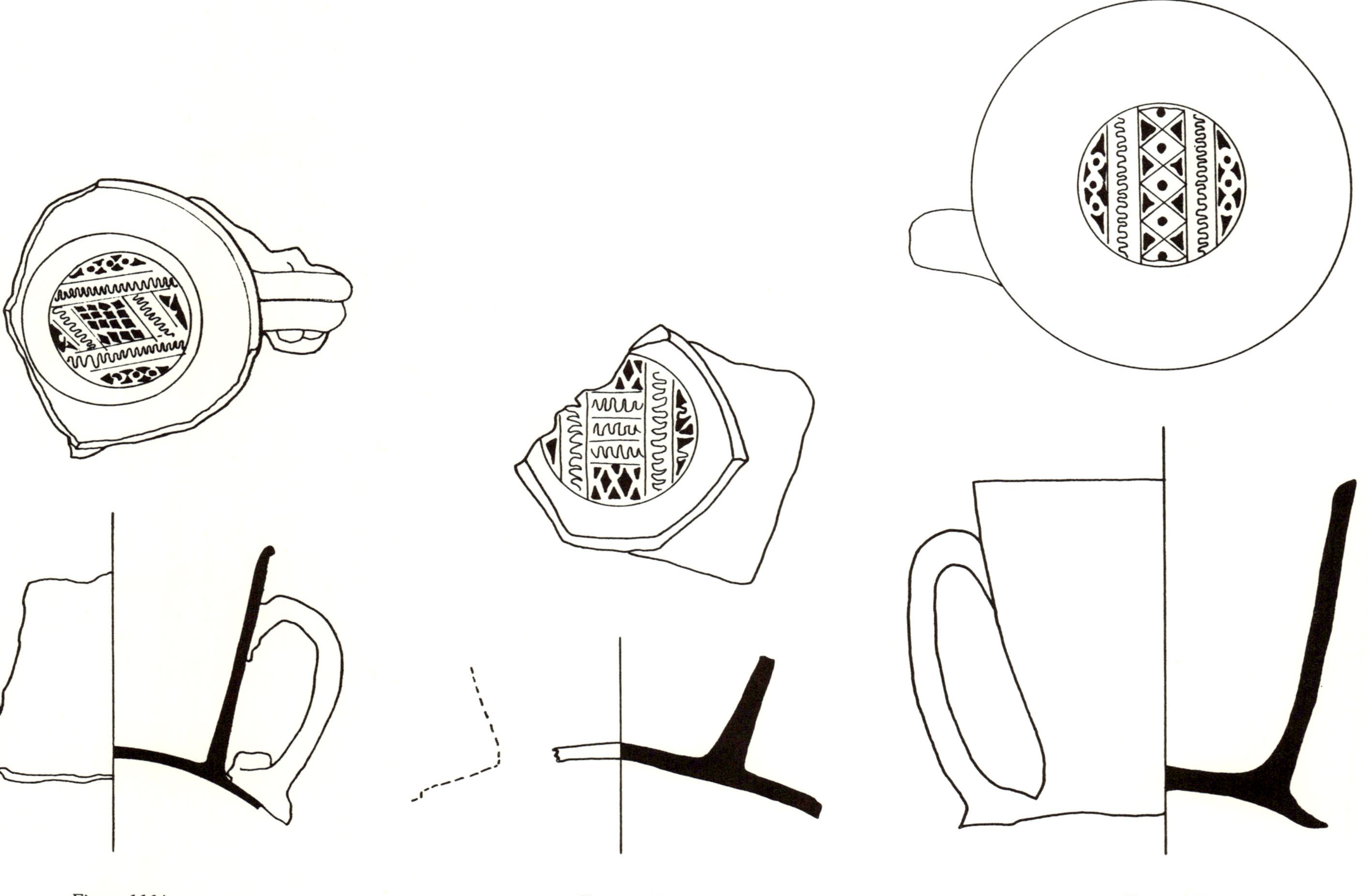

Figure 111*

Figure 112

Figure 113

126

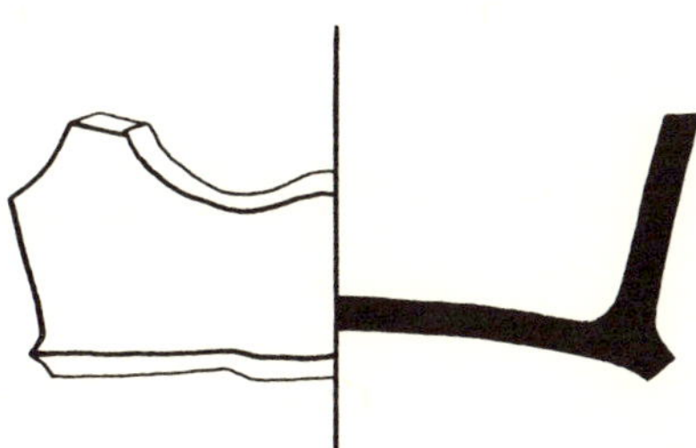

Figure 114

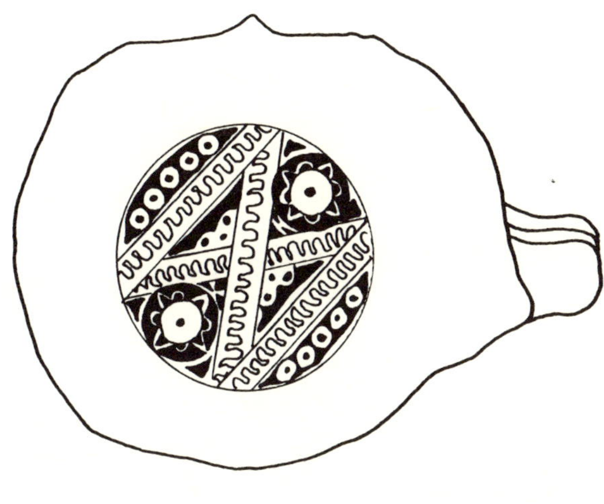

Figure 116

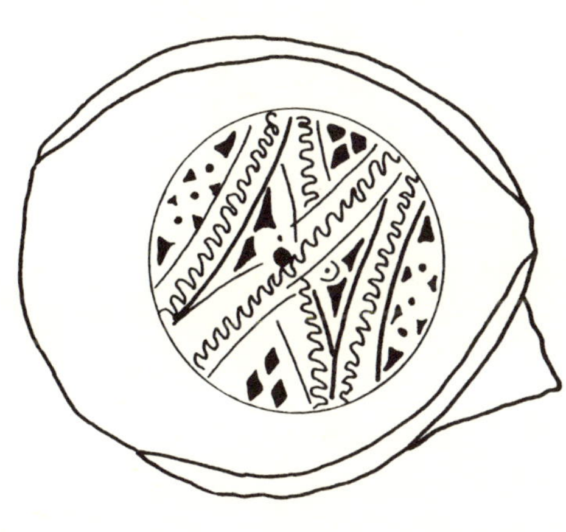

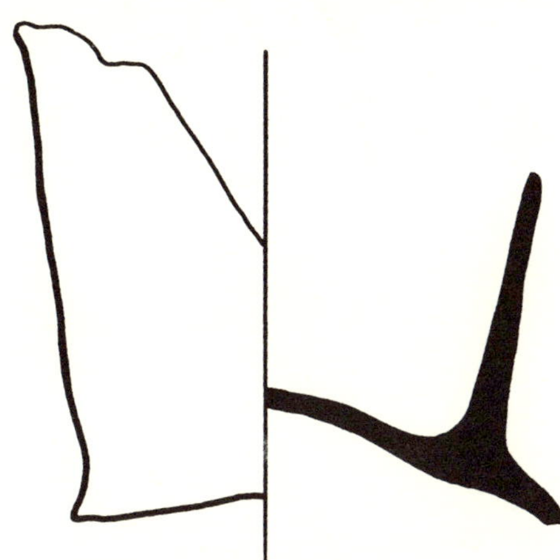

Figure 115

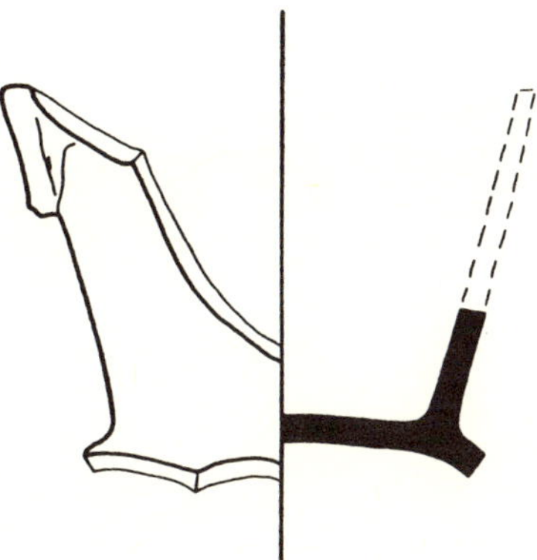

Figure 117

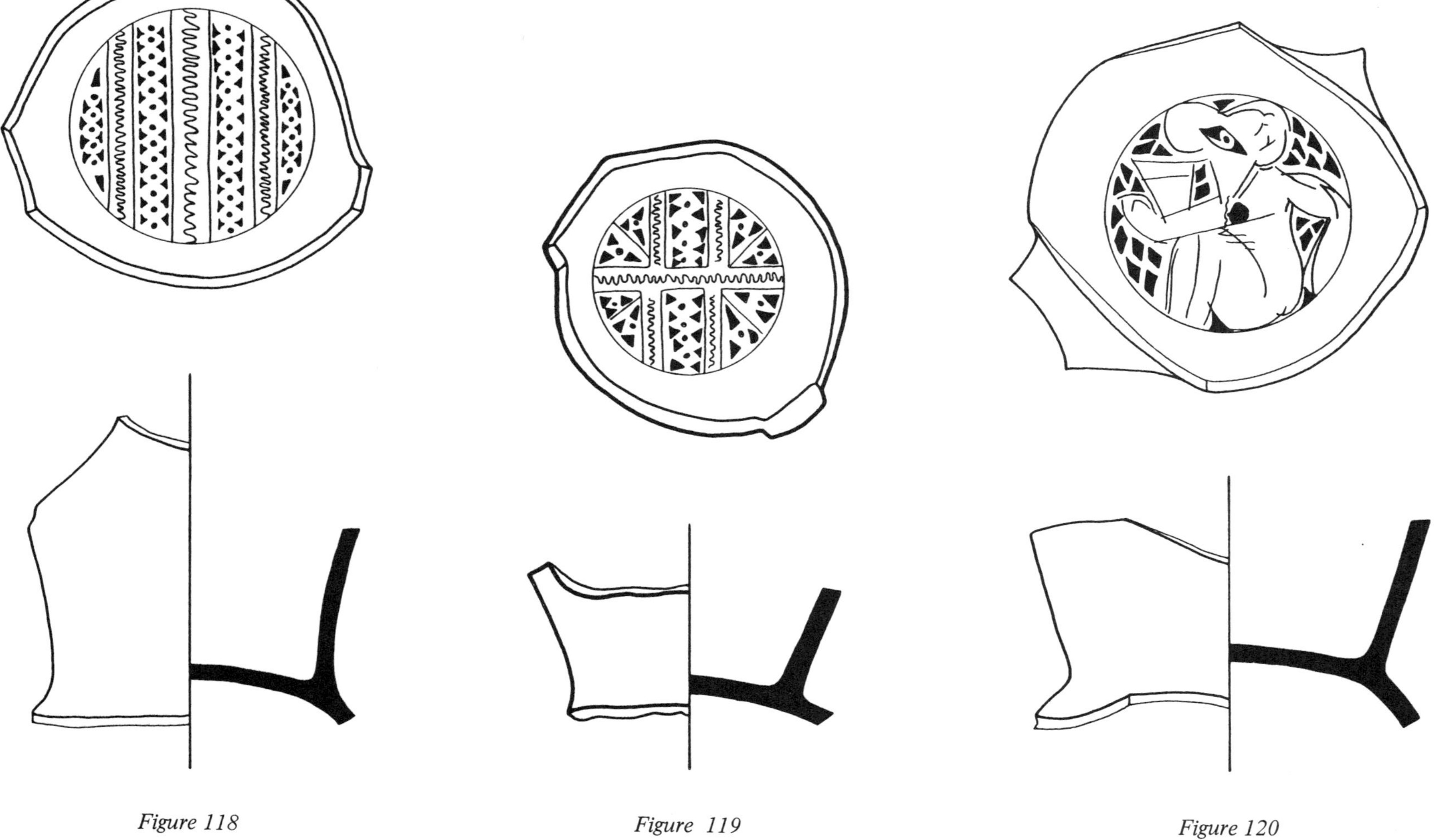

Figure 118

Figure 119

Figure 120

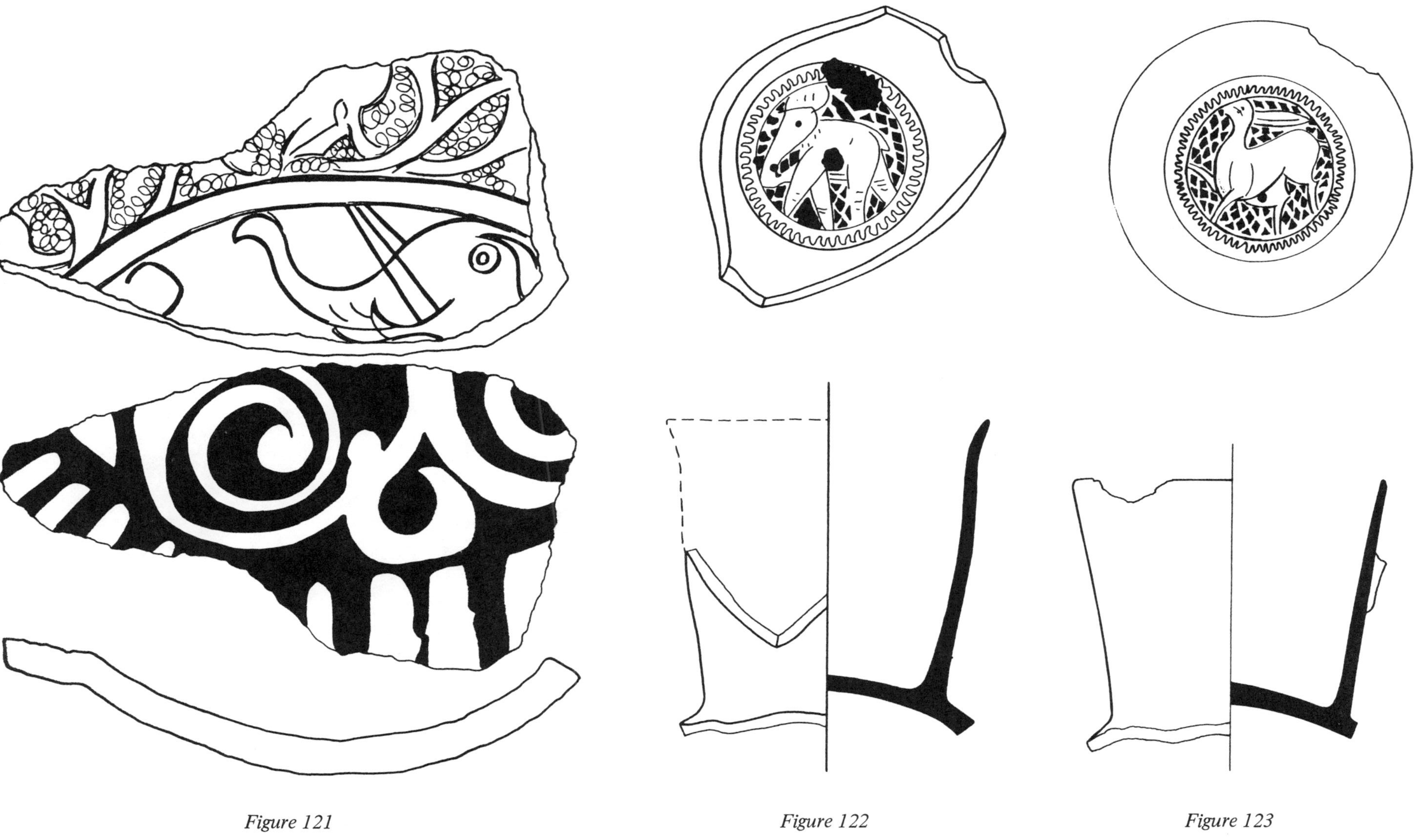

Figure 121

Figure 122

Figure 123

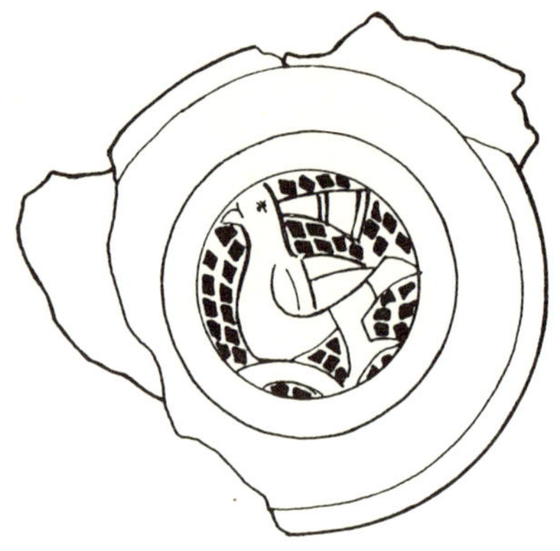

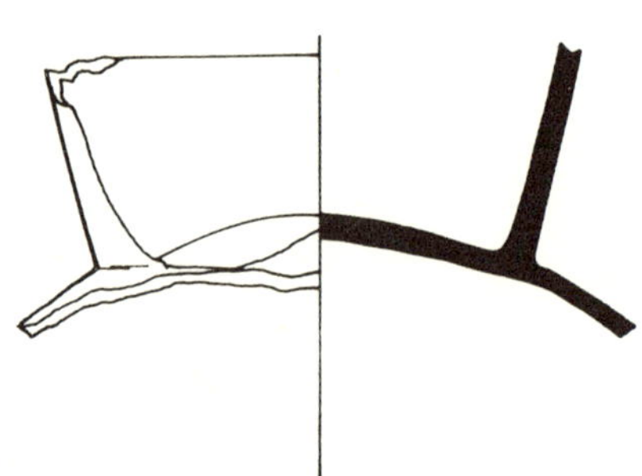

Figure 124

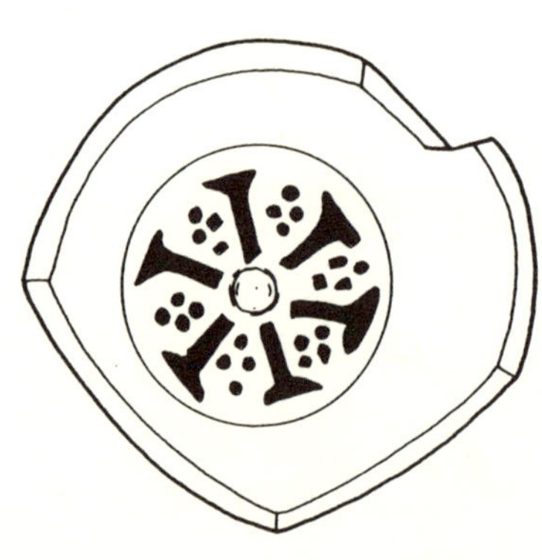

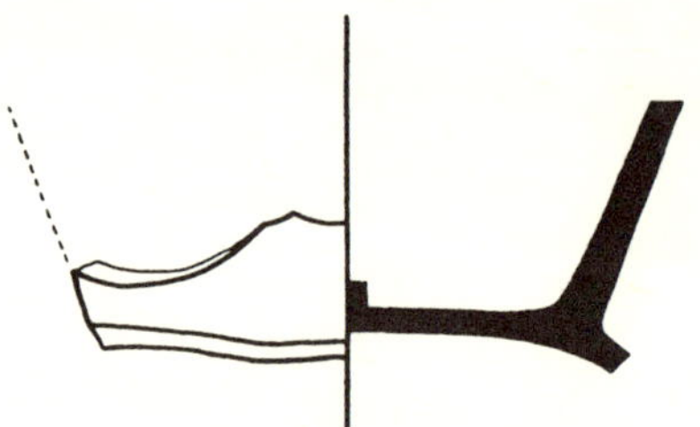

Figure 125

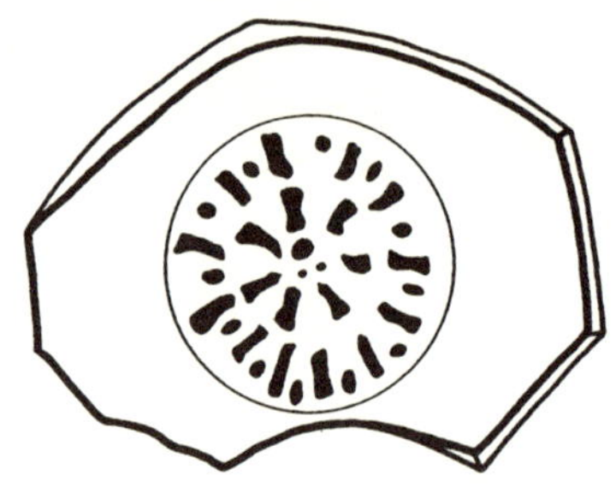

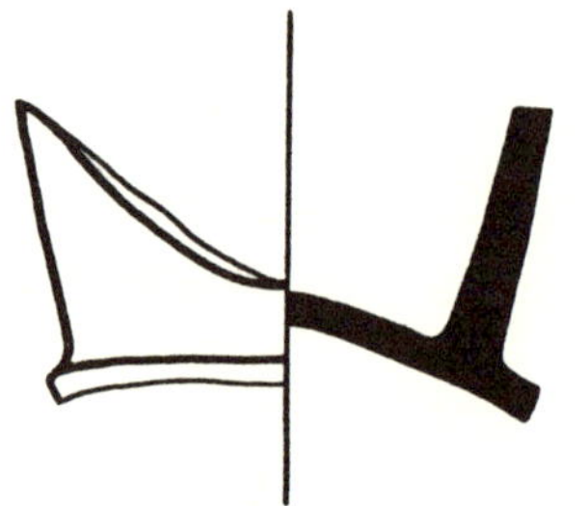

Figure 126

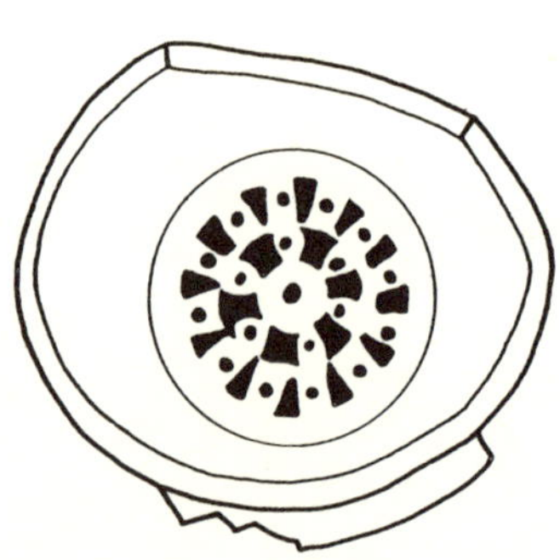

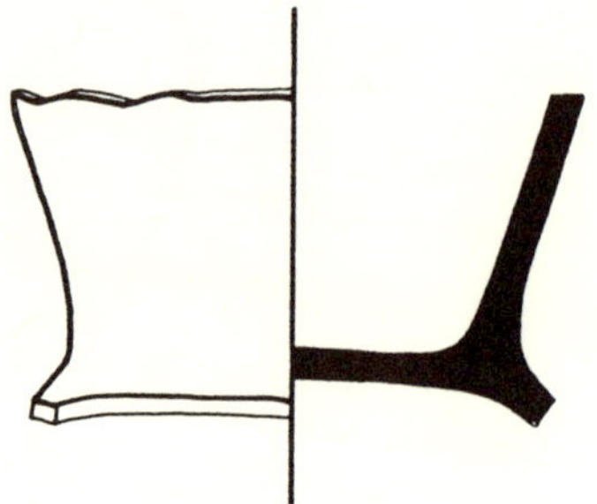

Figure 127

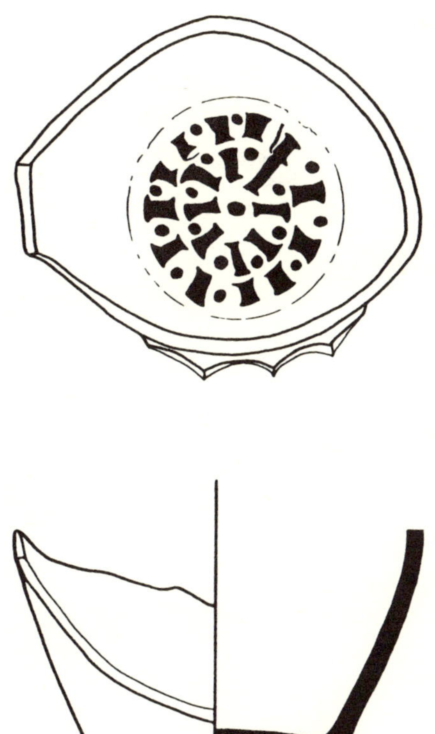
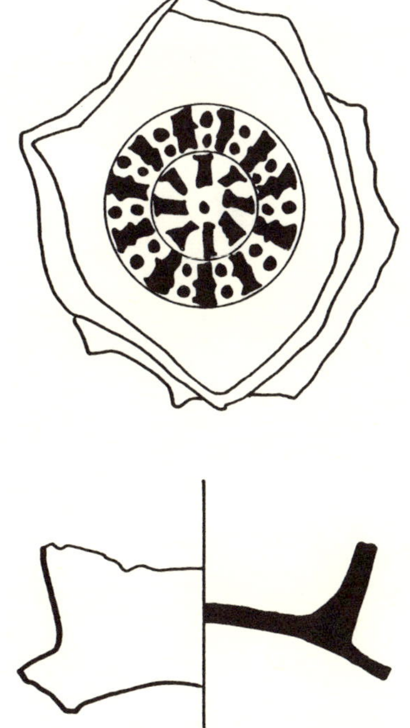

Figure 128

Figure 129

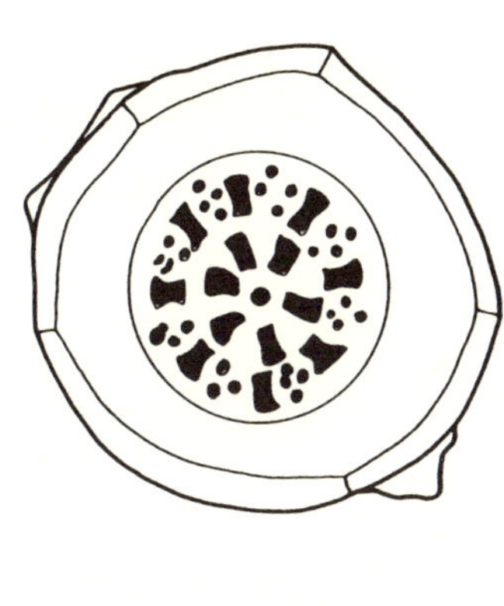
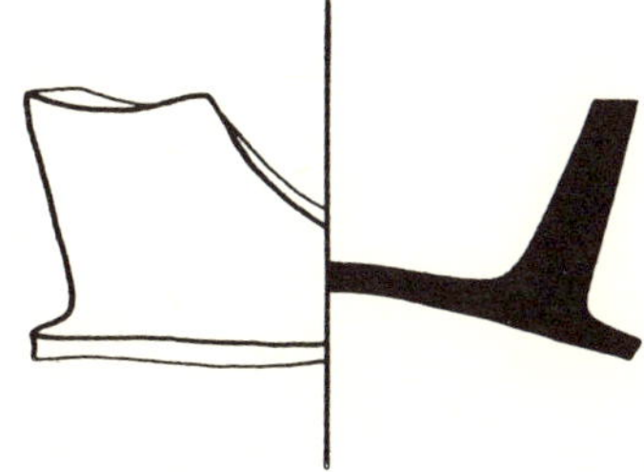

Figure 130

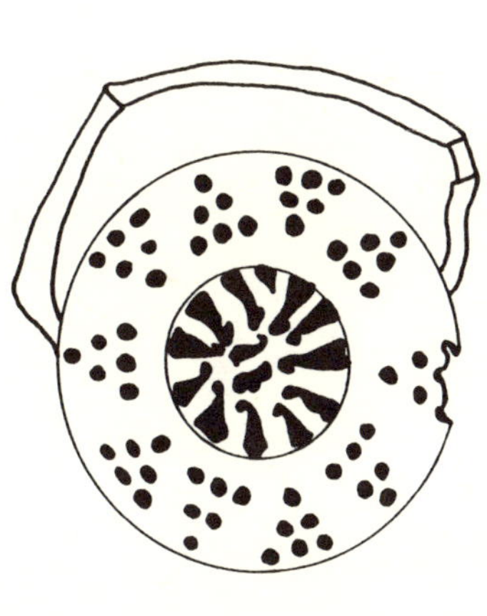
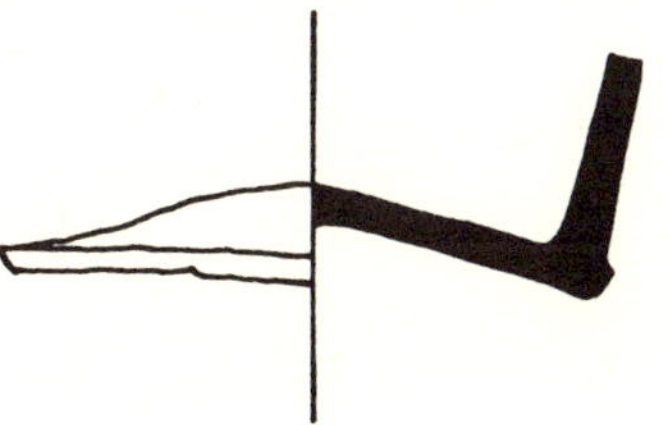

Figure 131

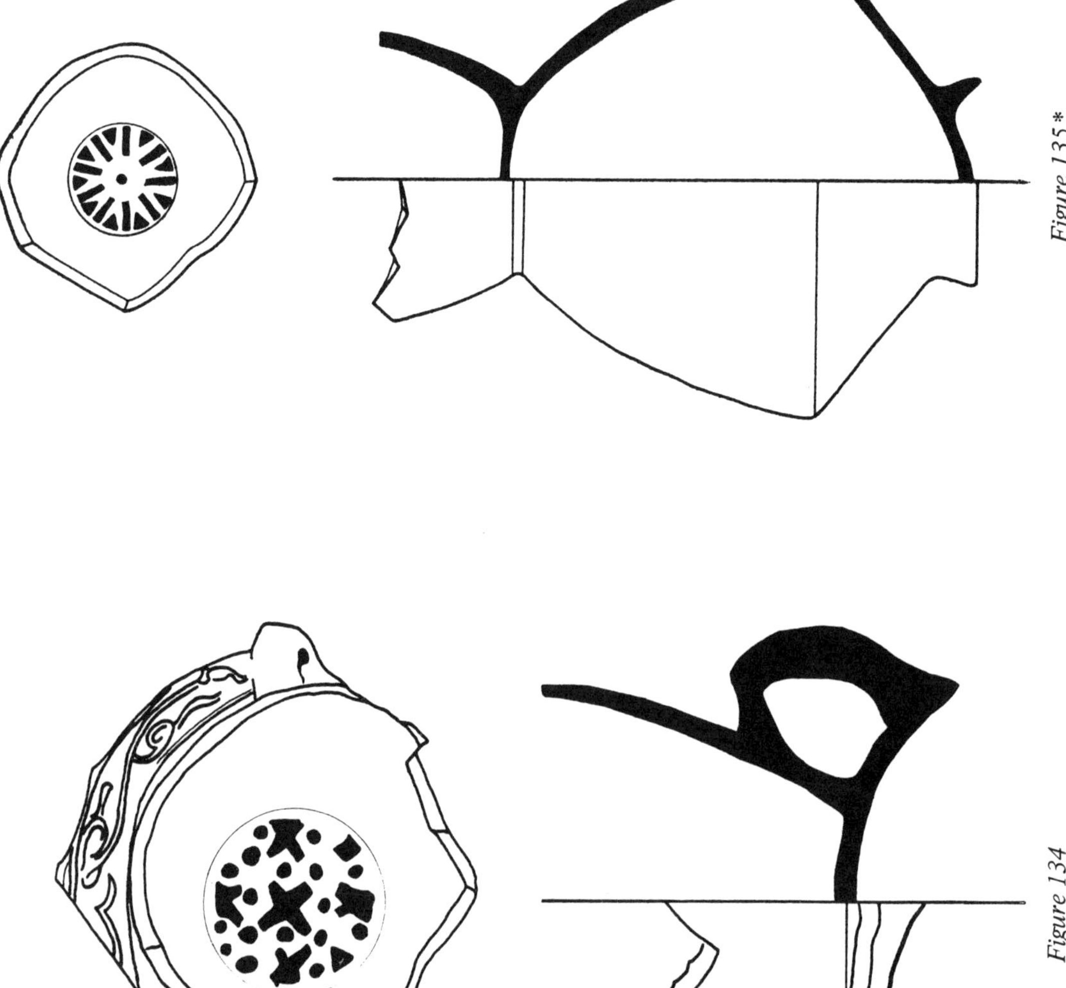

*Figure 135 ***

Figure 134

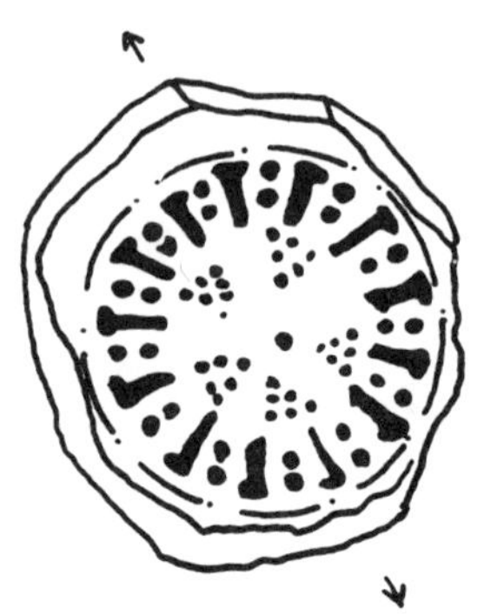

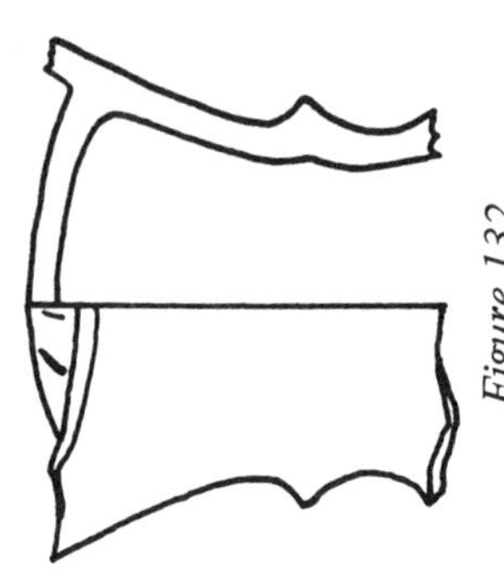

Figure 132

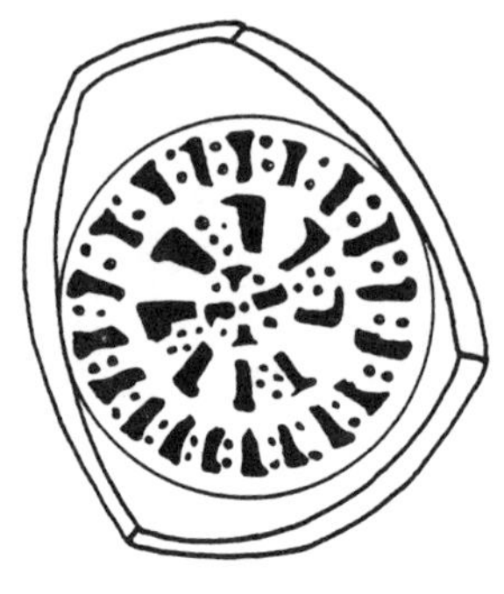

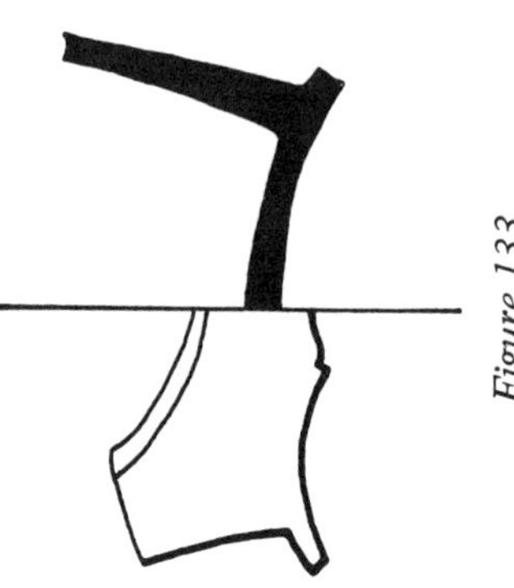

Figure 133

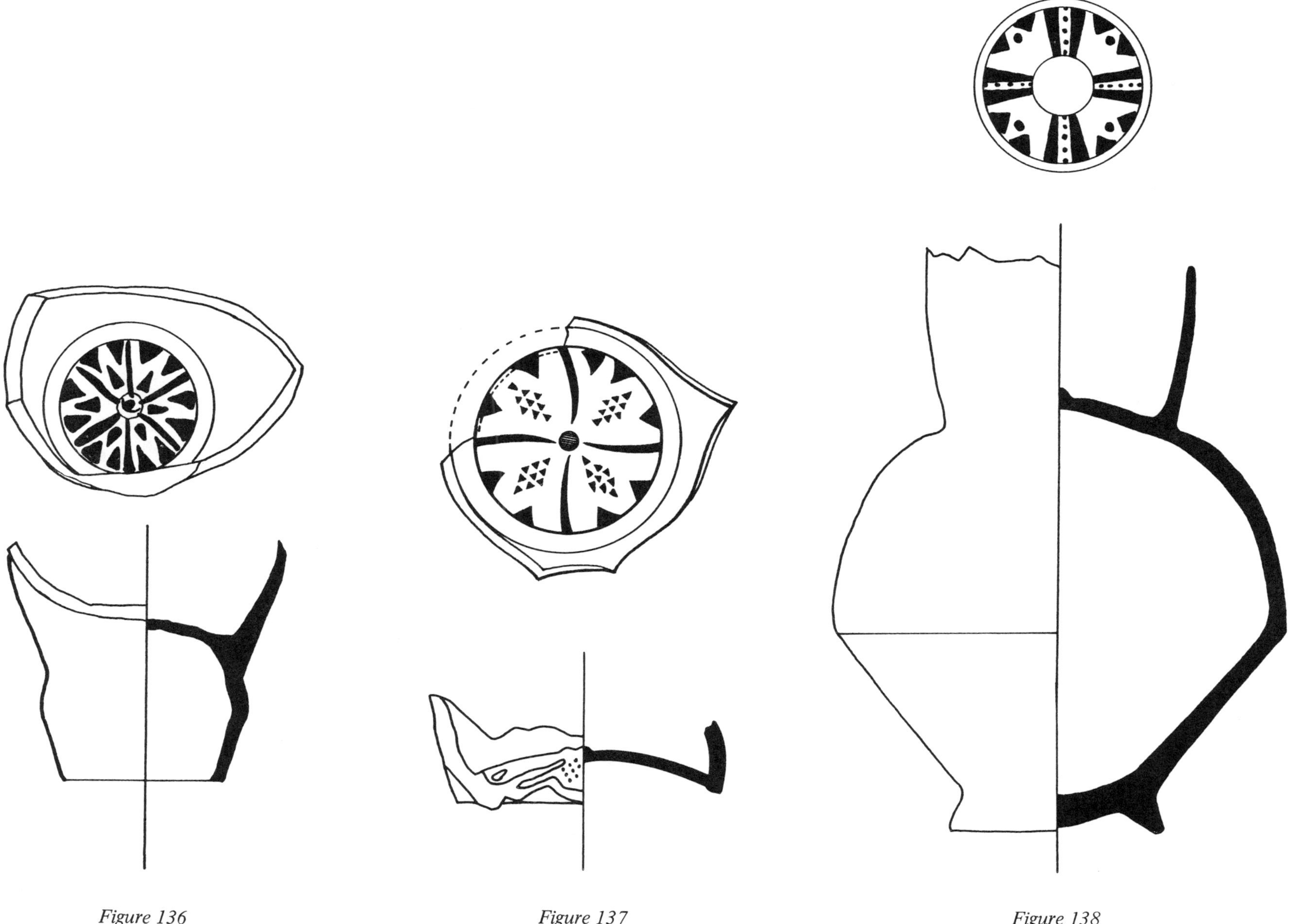

Figure 136

Figure 137

Figure 138

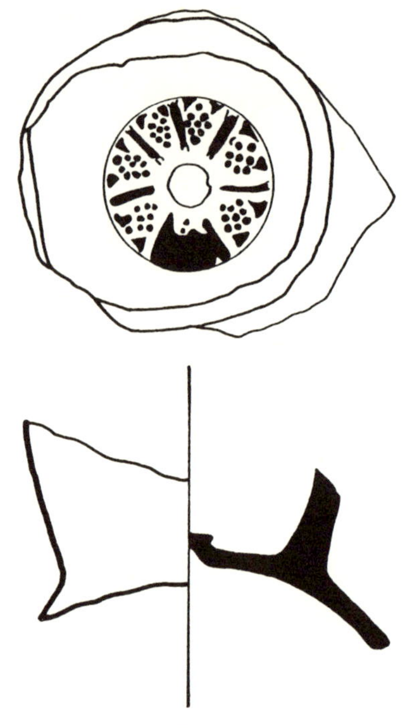

Figure 139

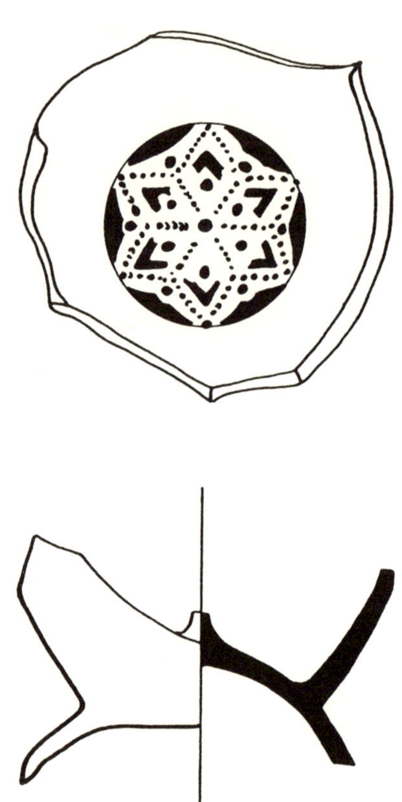

Figure 141

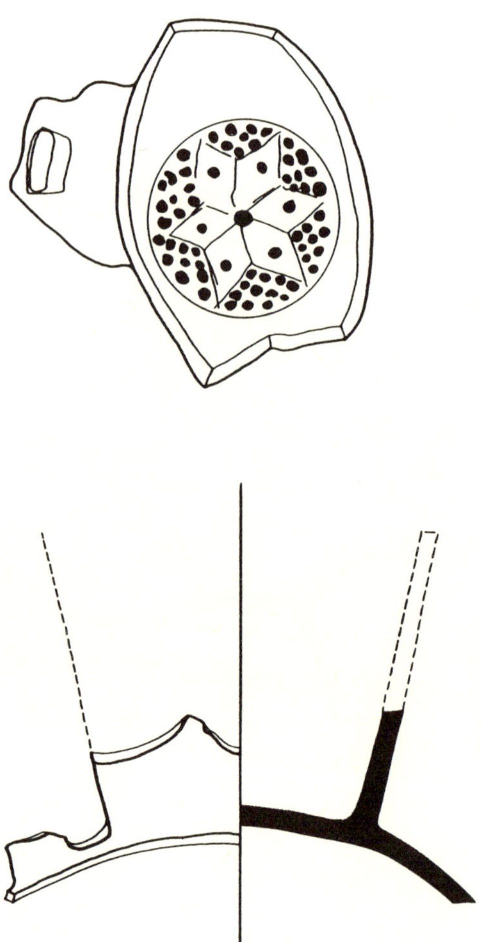

Figure 140

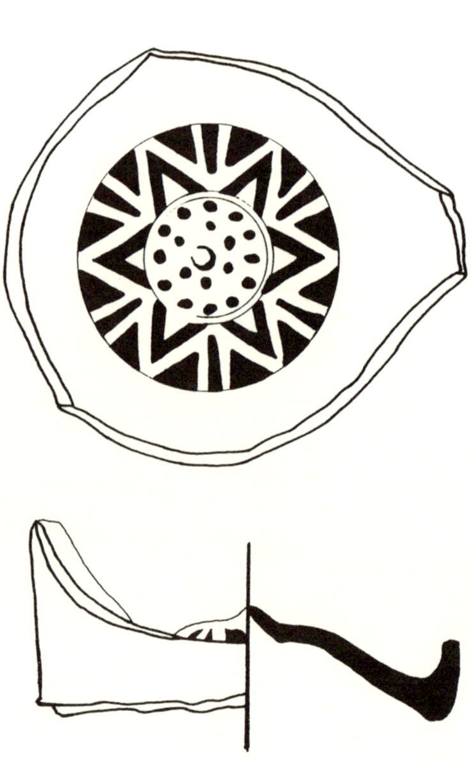

Figure 142

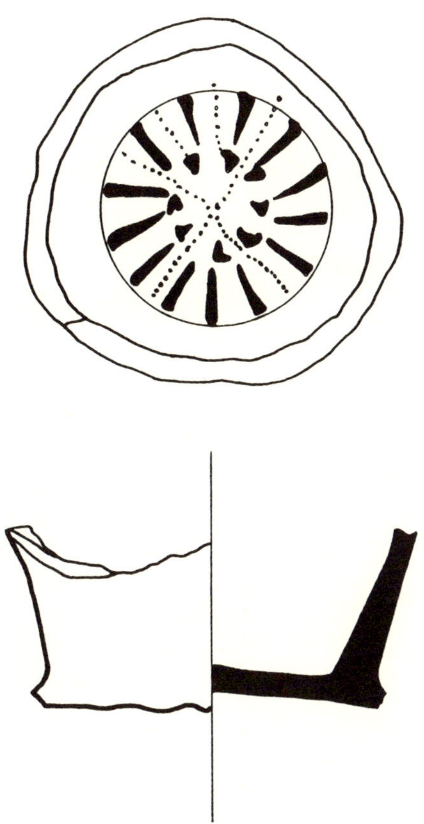
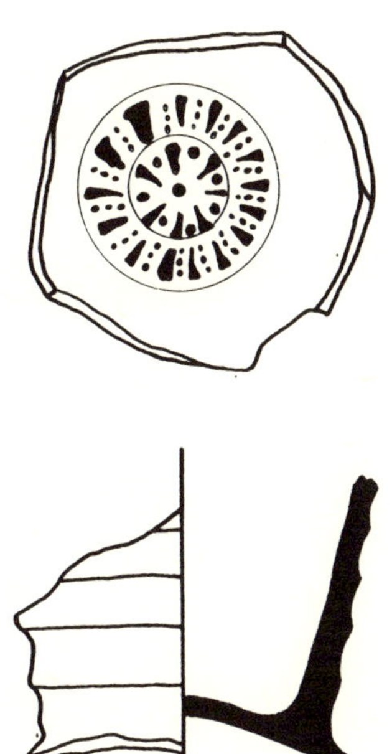

Figure 145

Figure 143

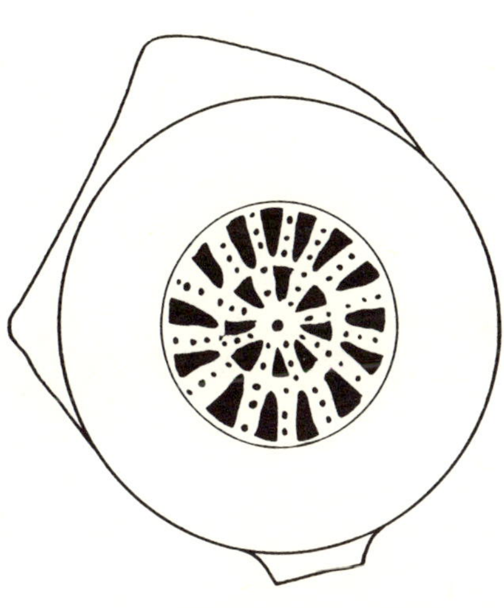

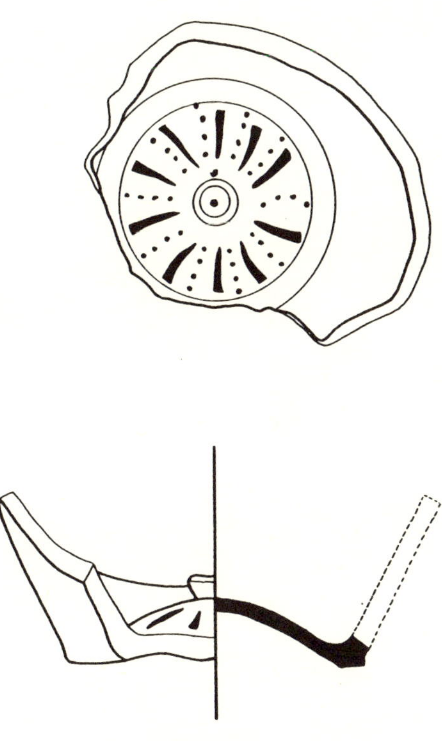

Figure 144

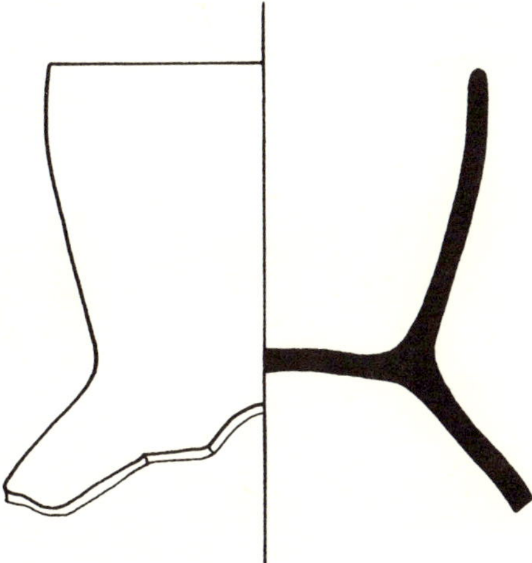

Figure 146

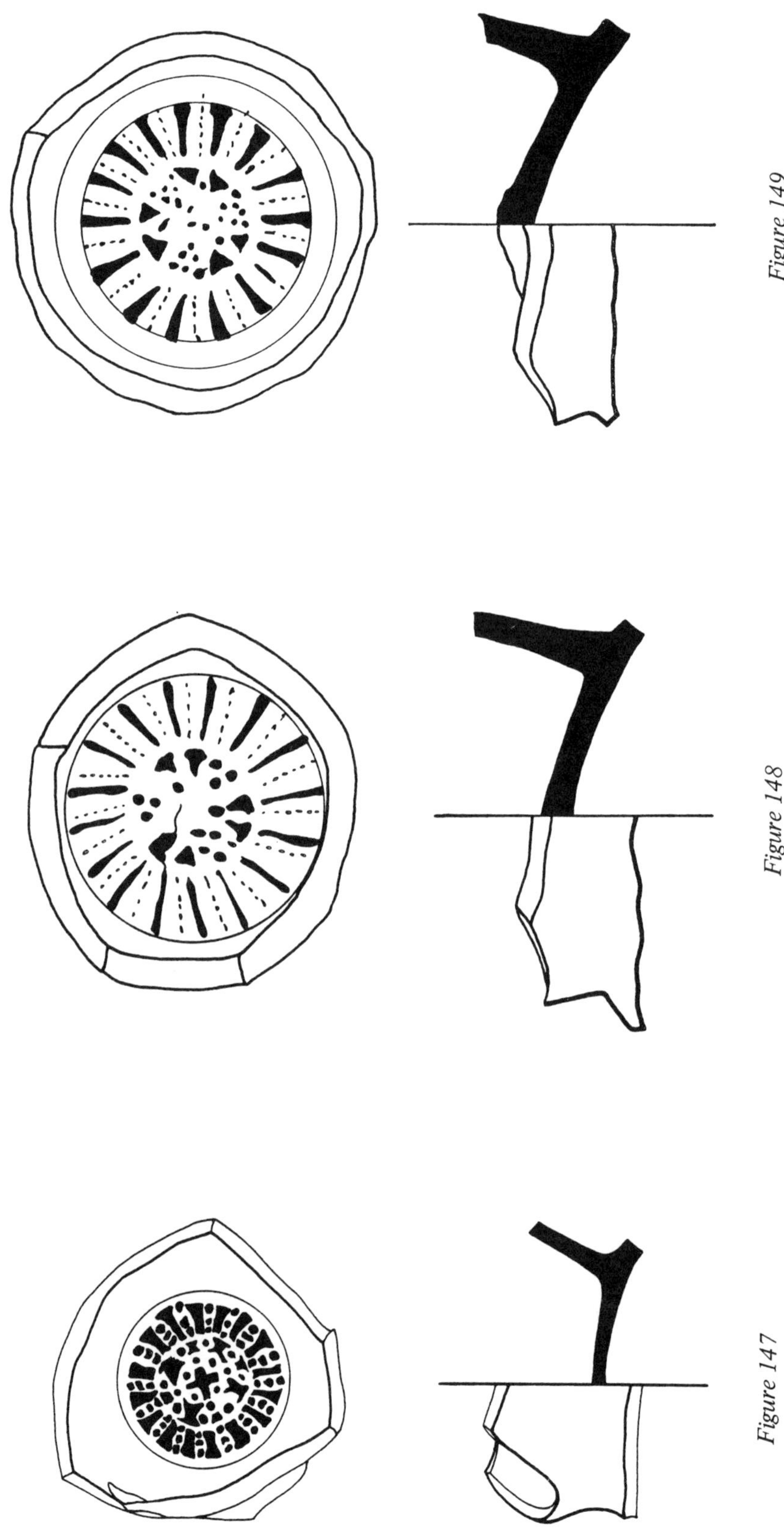

Figure 149

Figure 148

Figure 147

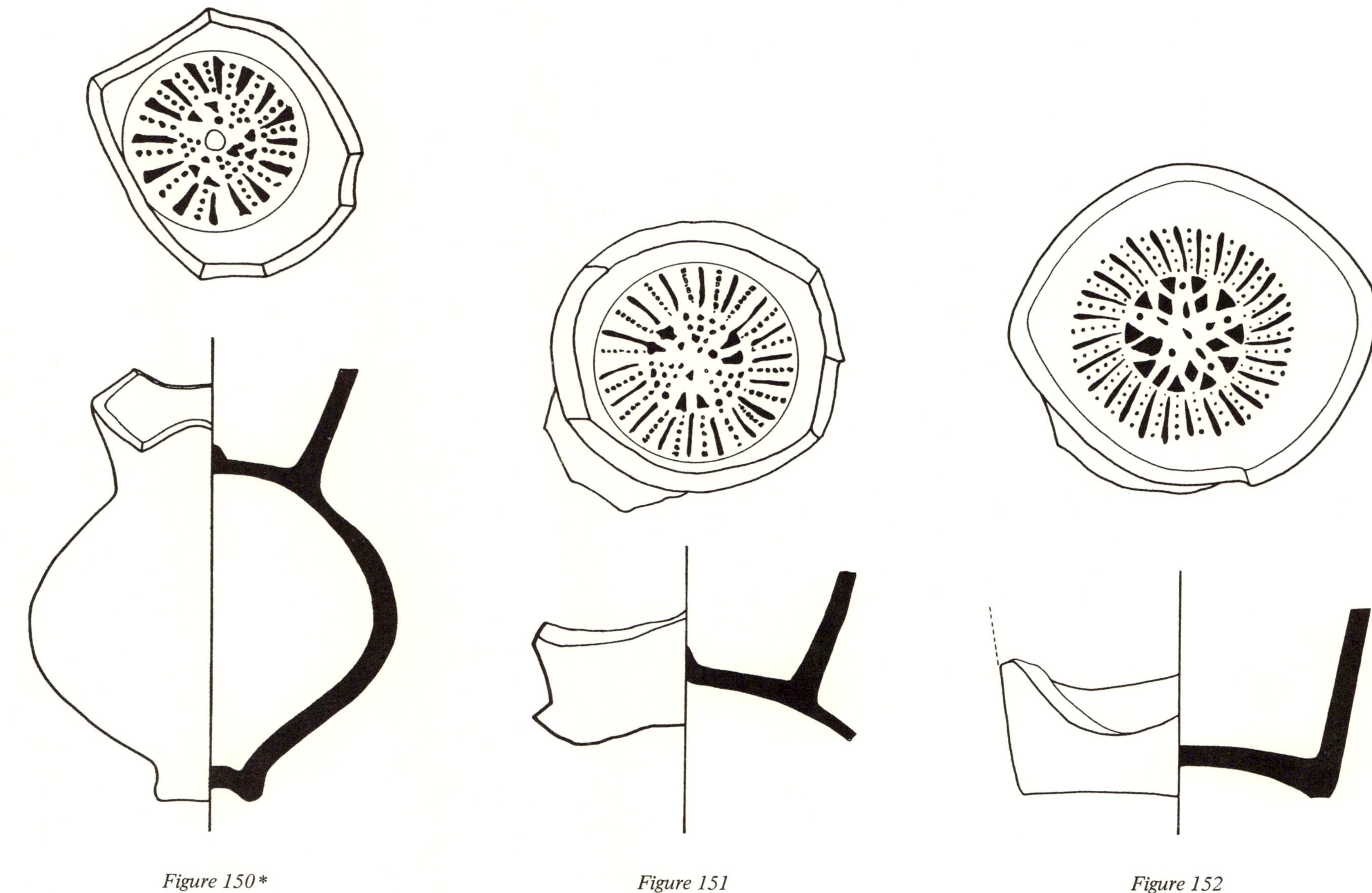

Figure 150*

Figure 151

Figure 152

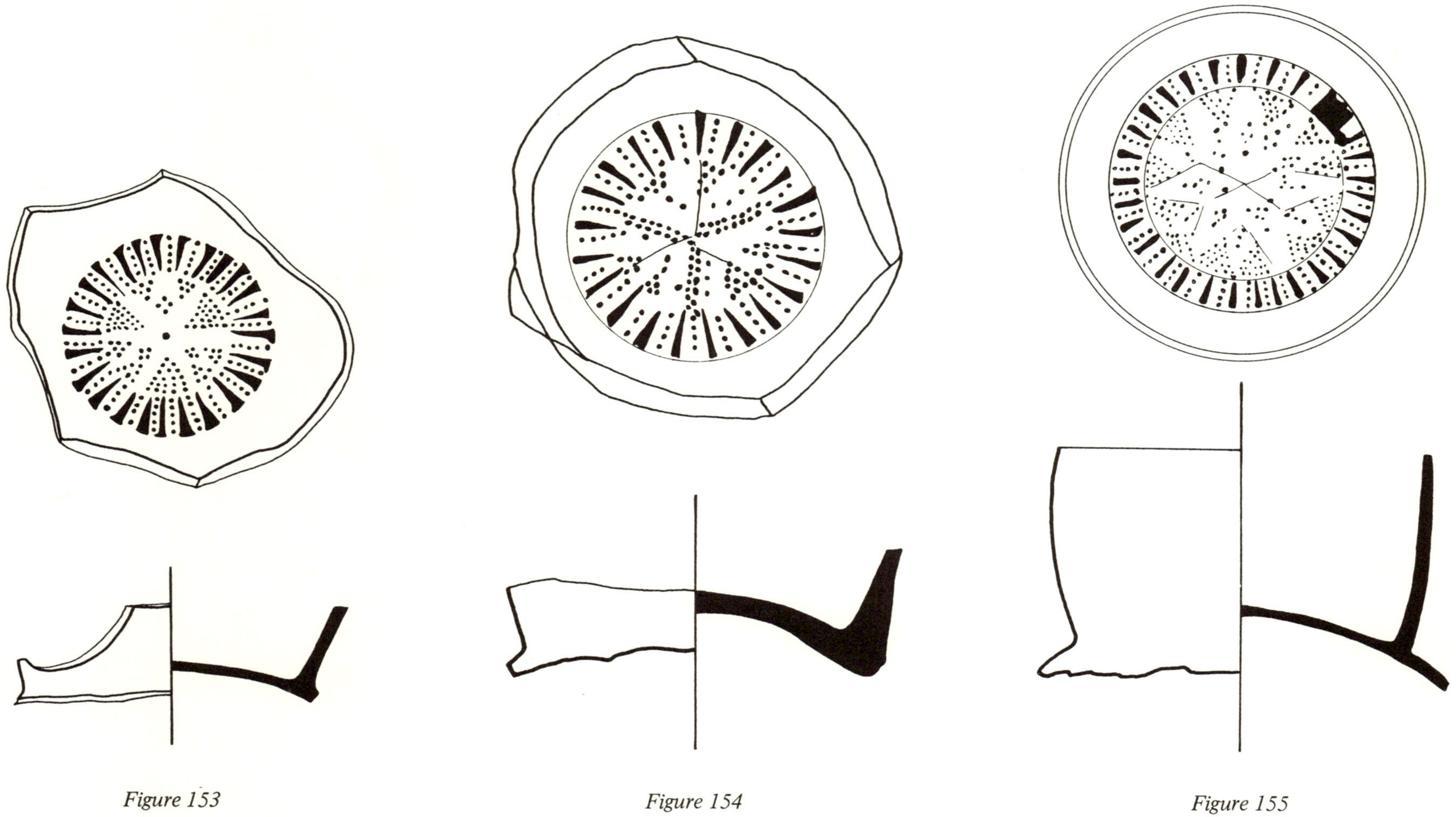

Figure 153

Figure 154

Figure 155

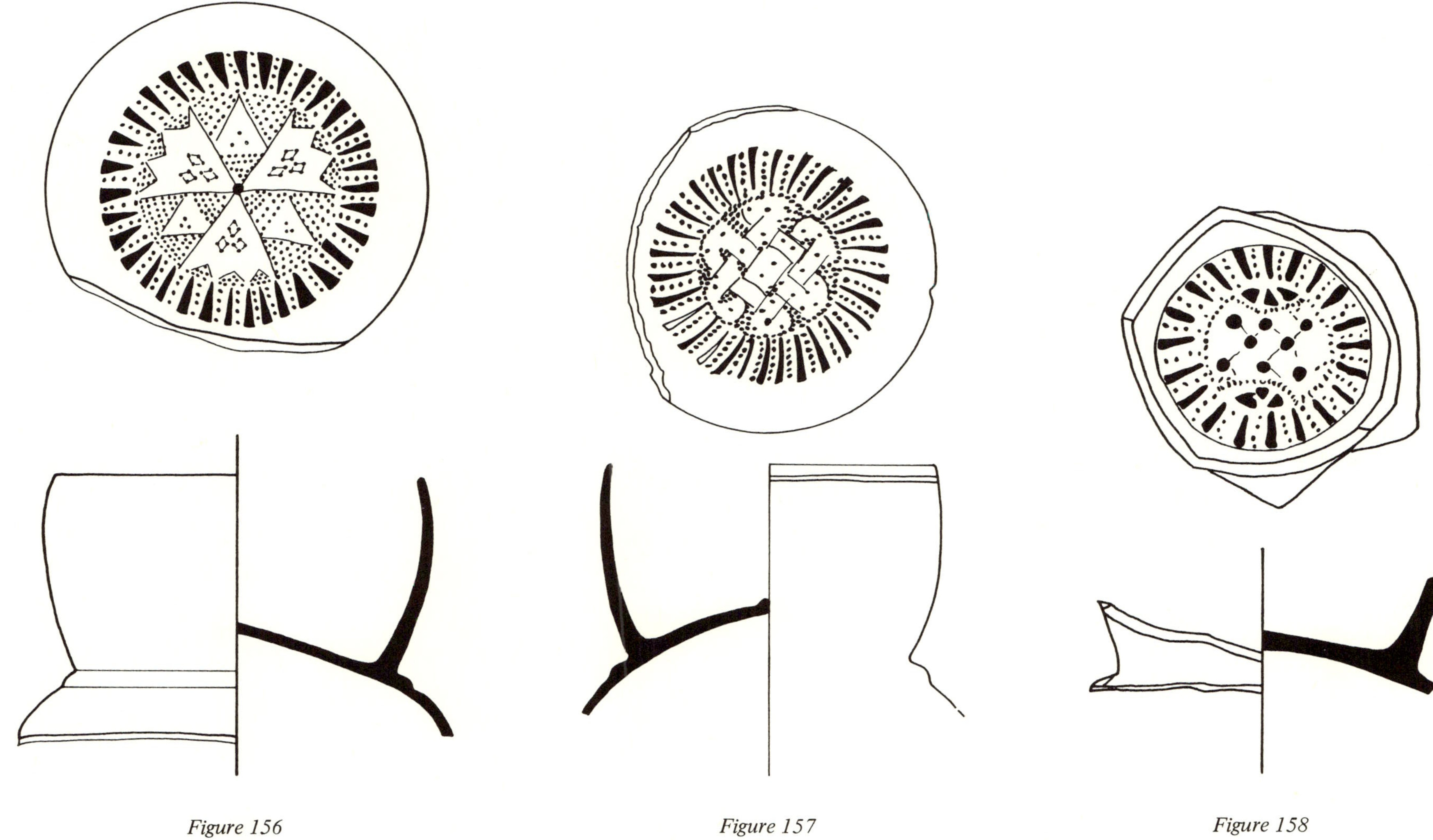

Figure 156

Figure 157

Figure 158

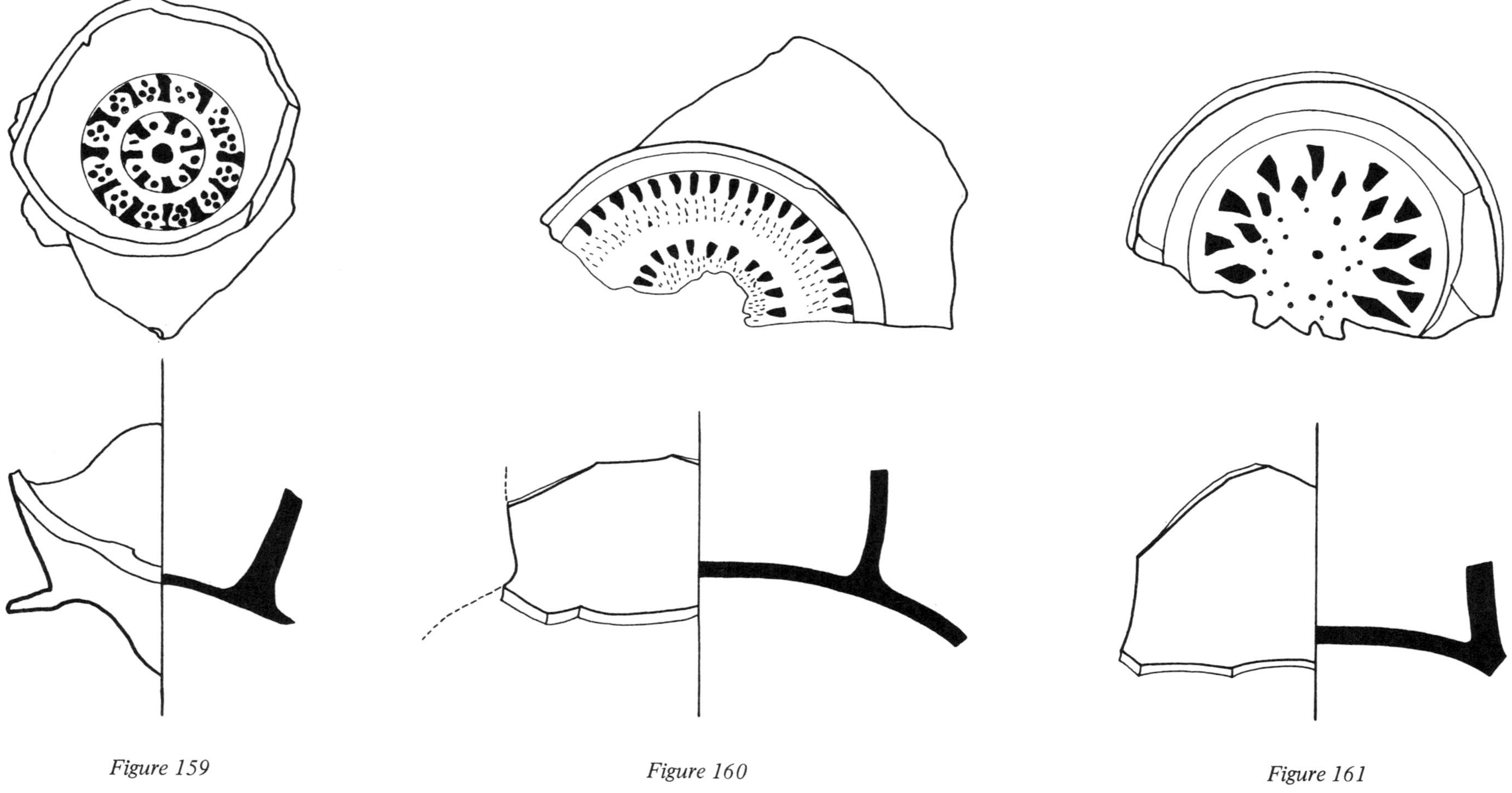

Figure 159

Figure 160

Figure 161

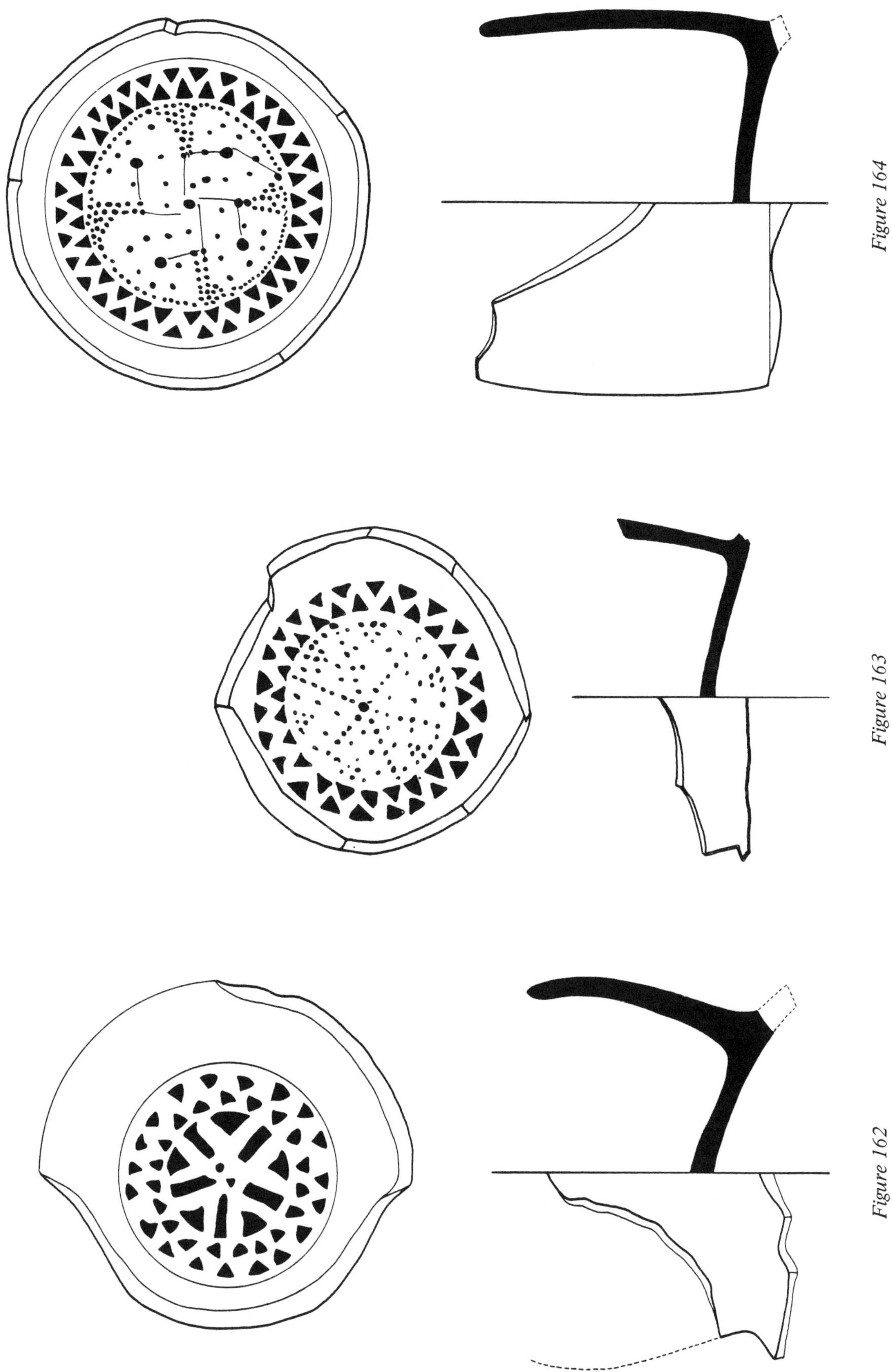

Figure 164

Figure 163

Figure 162

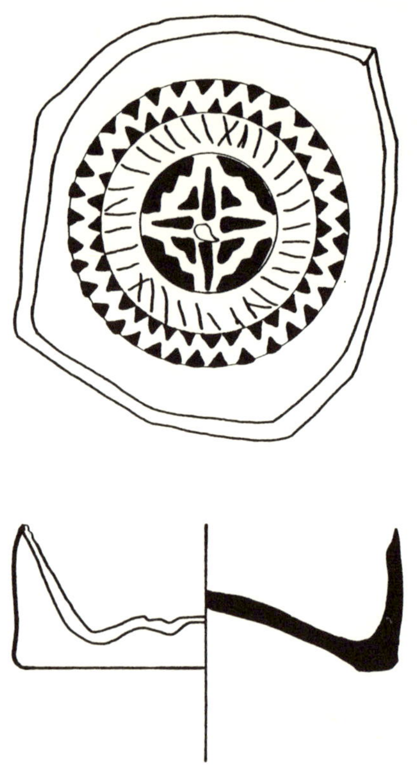

Figure 165

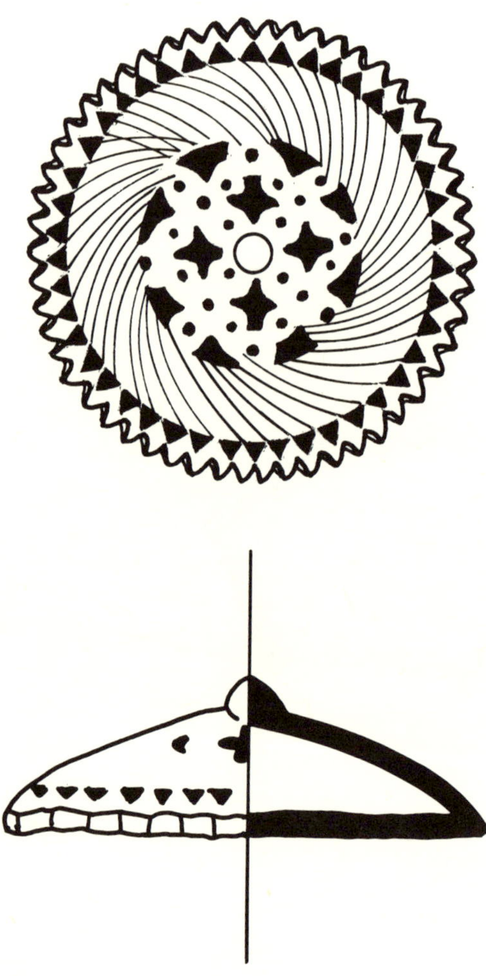

Figure 166

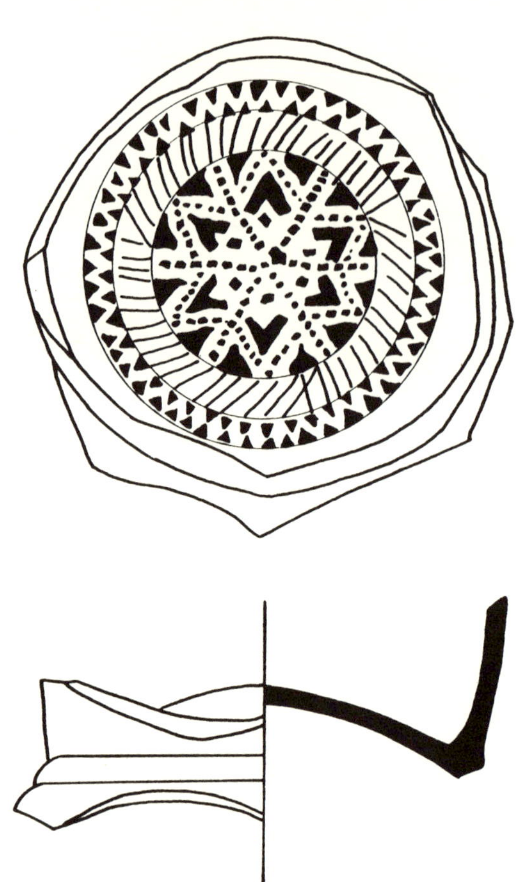

Figure 167

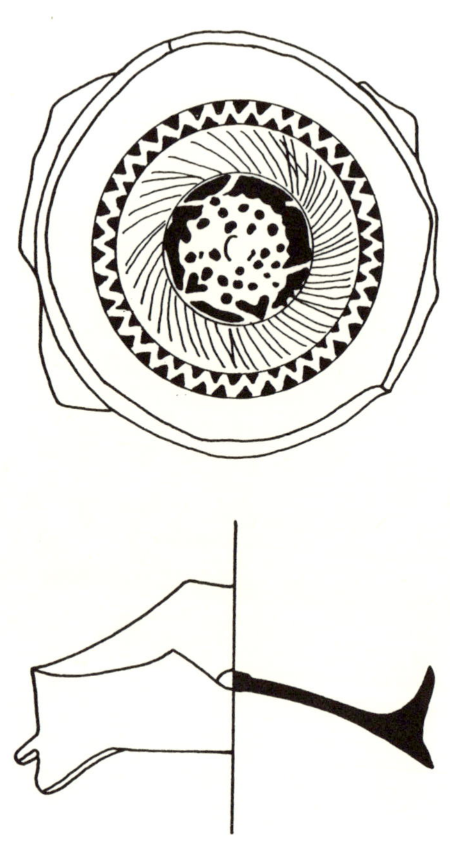

Figure 168

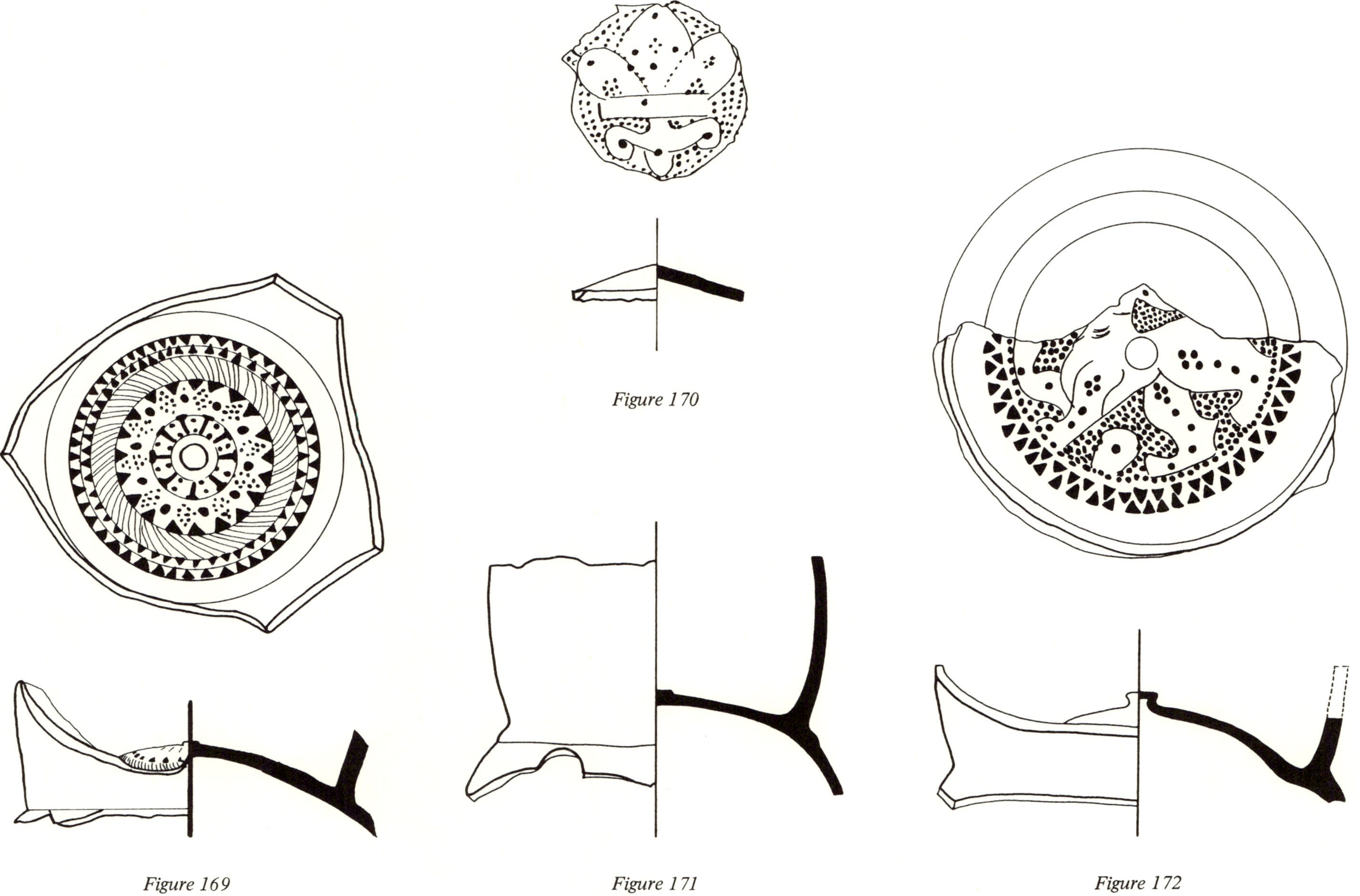

Figure 170
Figure 169
Figure 171
Figure 172

Figure 173

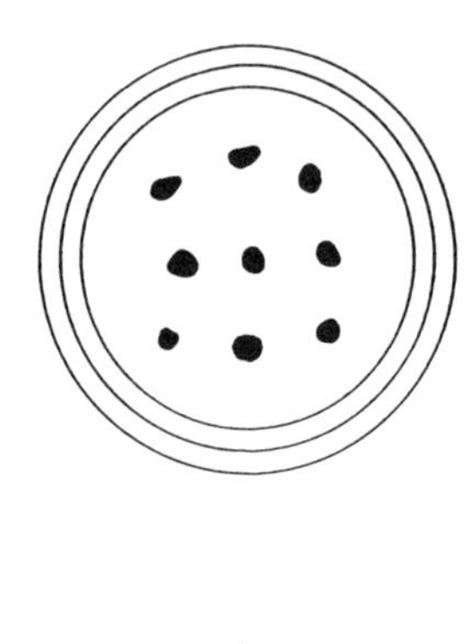

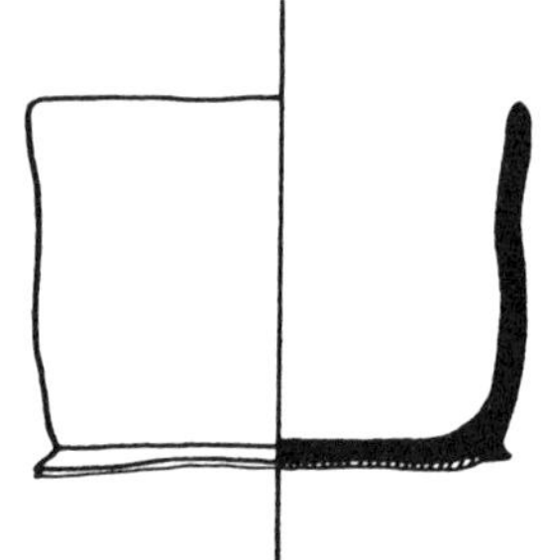

Figure 175

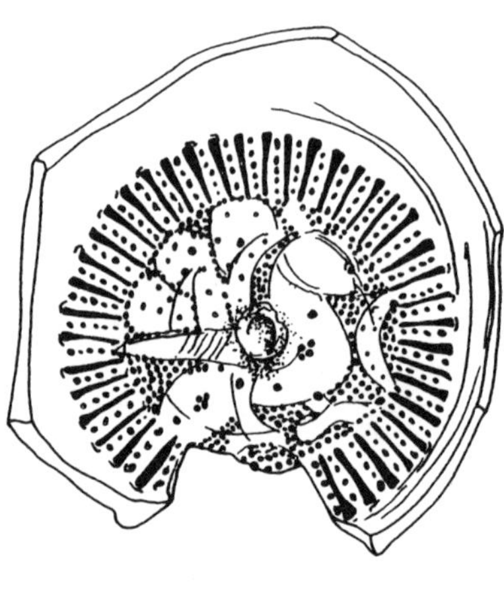

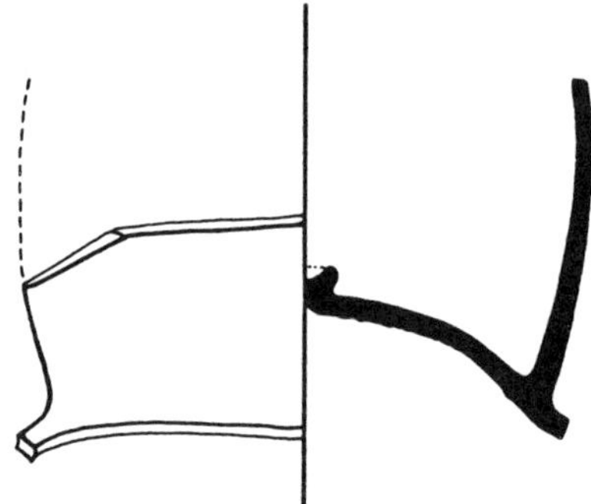

Figure 174

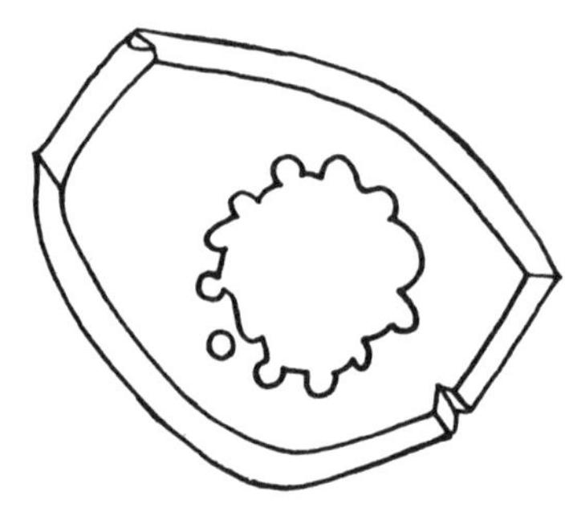

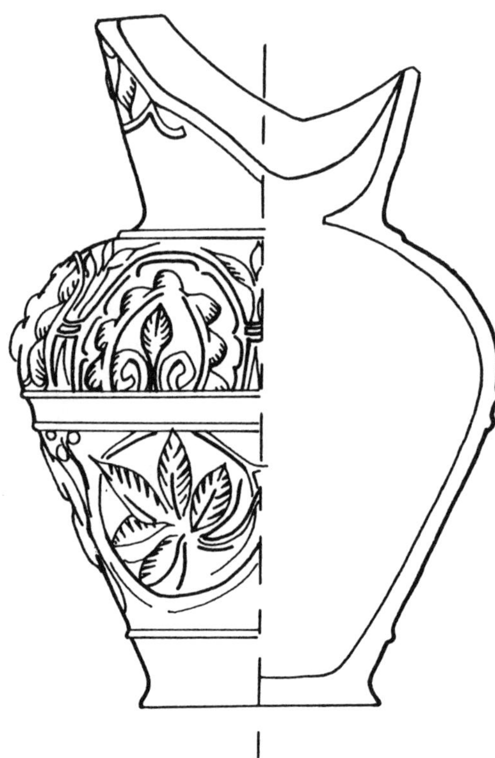

Figure 176

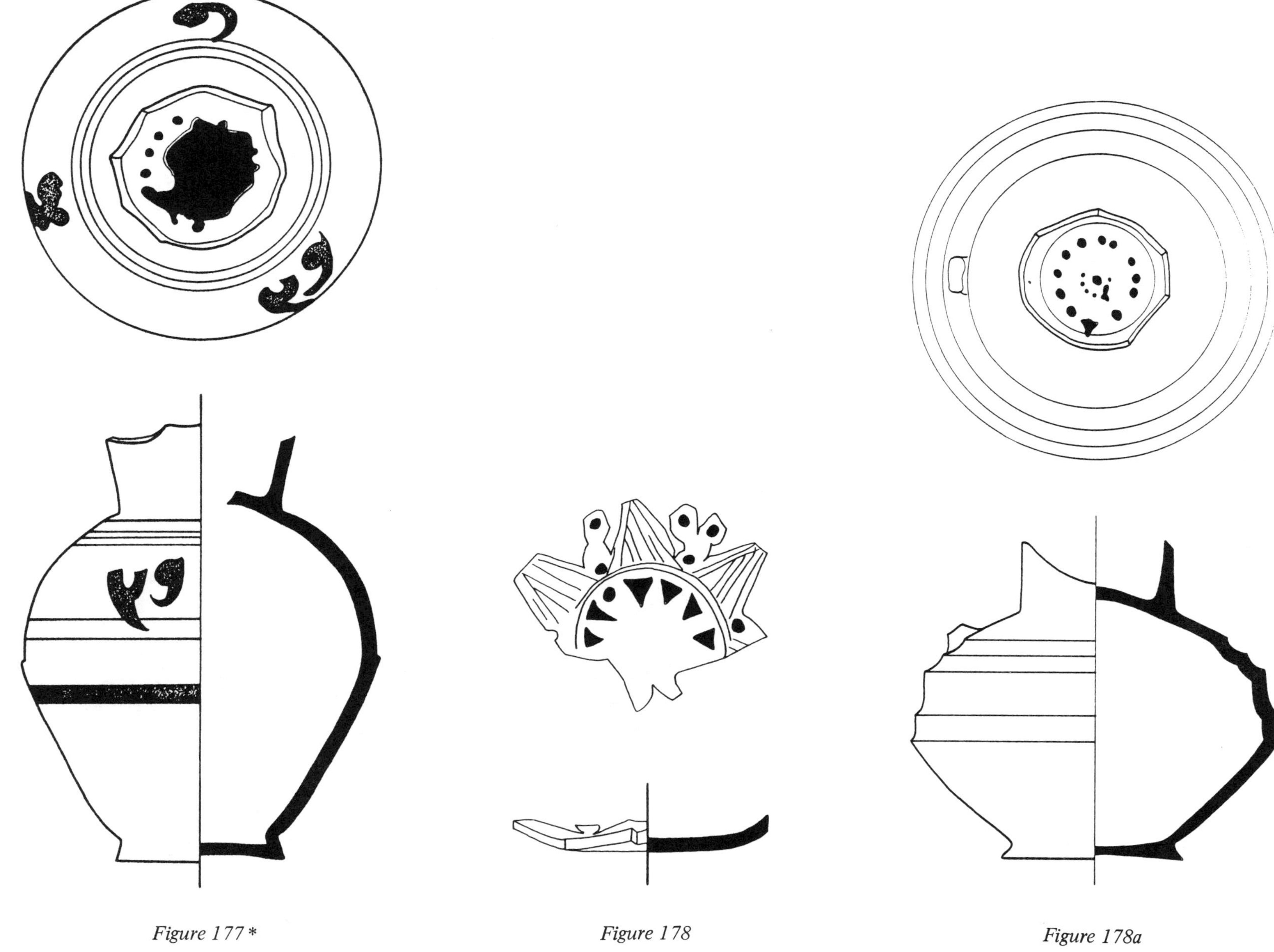

145

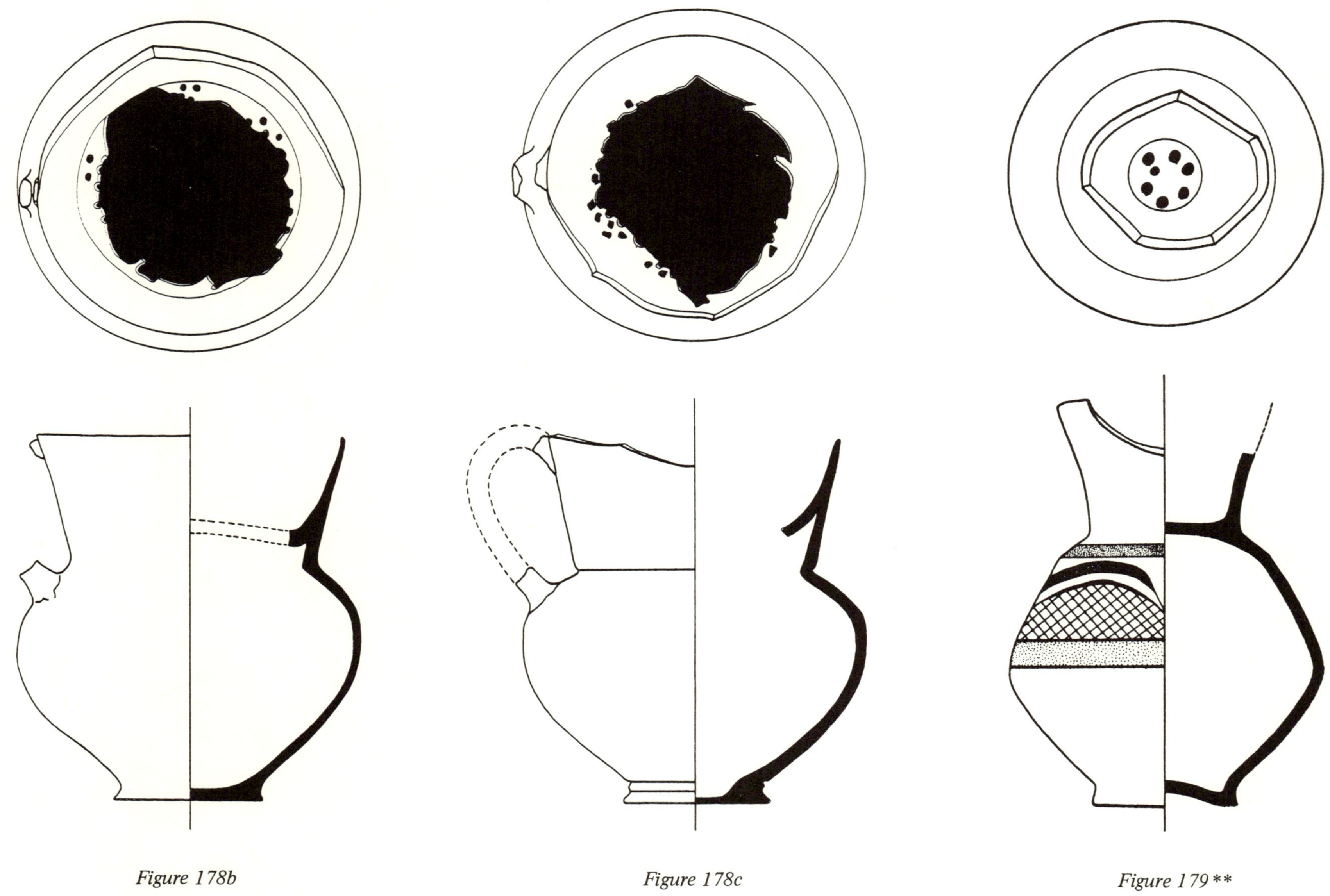

Figure 178b

Figure 178c

Figure 179 **

146

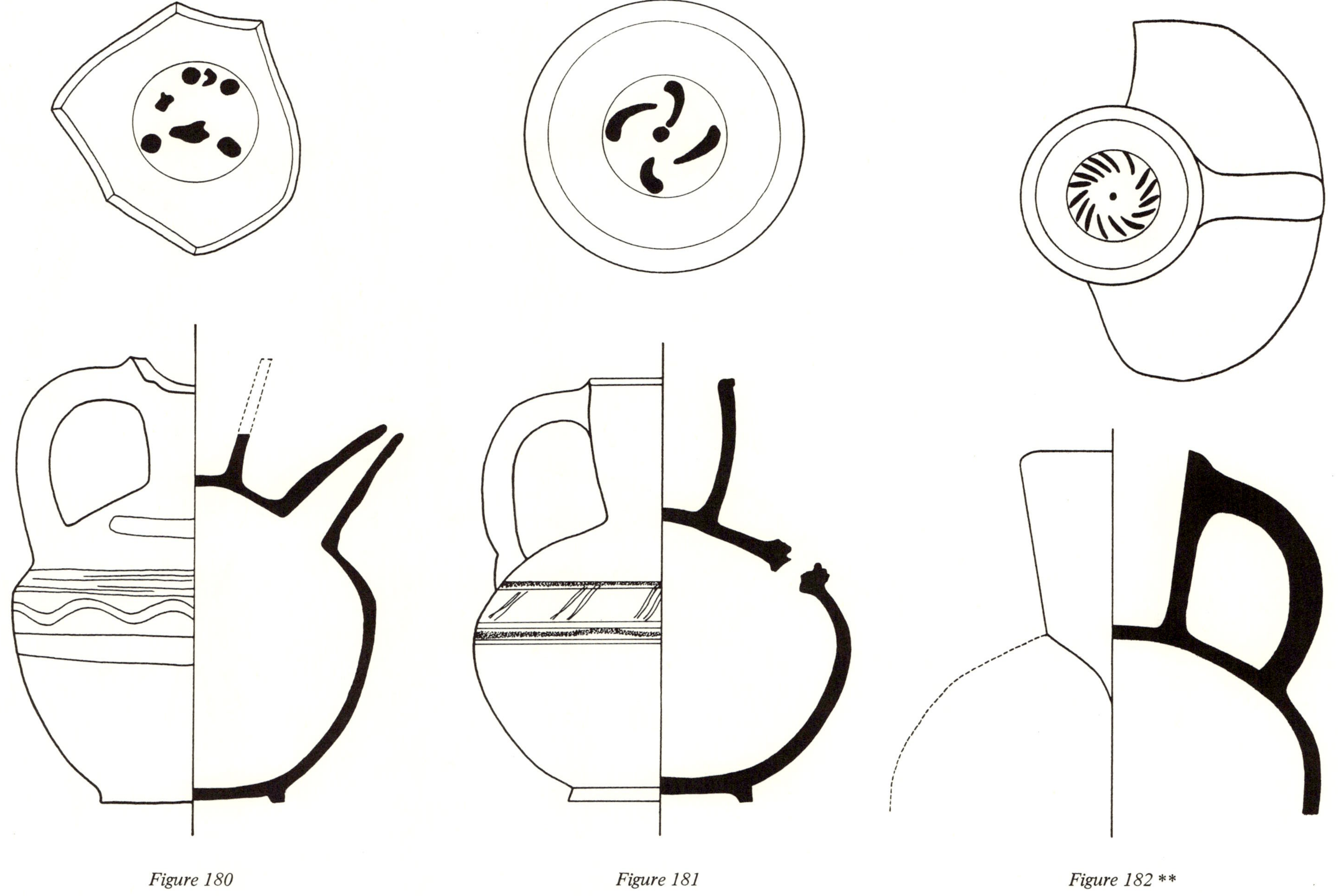

Figure 180   *Figure 181*   *Figure 182* **

147

Figure 183

*Figure 184 ***

*Figure 185 ***

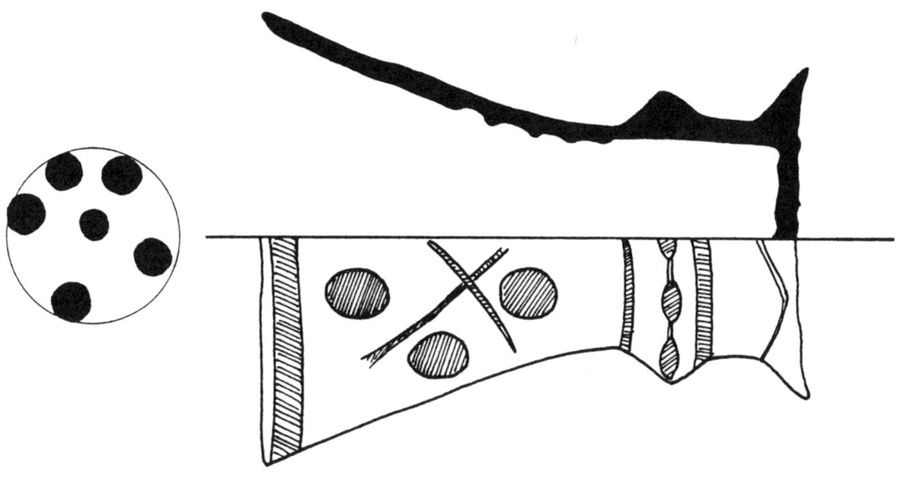

Figure 188

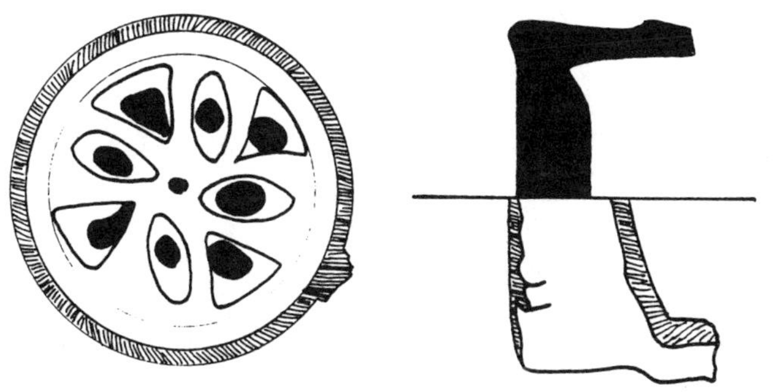

Figure 187

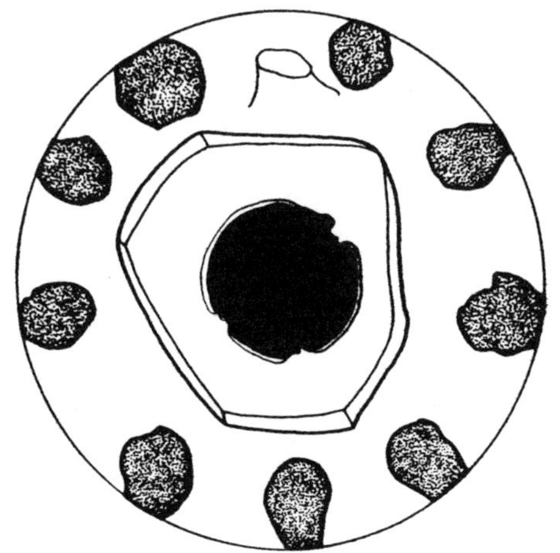

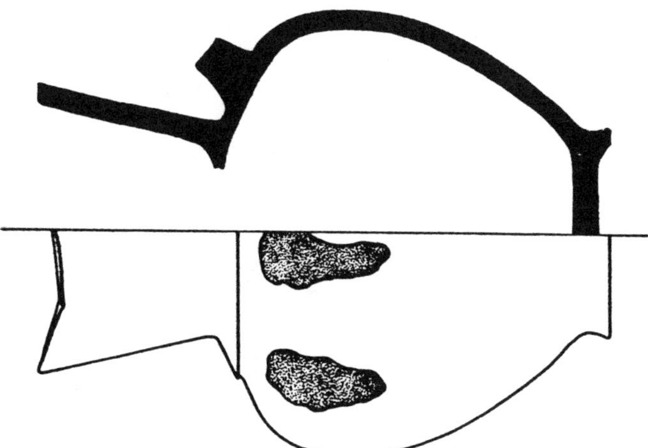

*Figure 186 **

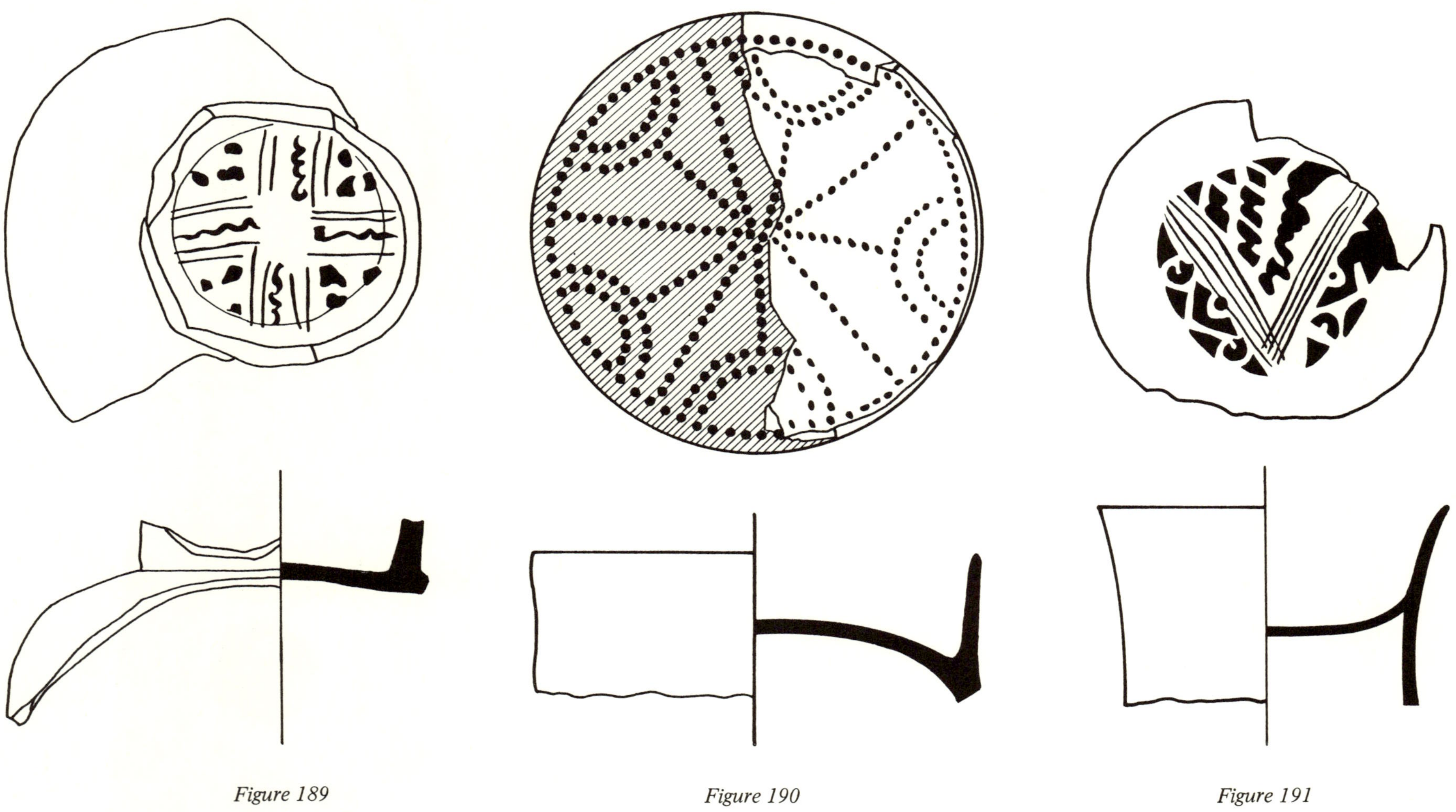

Figure 189   Figure 190   Figure 191

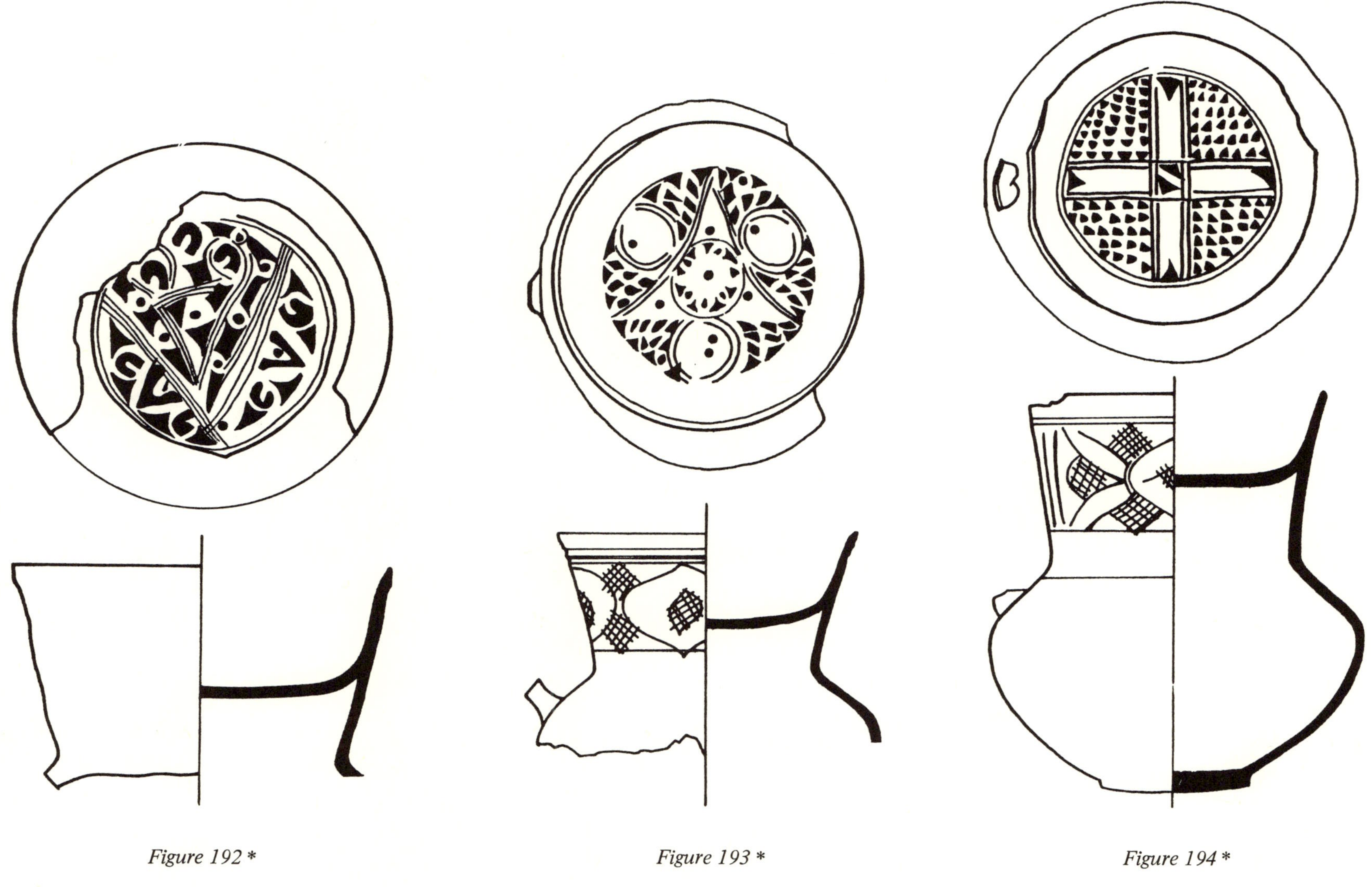

Figure 192 *

Figure 193 *

Figure 194 *

151

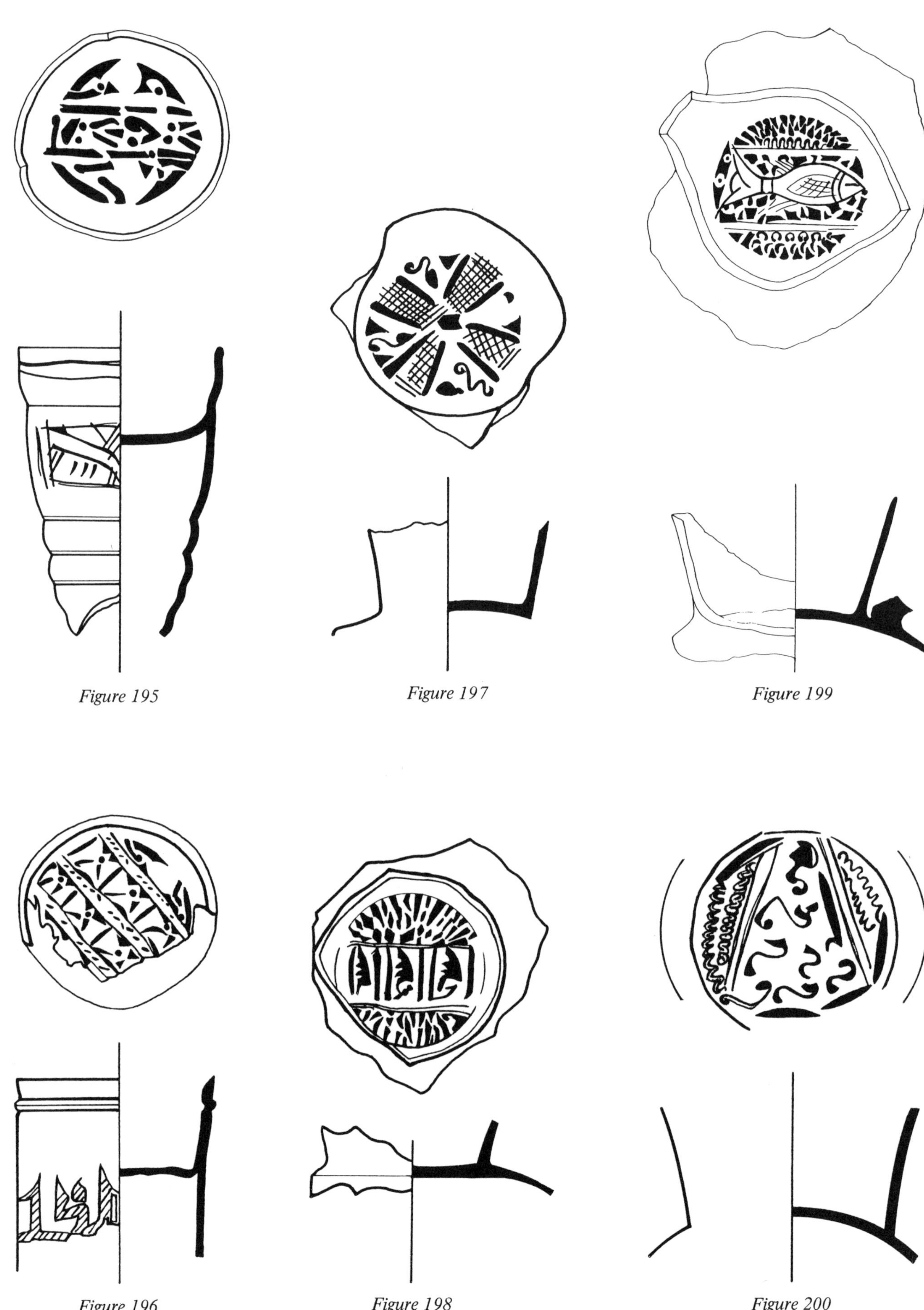

Figure 195

Figure 197

Figure 199

Figure 196

Figure 198

Figure 200

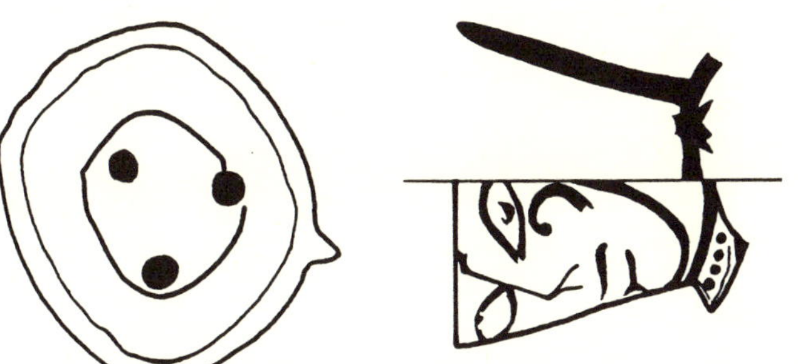

Figure 204

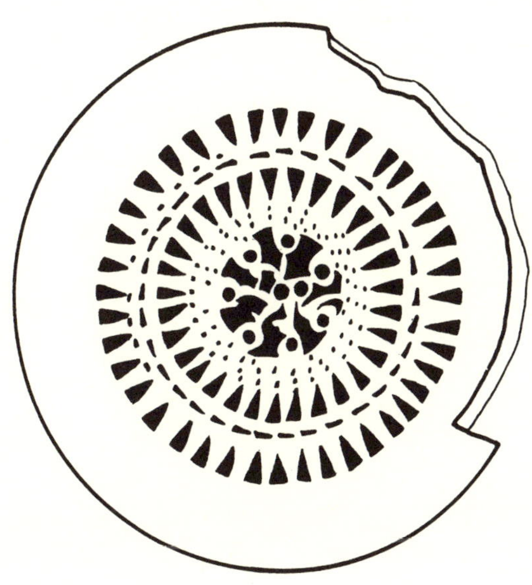

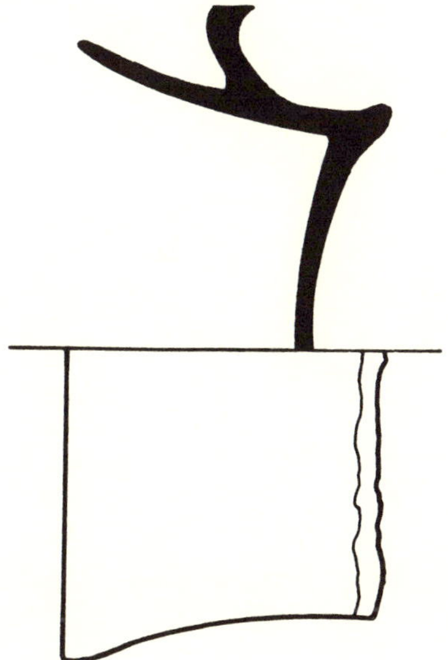

Figure 203

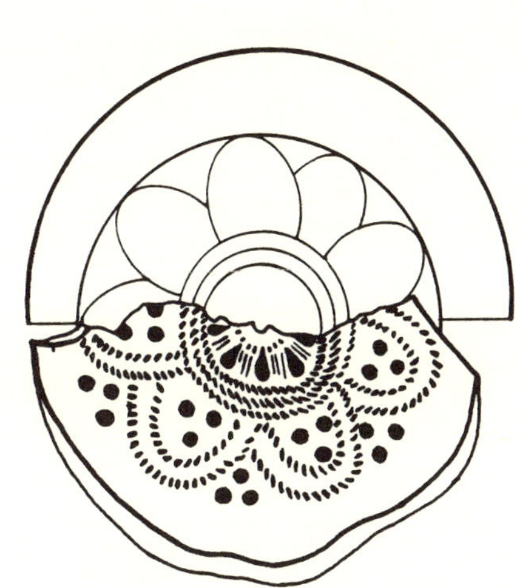

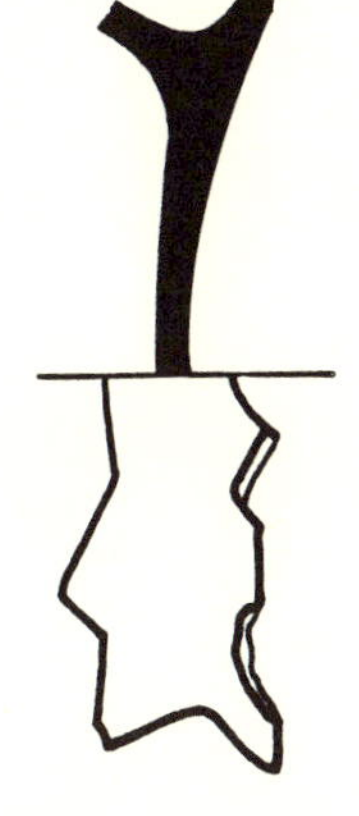

Figure 201

Figure 202

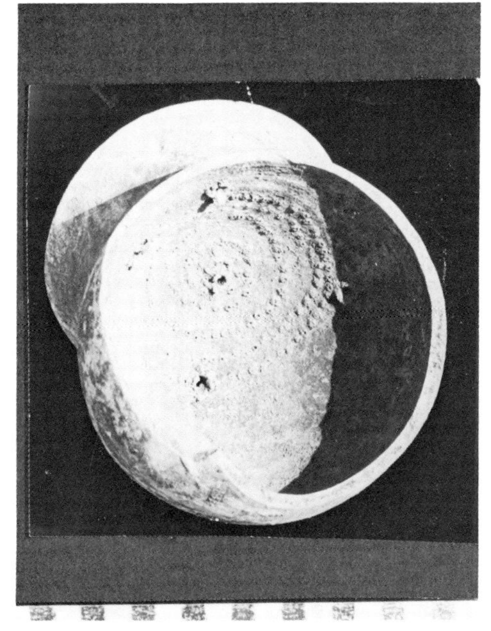

a

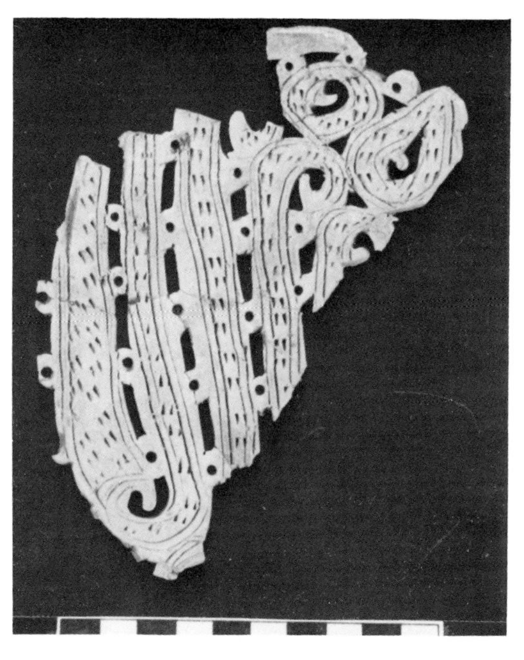

b

c

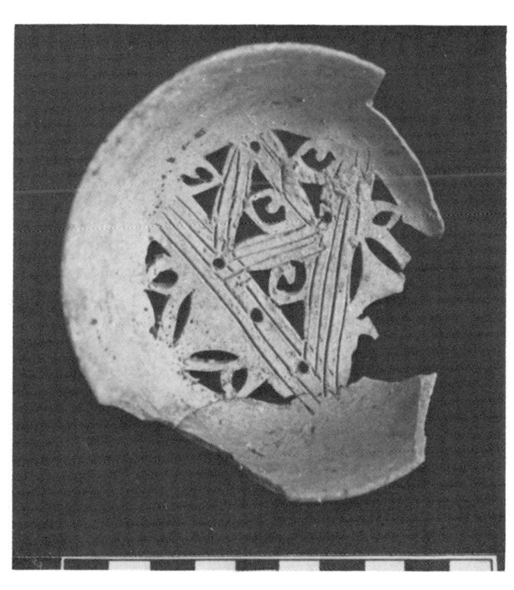

d

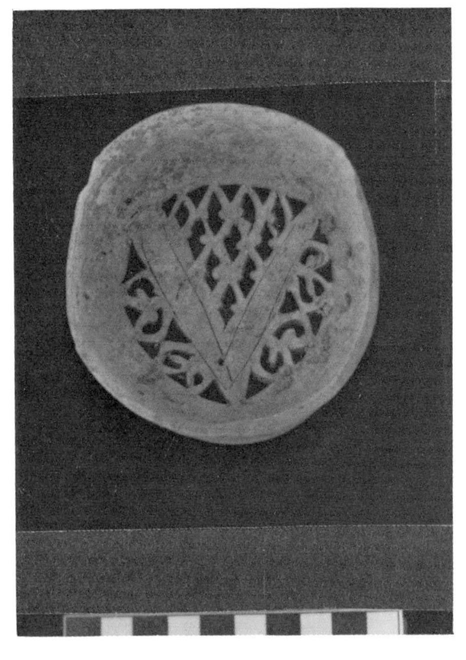

a

b

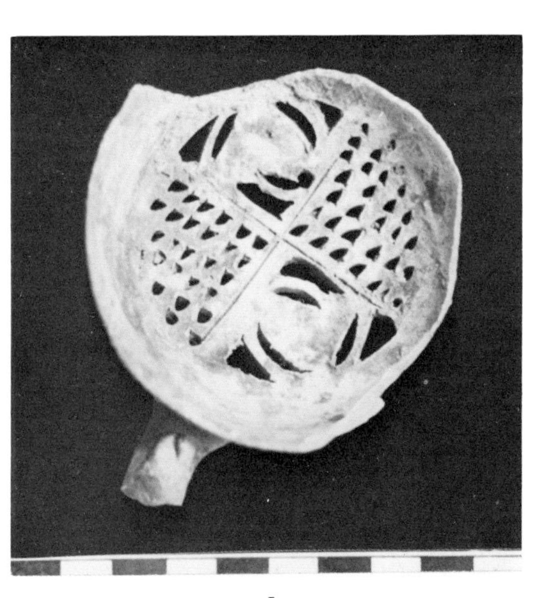

c

d

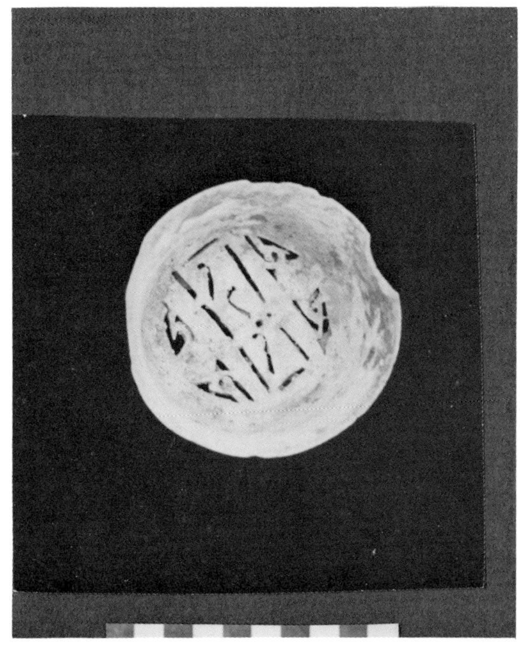

a

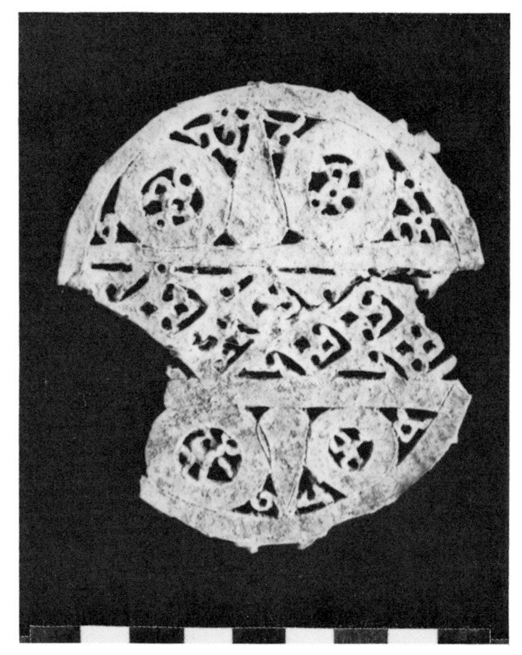

b

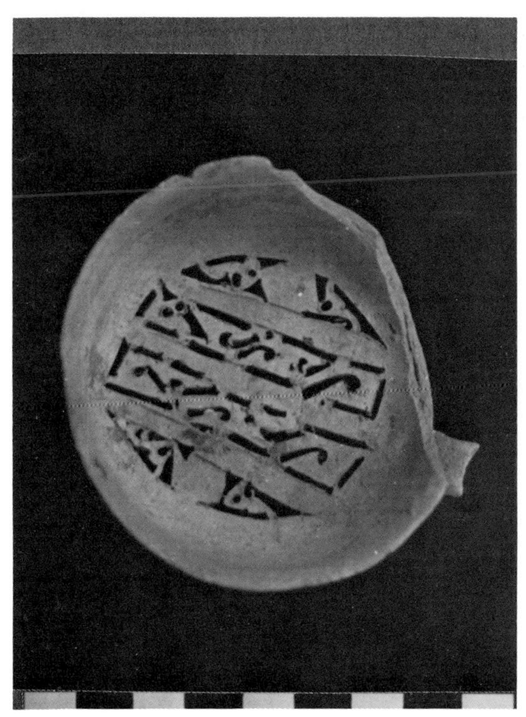

c

d

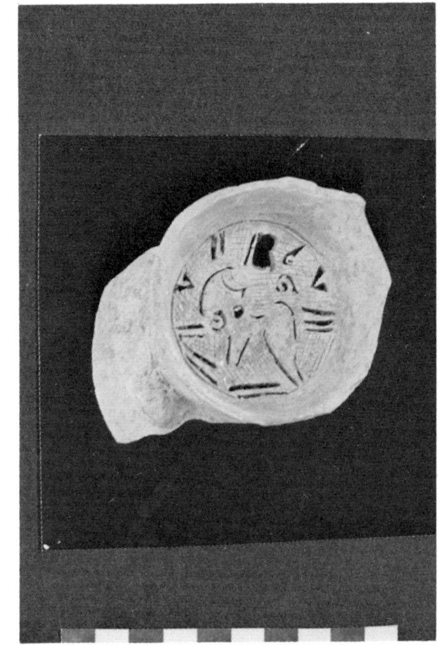

a

b

c

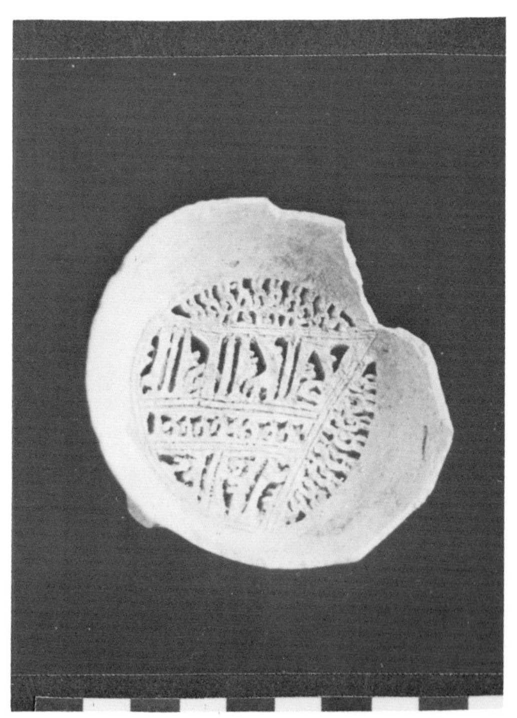

d

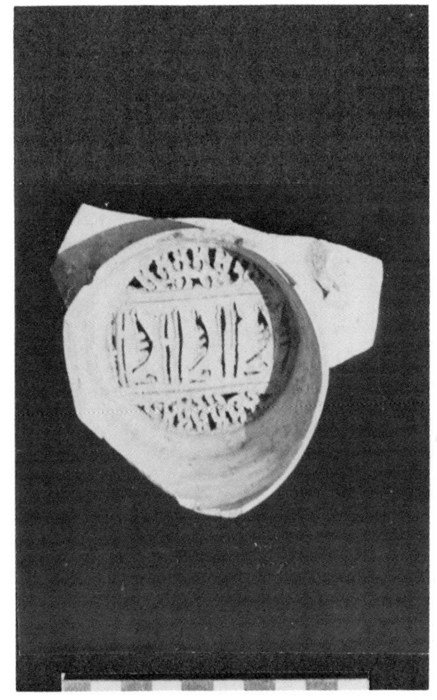

a

b

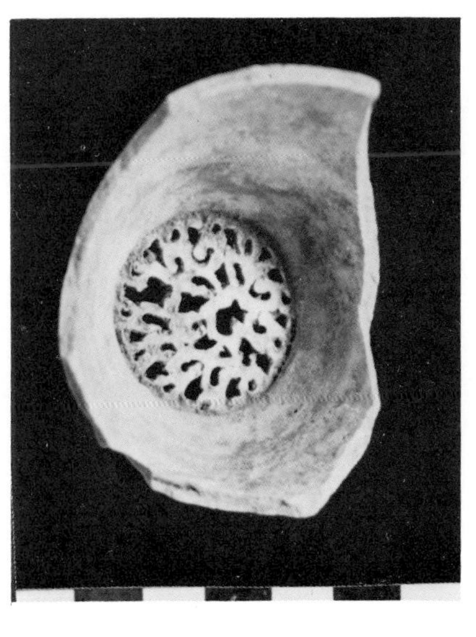

c

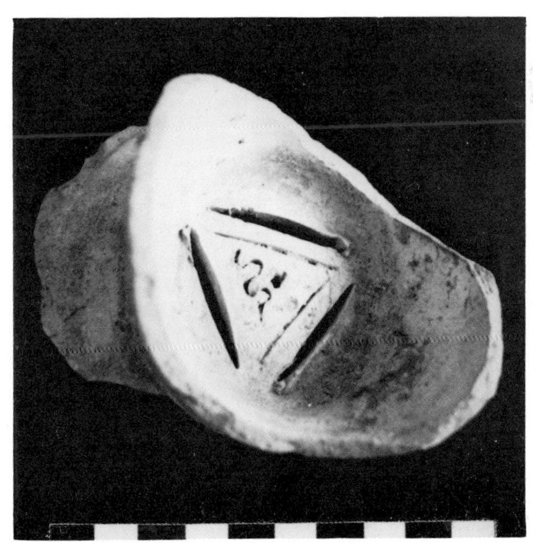

d

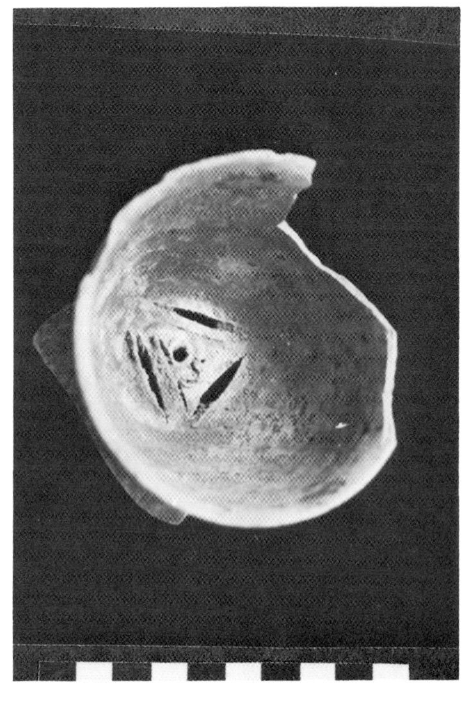

a

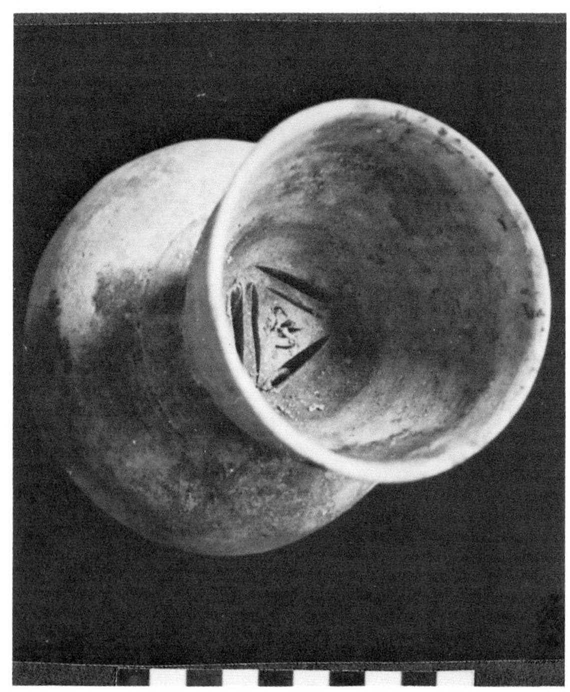

b

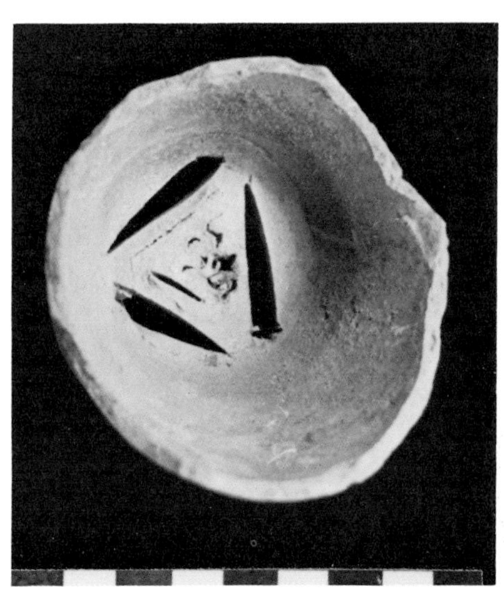

c

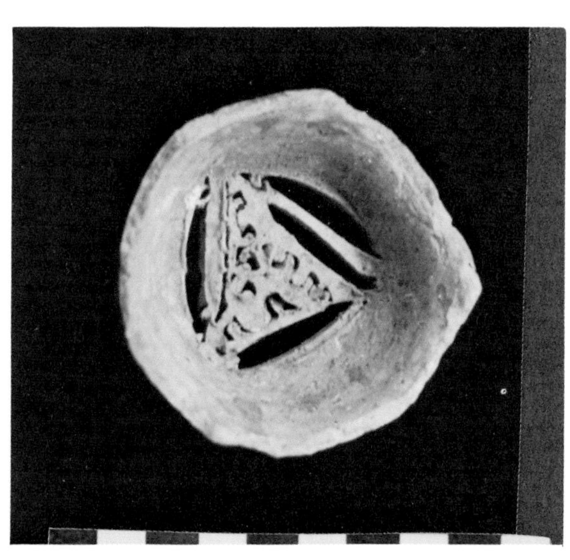

d

a

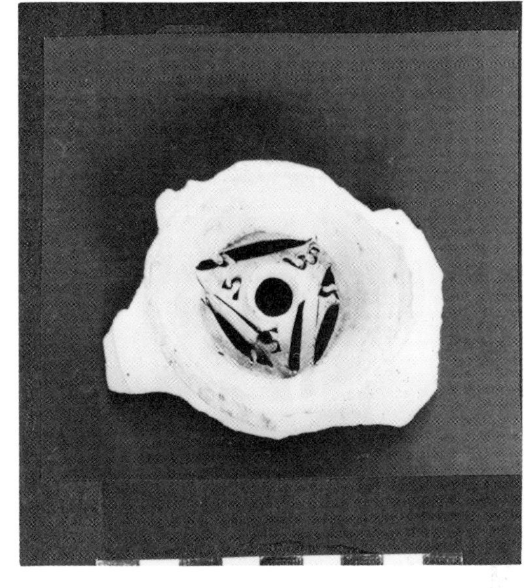

b

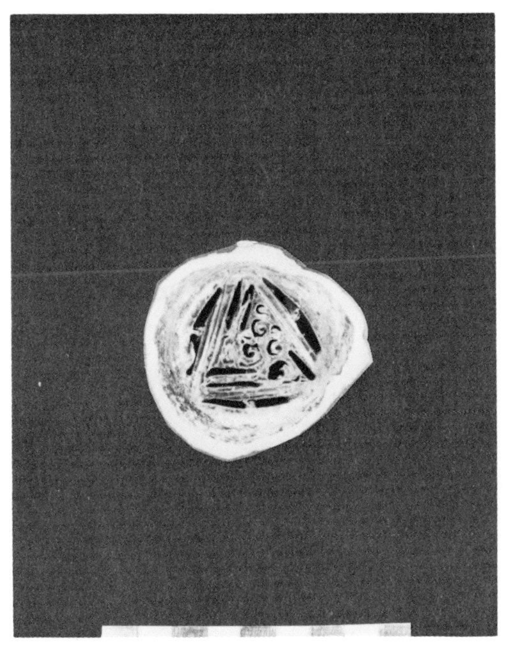

c

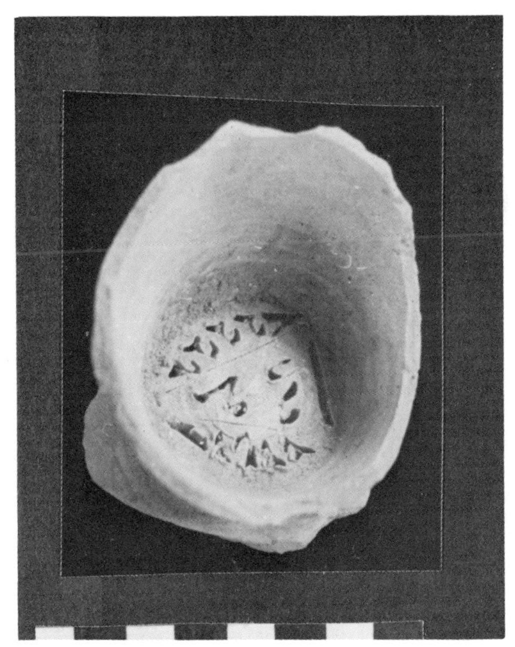

d

a

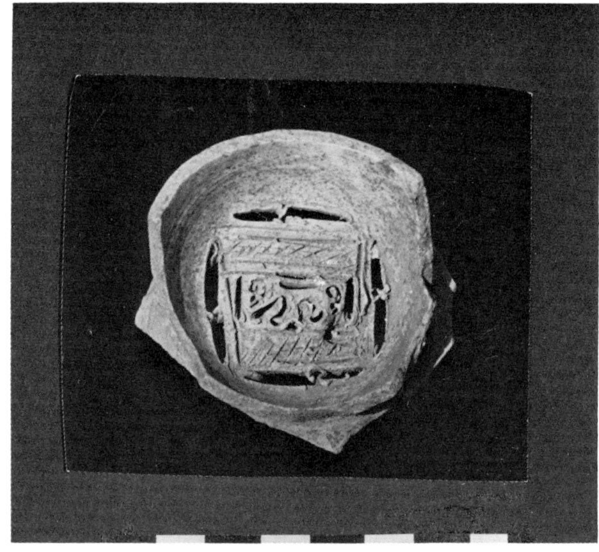

b

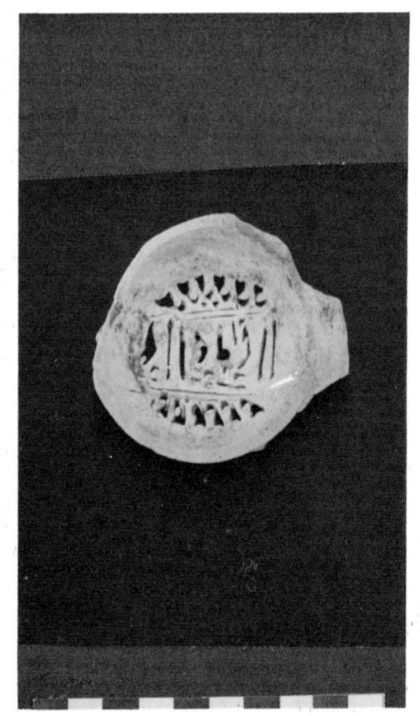

c

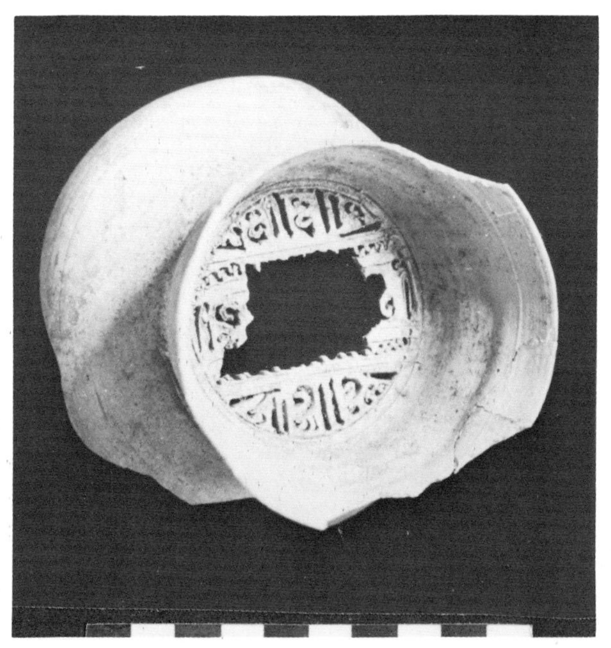

d

a

b

c

d

a

b

c

d

a

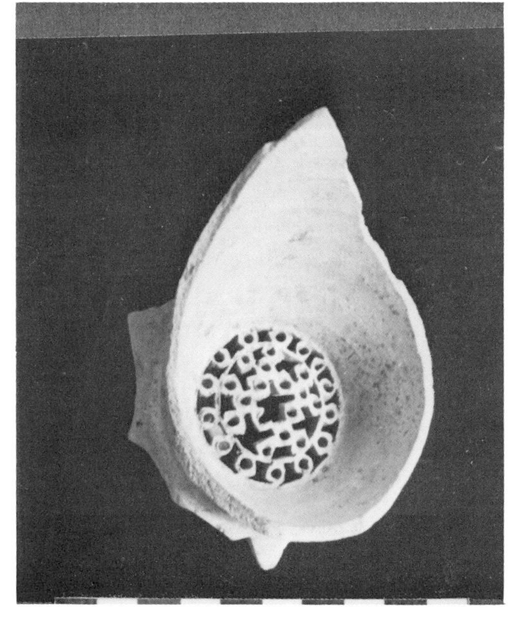

b

c

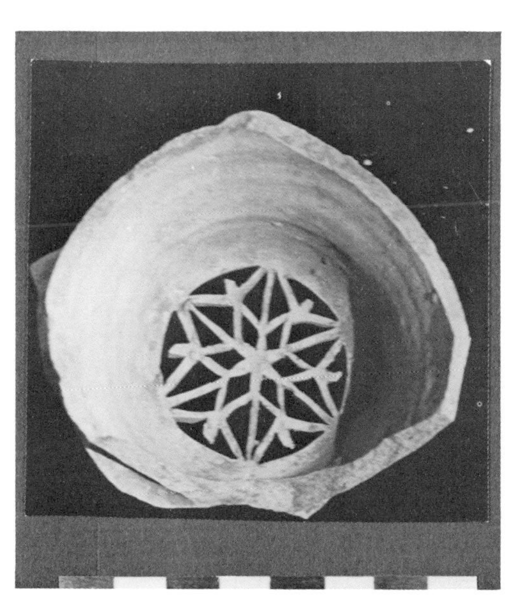

d

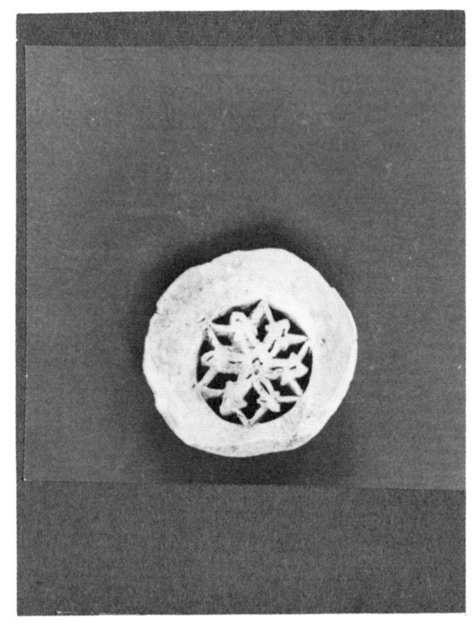

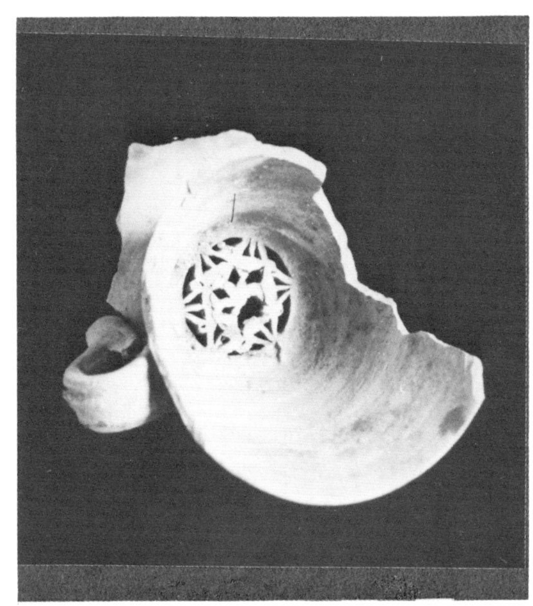

a

b

c

d

a

b

c

d

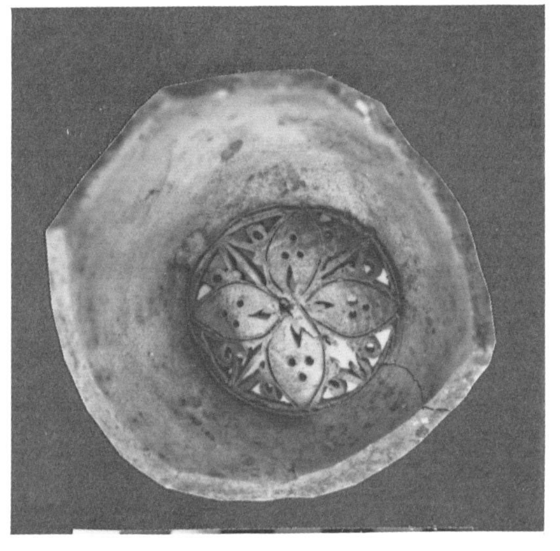

a

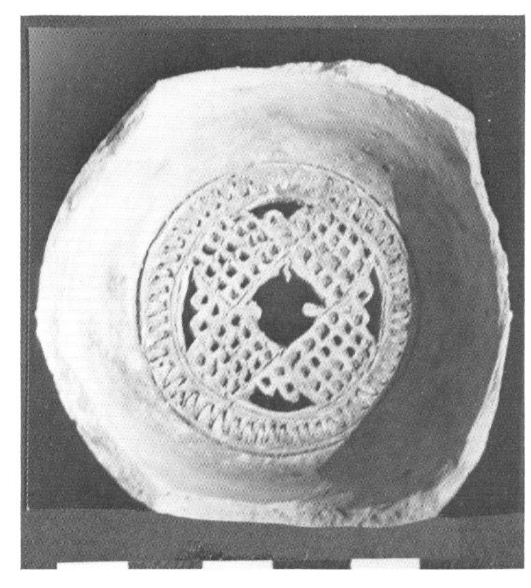

b

c

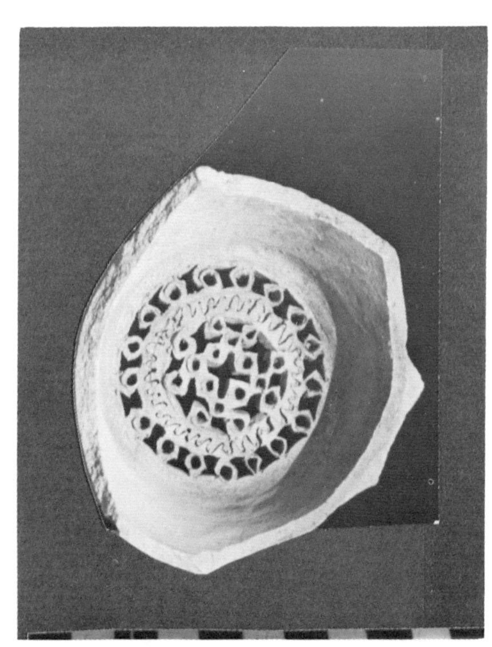

d

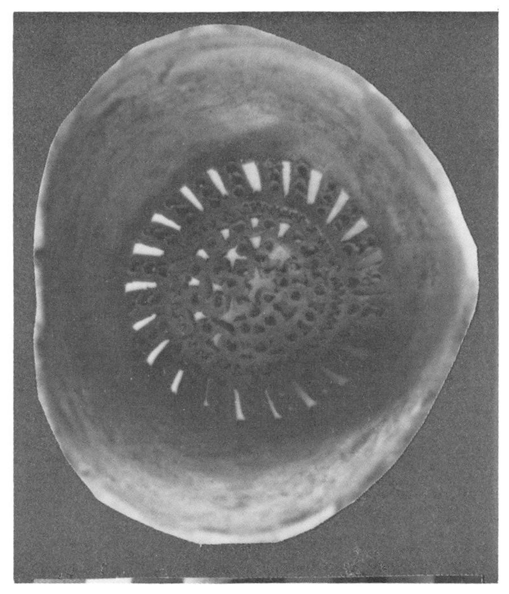

a

b

c

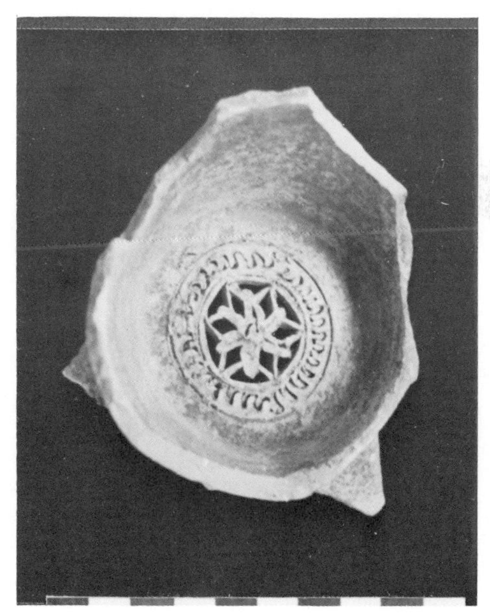

d

a

b

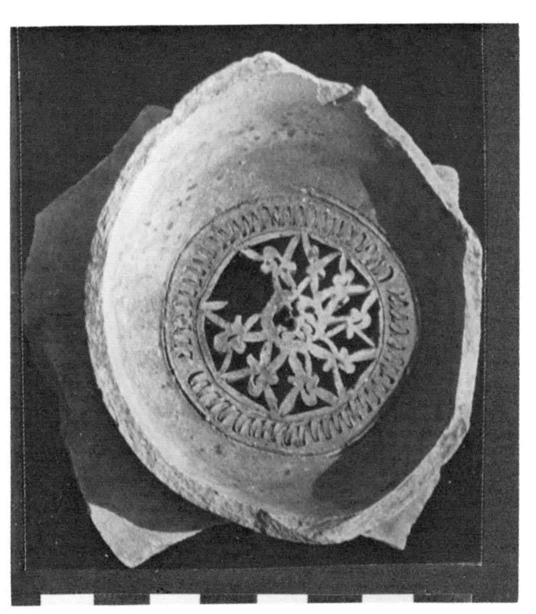

c

d

a b

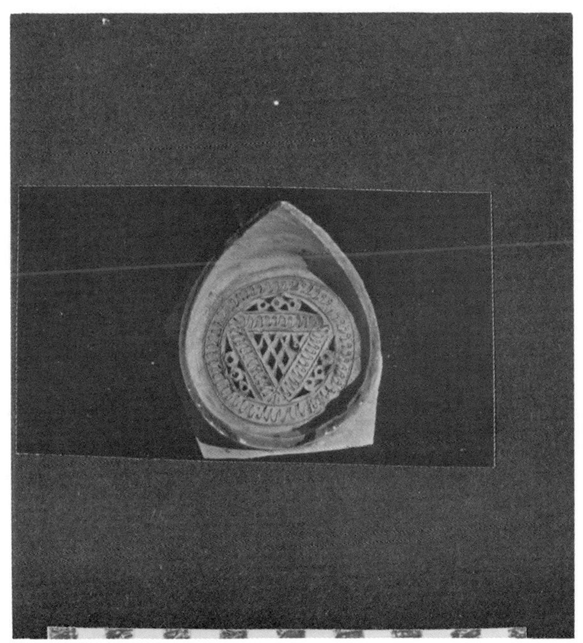

c d

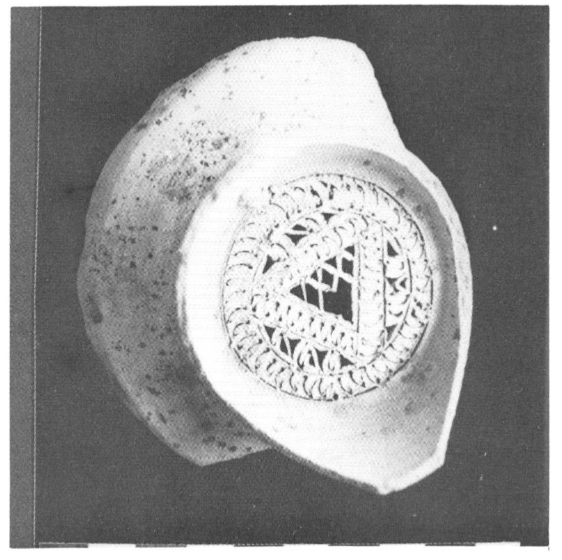

a

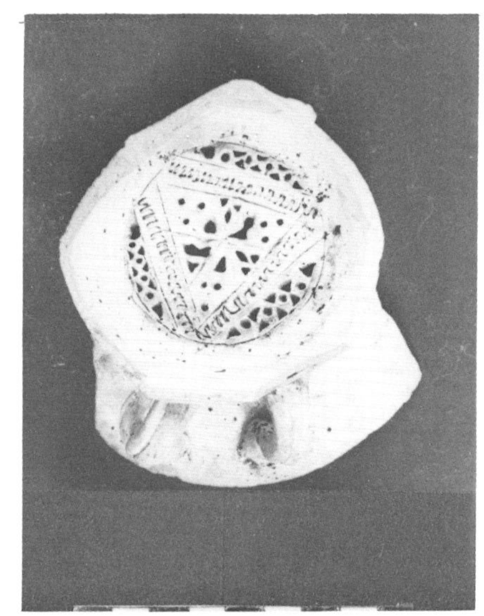

b

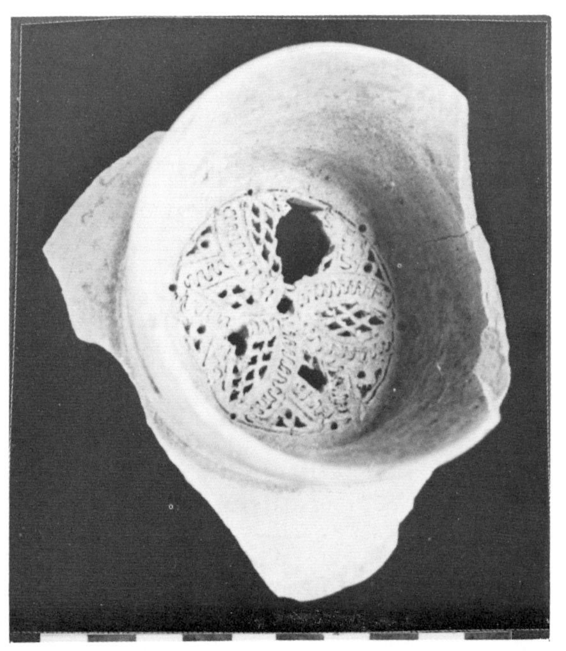

c

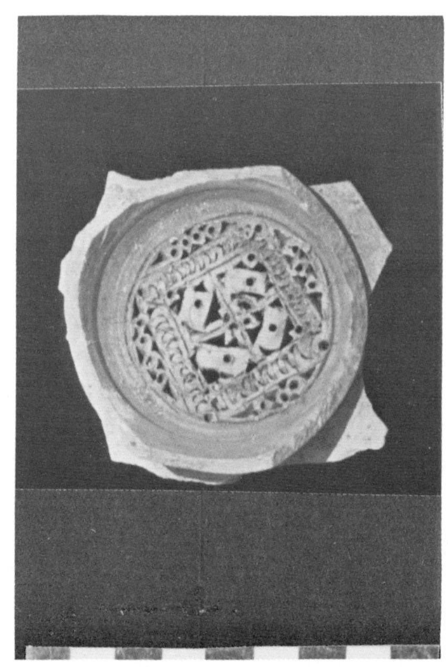

d

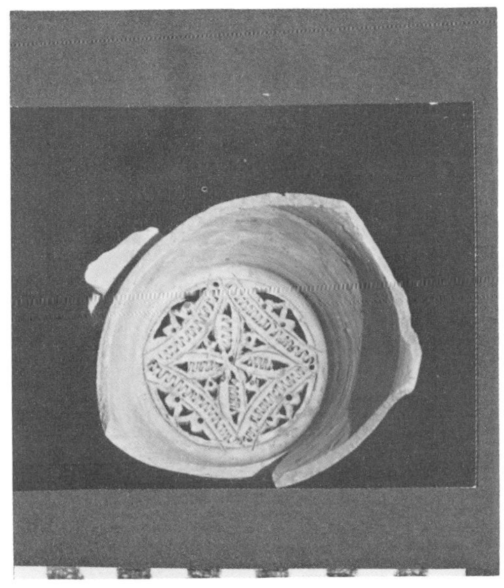

a

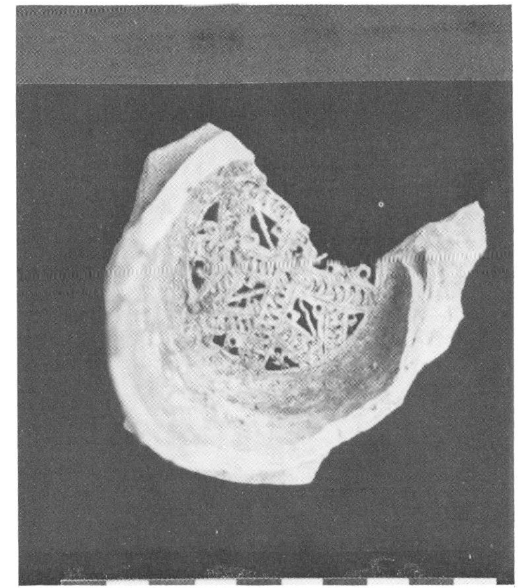

b

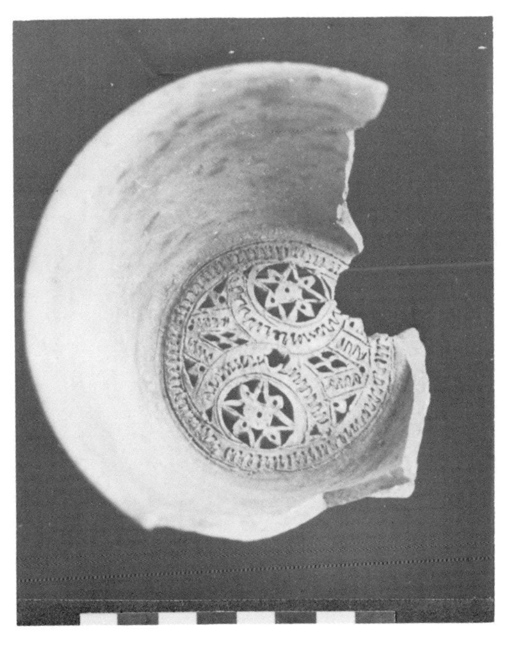

c

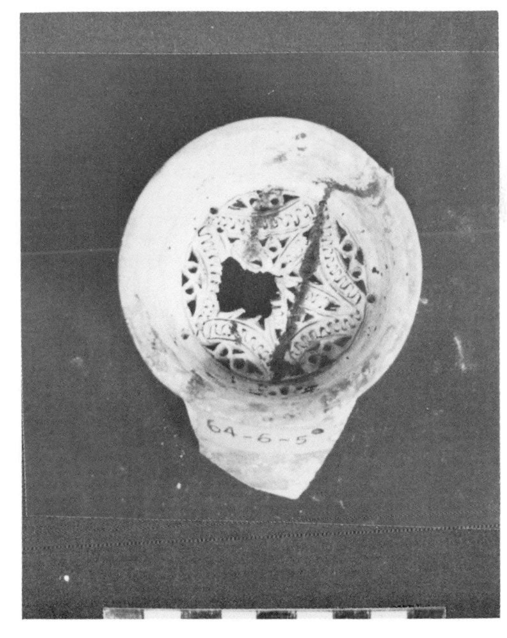

d

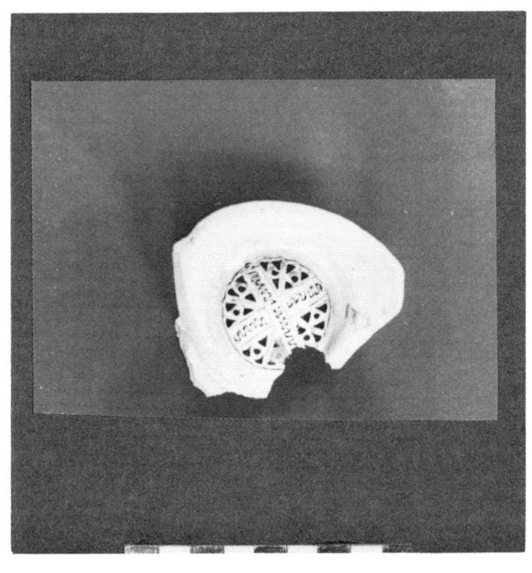

a

b

c

d

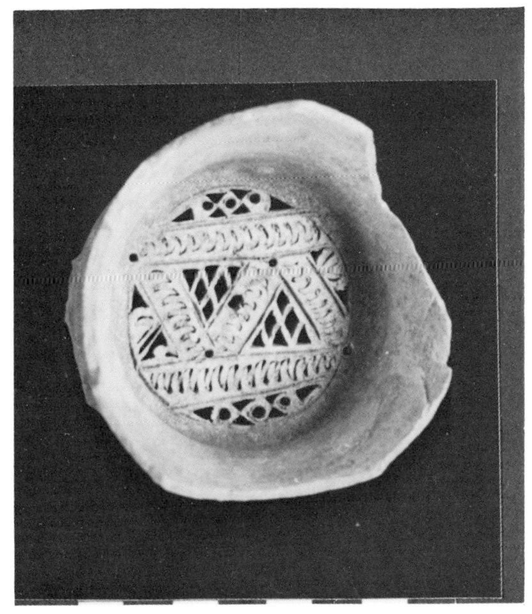

a

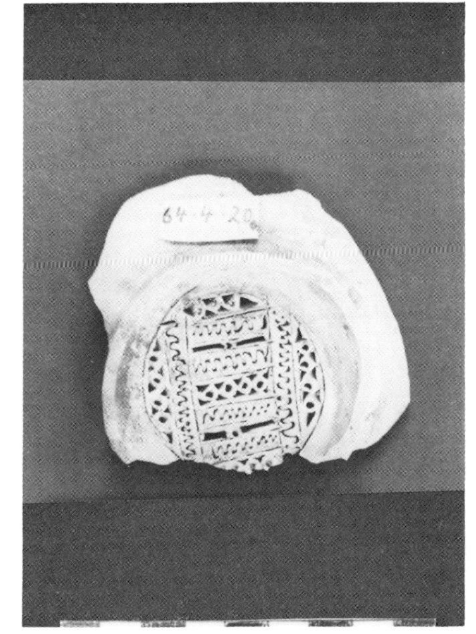

b

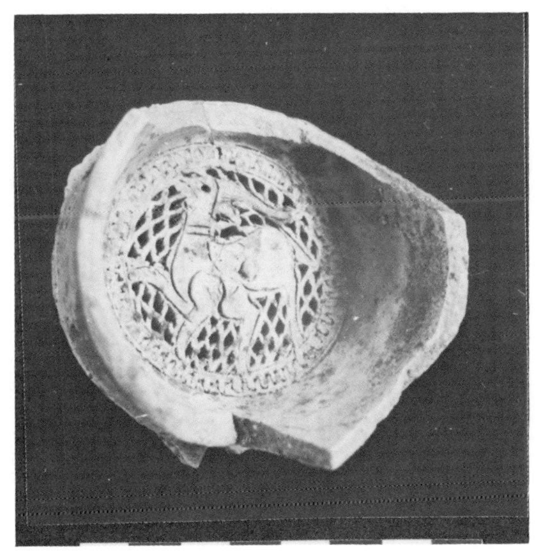

c

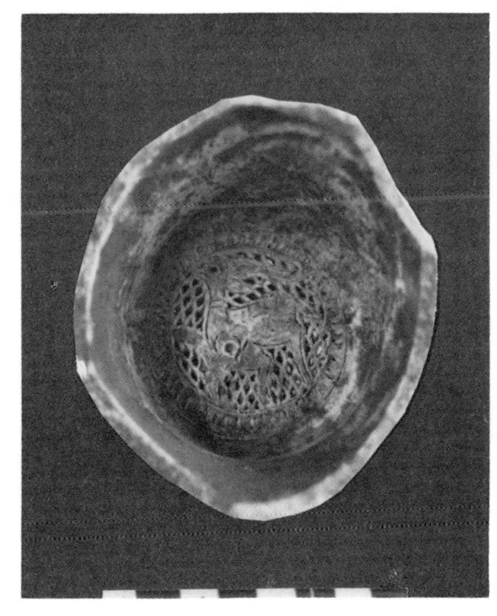

d

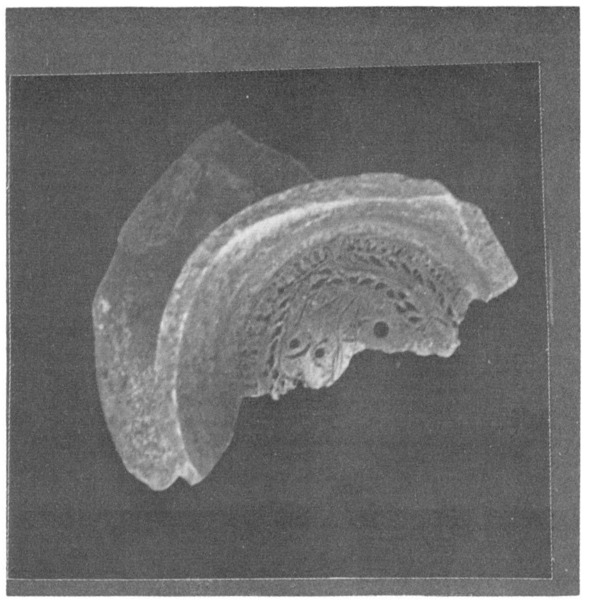

a

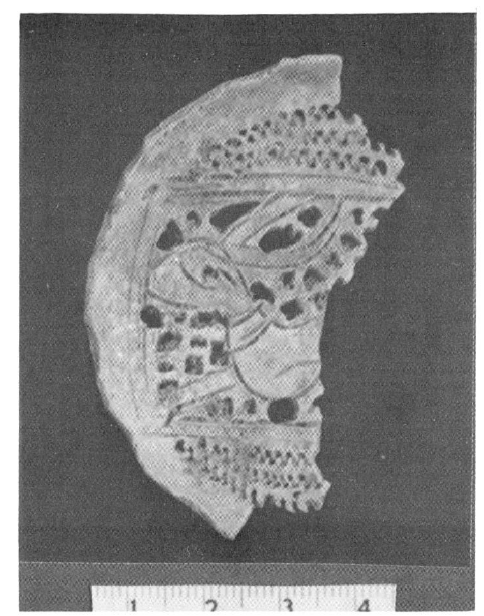

b

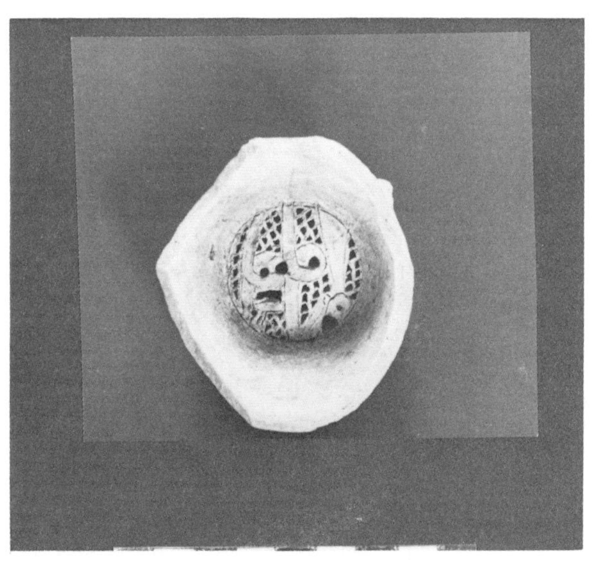

c

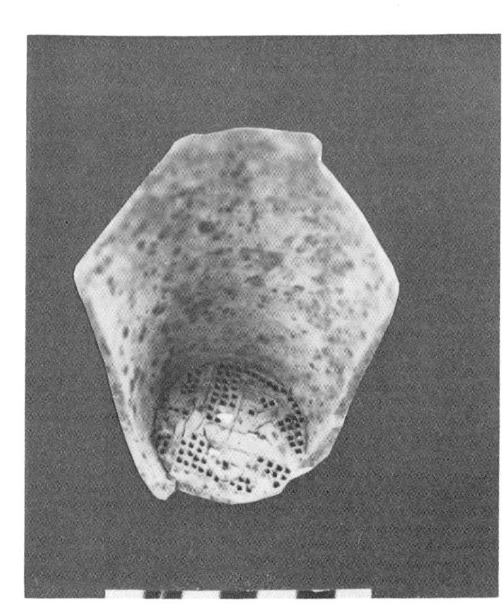

d

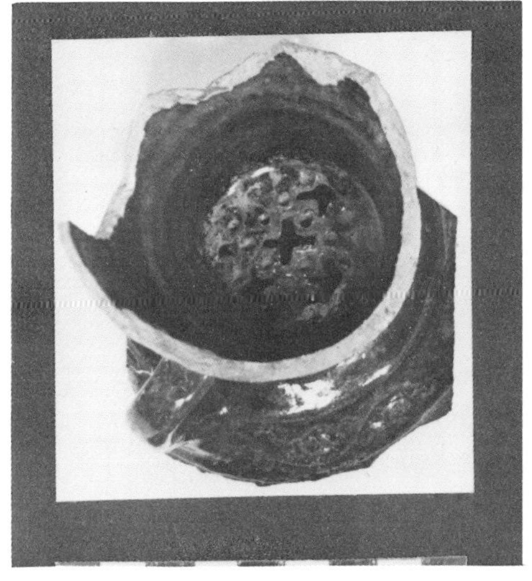

a

b

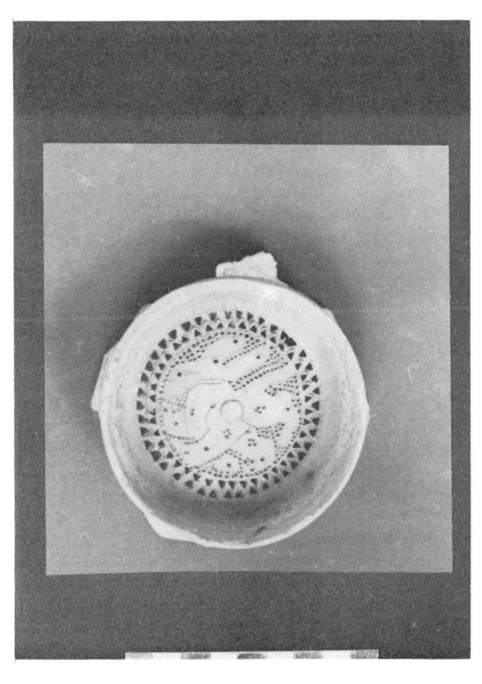

c

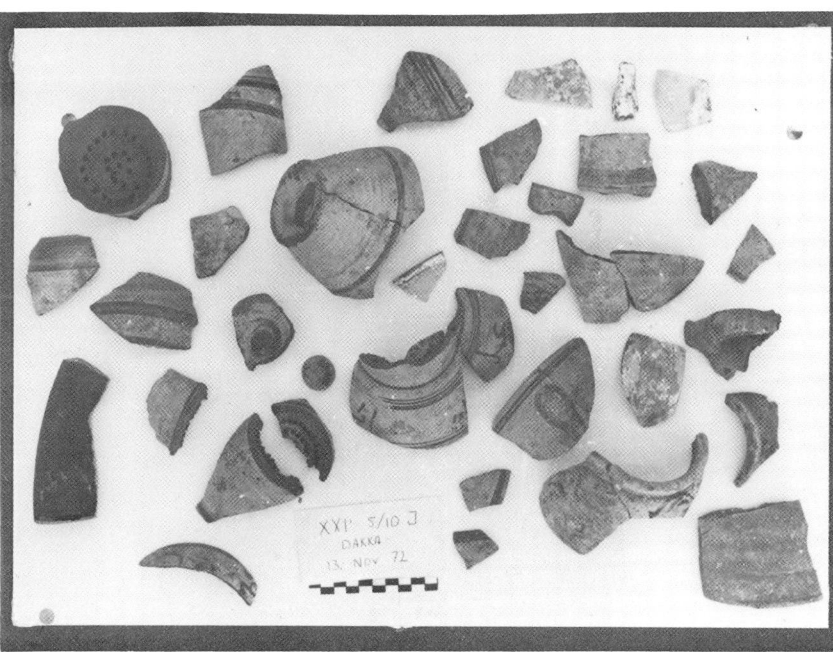

d

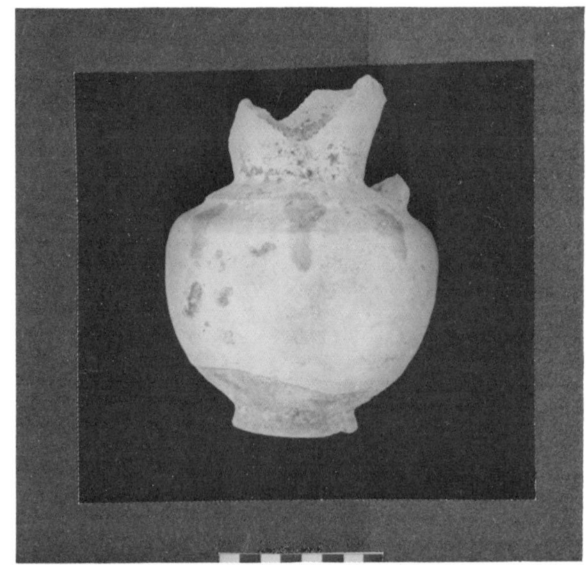

a

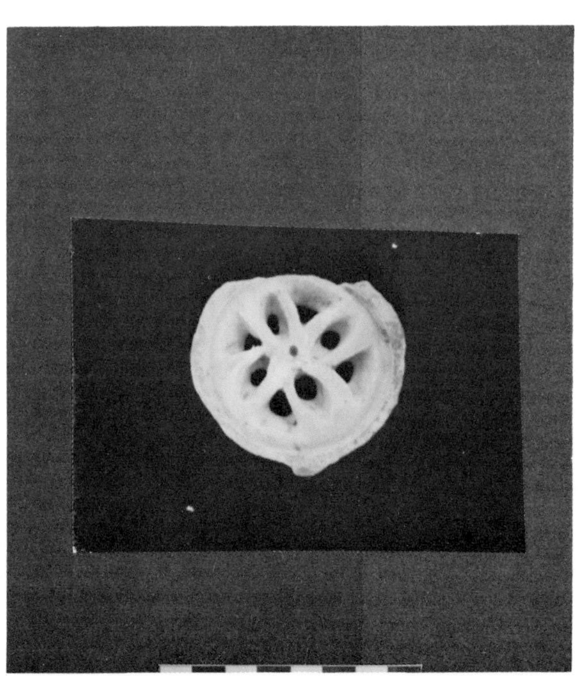

b